CARRIER AVIATION IN THE 21ST CENTURY, Aircraft carriers and their units in detail

Thomas Newdick (editor)

I0869160

CARRIER AVIATION IN THE 21ST CENTURY

Aircraft carriers and their units in detail

Thomas Newdick (editor)

HARPIA PUBLISHING

2803 Sackett Street, Houston, TX 77098-1125, U.S.A.
enquiries@harpia-publishing.com

Consulting and inspiration by Kerstin Berger

Front cover artwork by Ugo Crisponi showing a US Navy F/A-18F Super Hornet from Strike Fighter Squadron (VFA) 103 'Jolly Rogers'.

Rear cover artworks by Ugo Crisponi and Bertrand Brown/AviationGraphic.com (from top to bottom): Spanish Navy EAV-8B+ Harrier II, Indian Navy MiG-29K and a French Navy Rafale M.

Drawings by James Lawrence

Editorial by Thomas Newdick

Layout by Norbert Novak, www.media-n.at, Vienna

Printed at finidr, Czech Republic

Harpia Publishing, L.L.C. is a member of

ISBN 978-0-9973092-2-5

Contents

Introduction

With the end of World War II in the Pacific in 1945, the aircraft carrier was left among the victors. In a series of large-scale naval battles, the carrier had proven itself the most important capital ship, even eclipsing the battleship. Thanks to its rapidly expanding carrier fleet, the United States was able to project air power over thousands of miles and to operate aircraft where only minimal infastructure existed. Throughout the course of the war, the carrier had got bigger, and their air wings expanded. Aircraft flying from carrier decks also began to take on new roles, including air support for amphibious operations and anti-submarine warfare.

In the years since the end of World War II, the aircraft carrier's potential to deliver air power across vast distances, without the need for land-based infrastructure, has remained its key reason for existence. Even during the Cold War, when much of the world was conveniently divided up according to superpower-led alliances, the aircraft carrier was prized for its ability to intervene or to 'fly the flag' in areas where land-based airfields were unavailable or subject to threat. Today, this remains the case, but in most recent cases carrier-based air power has been used as an adjunct to land-based aircraft.

By the end of 1945 only the United Kingdom and the United States were in possession of carrier fleets, and today the US Navy's carrier power is unmatched. The UK's Royal Navy is only beginning to return to fixed-wing aircraft carriers, while the US Navy operates 10 *Nimitz*-class aircraft carriers and has introduced the first example of a new class of supercarriers, the USS *Gerald R. Ford* (CVN 78).

The Cold War years saw a number of important developments relating to carrier air power. With the arrival of jet aircraft on deck, carrier design was refined to improve operational efficiency. Three British innovations in particular were to have a significant impact on future operations: the angled deck, steam catapult launch system and mirror/projection landing system. While the 1950s and 1960s saw aircraft carriers increase in size, they also began to take on new roles. The anti-submarine warfare (ASW) carrier was a further development of the escort carriers that undertook convoy protection duty in World War II. Together with carrier-based nuclear strike aircraft, the purpose-designed ASW carrier no longer has a place in the world's navies. On the other hand, the 1950s also saw the emergence of the amphibious assault ship. These were initially based on the hulls of smaller fleet and escort carriers, but such was their success that dedicated designs began to be drawn up. While the US Navy is the only force that maintains a dedicated fleet of fixed-wing-capable amphibious assault vessels, outside America the demand for multipurpose ships has seen traditional aircraft carriers increasingly take on secondary amphibious or humanitarian taskings.

The supercarrier was born with the *Nimitz*-class of nuclear-powered vessels, which at the time of their appearance were the largest warships ever constructed. US aircraft carrier design continues to emphasise the primacy of size at all costs. Only the largest vessel is able to support a huge conventional take-off and landing (CTOL) air wing suitable for America's power projection requirements. France has followed a similar mode, albeit on a much smaller scale. As the only carrier in its navy, the *Charles de Gaulle* is nuclear powered and embarks CTOL aircraft. However, the cost of acquiring and running another carrier has proven to be prohibitive, and whever the *Charles de Gaulle* undergoes a regular refit it is unavailable to commanders in theatre. China's aircraft carrier revolution is in its infancy, but it too has opted for conventional take-off and landing aircraft. Beijing ultimately looks set to follow the US as it sets about establishing its carrier fleet. Its development path seems set to follow a 'building block' approach, with ships of increasing size and capability perhaps ultimately leading to a nuclear-powered supercarrier.

An alternative to conventional carriers with CTOL aviation can be found in short take-off and vertial landing (STOVL) carriers. These emerged during the latter half of the Cold War in response to the development by the UK and US of the Hawker Siddeley Harrier (later British Aerospace/McDonnell Douglas) 'jump jet'. This small but versatile warplane first went to sea operationally with the US Marine Corps (USMC), as the AV-8A Harrier, aboard amphibious assault ships. Development continued in the UK and led to the BAe Sea Harrier, which was allied with a 'ski jump' take-off ramp. Flying from STOVL carriers, advanced versions of the Harrier remain the cornerstones of carrier air power in Italy and Spain, while the AV-8B Harrier II continues to serve with the USMC aboard US Navy assault ships.

Waiting in the wings to replace the Harrier is the Lockheed Martin F-35B Lightning II. It will serve aboard warships in Italy, the UK and the US, and may well find additional customers too. The UK's return to fixed-wing carrier operations has been predicated on the arrival of the F-35, and the design of the Royal Navy's two new carriers have been tailored to suit the aircraft. Carrier trials of the F-35B aboard HMS *Queen Elizabeth*, the first of a class of two warships, are due to begin in 2018.

The premise of this book is to describes the components of carrier aviation around the world, and the ships from which they operate. What constitutes an aircraft carrier is open to debate. It is noteworthy that Russia described its sole aircraft carrier, *Admiral Kuznetsov*, as a 'heavy aircraft-carrying cruiser', although it deploys CTOL aircraft from its deck, although these are launched using a ski jump rather than a catapult. The US Navy's largest amphibious assault ships are not aircraft carriers in the strictest sense, but they are able to embark significant aviation components – including fixed-wing aircraft – that are at least as capable as those of the navies operating 'true' aircraft carriers.

For the purposes of this book, an 'aircraft carrier' is a vessel able to regularly embark fixed-wing aviation assets. While there exist certain amphibious assault ships from which fixed-wing aircraft – and in particular those with STOVL capabilities – could potentially operate, these are excluded from this book, together with smaller helicopter-carrying vessels. Some of these latter are, in practice, little different from their fixed-wing-capable sisters. For instance, Australia's *Canberra*-class landing helicopter docks (LHD) are a derivative of the Spanish *Juan Carlos I* design, which routinely embarks Harrier IIs. For now, however, the Australian ships operate only rotorcraft. The same goes for the Japanese *Izumo*-class 'helicopter destroyer', the country's largest surface combatants. This reportedly incorporates some design elements that would enable the (future) deployment of fixed-wing aircraft. Meanwhile, the definition of 'fixed wing' excludes tiltrotor type aircraft – namely the Bell Boeing V-22 Osprey – which straddles the capabilities of a fixed-wing aircraft an a helicopter, and which can be increasingly be found operating from both traditional carrier decks and assault ships.

Acknowledgements

This book would not have been possible without the generous contributions and enthusiasm of the following contributors, who are listed alphabetically:

Stanislav Bazhenov, Luigino Caliaro, Giovanni Colla, Richard Cooper, Marco Dijkshoorn, Alexandre Galante, Salvador Marín González, Remo Guidi, Lt Col Dirk Heinzmann, Sergey Kuznetsov, Georg Mader, Salvador Mafé Huertas, Alexander Mladenov, João Paulo Moralez, Riccardo Nicoli, Carlos Filipe Operti, Wolfgang Pusztai, Santiago Rivas, Patrick Rogiues, Luigi Sani, Rob Schleifert, Angad Singh, Katsuhiko Tokunaga/ D.A.C.T., Christian Valverde, Cees-Jan van der Ende and Andreas Zeitler.

Thomas Newdick, November 2017

Abbreviations

AAM	air-to-air missile
AASM	Armement Air-Sol Modulaire, Modular Air-to-ground Armament, also known as Hammer, for Highly Agile, Modular Munition Extended Range
AB	Air Base
ACE	Aviation Combat Element (US Marine Corps)
AESA	active electronically scanned array
AEW	airborne early warning
AMRAAM	Advanced Medium-Range Air-to-Air Missile
AOO	area of operations
ARG	Amphibious Ready Group (US Marine Corps)
ASW	anti-submarine warfare
ASuW	anti-surface warfare
BVR	beyond visual range
CATOBAR	catapult assisted take-off but arrested recovery
CCD	charge coupled device
C-i-C	commander-in-chief
CMFD	colour multifunction display
COD	carrier on-board delivery
CSG	carrier strike group
CTOL	conventional take-off and landing
CVW	carrier air wing
Det./DET	detachment
EMALS	electromagnetic aircraft launch system
EW	electronic warfare
FAB	Força Aérea Brasileira, Brazilian Air Force
FLIR	forward-looking infrared
FOC	full operational capability
FRS	Fleet Replacement Squadron
FY	Fiscal Year (US), starting on 1 October
GAE	Groupe Aérien Embarqué, French carrier air group
HM	Helicopter Mine Countermeasures Squadron
HOTAS	hands on throttle and stick
HSC	Helicopter Sea Control Squadron
HSM	Helicopter Maritime Strike Squadron
IFF	identification friend or foe
INAS	Indian Naval Air Squadron
INS	Indian Navy Ship and Indian Naval Station
IOC	initial operational capability
kW	kilowatts
LAMPS	Light Airborne Multipurpose System
LDS	landing platform ship
LHA	amphibious assault ship
LHD	amphibious assault ship
LPD	landing platform dock

MAGTF	Marine Air-Ground Task Force (US Marine Corps)
MAW	Marine Aircraft Wing
MAWS	missile approach warning system
MCAS	Marine Corps Air Station
MEDEVAC	medical evacuation
MEU	Marine Expeditionary Unit
NAe	Navio Aeródromo, aerodrome ship (Brazil)
NAeL	Navio Aeródromo Leve, light aerodrome ship (Brazil)
NAS	Naval Air Station
nm	nautical miles
N/T	Navio Tanque, replenishment oiler/tanker
NVG	night vision goggles
OBOGS	on-board oxygen generating system
OCU	operational conversion unit
OKIAP	Otdelnyi Korabelnyi Istrebitelnyi Aviatsionnyi Polk, Independent Shipborne Fighter Aviation Regiment (Russia)
PEAMB	Plano de Equipamento e Articulação da Marinha do Brasil, Brazilian Navy's Equipment and Force Distribution Plan
PLAN	People's Liberation Army Navy (China)
RCOH	refueling complex overhaul
RN	Royal Navy (United Kingdom)
RWR	radar warning receiver
SAR	search and rescue
shp	shaft horsepower
SLEP	service-life extension program
STOBAR	short take-off but arrested recovery
STOVL	short take off and vertical landing
TACAN	tactical air navigation system
USD	US Dollar
USMC	US Marine Corps
VAQ	Electronic Attack Squadron
VAW	Carrier Airborne Early Warning Squadron
VFA	Strike Fighter Squadron
VMFA	Marine Strike Fighter Squadron
VMFAT	Marine Strike Fighter Training Squadron
VMM	Marine Medium Tiltrotor Squadron
VOD	vertical on-board delivery
VRC	Fleet Logistic Support Squadron (Composite)
VTOL	vertical take-off and landing
VX	Air Test & Evaluation Squadron

Chapter 1

BRAZIL

Felipe Salles

On 14 February 2017 the Brazilian Admiralty announced that the aircraft carrier NAe *São Paulo* (A12) would not undergo the large-scale upgrade programme originally planned. The proposal would have allowed it to soldier on for another 30 years. According to the announced, the cost of the upgrade would have been similar to buying a brand-new carrier besides requiring around 10 years to be completed. But at the same time the admirals made clear that this change of plan by no means implied the end of carrier aviation for the Brazilian Navy. Instead, they confirmed that an acquisition plan for new carriers had been moved up the naval service's priorities list and that fixed-wing aviation squadrons would continue with their training programmes. Their work would be carried out both from the naval air station at São Pedro d'Aldeia and using 'carriers from friendly nations'.

Marinha do Brasil
(Brazilian Navy)

Aviação Naval Brasileira
(Brazilian Naval Aviation)

Roundel of Brazilian
Naval Aviation

Historical ambitions

Throughout most of its almost 200 years of history the Brazilian Navy has harboured blue-water naval ambitions. For this reason Brazil managed to join the select club – together with France and the United States – of navies with a commissioned steam-catapult-equipped carrier in its fleet. These bold ambitions, as it turned out, have exceeded both Brazil's national political and geopolitical ambitions as well as the economic, technological and human means to support them. Today, however, the greatest threat to Brazilian carrier aviation might come from 'friendly fire' as Brazilian Navy proponents of the country's nuclear-powered attack submarine programme began to see the NAe *São Paulo* and its fixed-wing naval aviation as a key competitor for the scarce available funding. After 2014 this situation became critical when the disastrous effects of the 2008 global economic crisis finally hit the Brazilian government in full.

The complicated political and economic environment in which the carrier and fixed-wing naval aviation exist in is no way a recent development for the Brazilian Navy. In 1904 the Brazilian naval equipment plan decided in favour of the acquisition from British shipyards of three state-of-the art 19,250-ton dreadnoughts. This was to be the opening salvo in a regional naval arms race waged against Argentina and Chile to determine which country would have naval pre-eminence in South America. At the time, these ships then even larger than those being supplied to the Royal Navy. Two of these giants[1] made it to Brazil where the Brazilian Navy painfully discovered it lacked

◄ NAe *São Paulo* (A12)
(Cees-Jan van der Ende)

The NAeL *Minas Gerais* (A11) underway in 1996. (Rob Schleiffert)

the trained human resources as well as the local technical infrastructure to operate them to the fullest.

Four decades later, with Brazil having fought against the Axis powers on the side of the Allies, the process repeated itself in the aftermath of World War II. Having seen the critical contribution of modern aircraft carriers in the Pacific theatre, the Brazilian Navy seized the opportunity to acquire its first carrier vessel when the British decided to sell off most of the Royal Navy's wartime carrier fleet. The Brazilian Navy saw the carrier as the natural substitute for the dreadnoughts at the top of the naval hierarchy but it had to fight off multiple opponents to the idea in order to make it happen. Internally, the 1941 creation of the independent Força Aérea Brasileira (FAB, Brazilian Air Force) was responsible for the traumatic excision of navy aviation and its subsequent consolidation with the army's air units, taking with it the navy's pilots and maintainers. Within the Brazilian Navy at the time, the officers and ratings that chose to transfer to the new military branch were billed as 'traitors'. Because of this the FAB and Brazilian Navy endured a difficult relationship in those early years. During one occasion, on 5 December 1964, FAB infantry shot at a refuelling Brazilian Navy helicopter and arrested its crew.

Ironically, old regional rivalries also emerged at the same time in support of the admirals' plans when in 1958 the Argentine Navy acquired HMS *Warrior*, a surplus British Colossus-class carrier. The US government in general and the US Navy in particular failed to embrace Brazilian interest in carriers, in a bid to block the possible start of a new arms race between its local military partners. This in spite of the close working relationship between the US Navy and the Brazilian Navy combatting German submarines in the South Atlantic during World War II.

In response the Brazilian Navy cleverly played the 'specialist navy' card by proposing in return that its carrier would be no more than a heavy ASW platform equipped exclusively with the then brand-new Grumman S2F-1 Tracker anti-submarine aircraft. Much more complicated was the need to balance the internal conflict, namely the ongoing turf wars between the FAB and the Brazilian Navy.

The Brazilian aircraft carrier NAe *São Paulo* accompanied by its dedicated tanker N/T *Marajó*. (Carlos Filipe Operti)

The surplus Royal Navy carrier HMS *Vengeance* was purchased by Brazil in 1956 and the new NAeL *Minas Gerais* (A11) was commissioned at the beginning of 1961 after a major refurbishment period by the Dutch Verolme Shipyards. Work included the fitting of a new angled deck as well as other improvements.

Along with the new carrier the Brazilian Navy bought six Pilatus P.3 trainers, three Grumman TBM Avenger and eight second-hand North American T-28 Trojans. The tense situation can be measured by the fact that aircraft of the Brazilian Navy's first helicopter unit (HU-1) were described as 'unidentified flying objects' by the Brazilian Air Force and were also charged with being a 'menace to commercial traffic' at the nearby Galeão Airport. Eventually it was left to General Castello Branco, the first Brazilian post-coup president, to decide in 1965 that fixed-wing aircraft flown from the carrier would be owned and operated by the Brazilian Air Force, while helicopters would belong to the Brazilian Navy. For that reason six FAB Sikorsky H-34 (HSS-1) ASW helicopters were transferred to naval control that year. This was a political settlement that only managed to promote the inter-force conflict since in the end it actually displeased both sides.

The NAeL *Minas Gerais* underwent a major technological overhaul period at the Rio de Janeiro Navy Arsenal (AMRJ) between 1975 and 1979 allowing the Brazilian Air Force to further postpone their upgrade plans for its carrier aircraft. In the end, mostly due to the lack of spares for its obsolete radial engines, the venerable Trackers (designated P-16 by the FAB) were finally removed from service in 1996 with no substitute being available or procured. From 1965 until their demise in 1998, the FAB P-16s of the 'Cardeal' Squadron spent 1,382 days at sea totalling 14,072 day-time and 2,764 night-time landings on board, as well as 2,944 catapult-assisted take-offs.

At that time only the US was developing new carrier aircraft, making it hard to find new fixed-wing platforms able to operate from the small-decked *Minas Gerais*. The Brazilian Air Force budget spent on carrier aviation was seen by its generals[2] as an unjustifiable waste at a time when there were simply no funds available for its own core missions. The FAB's inability to comply with its side of the 1965 deal turned the

Minas Gerais into an exclusive helicopter carrier. This was also seen as a tacit 'green light' for the navy to rekindle its efforts for the recreation of fixed-wing naval aviation.

On 19 December 1997 the navy signed a Memorandum of Understanding with the Kuwait Air Force for the acquisition of 23 surplus McDonnell Douglas A-4KU/TA-4KU Skyhawk attack aircraft; the definitive contract was signed on the 30th of that month. Before these aircraft were delivered to Brazil both the *Minas Gerais* and the naval air station at São Pedro d'Aldeia would undergo their own modification programmes to be able to support the new aircraft. The navy knew from the beginning that in operational terms the small-decked *Minas Gerais* was only marginally suited for the Skyhawk. The maximum speeds attainable by the old steam plant and the reduced size of the deck meant that on wind-less days flight operations would be impossible with the A-4 at its maximum take-off weight. In fact, this very limitation would soon end up being employed by the navy as an argument for its replacement by a larger carrier.

Plans to build a new carrier were soon trumped by a French offer for the sale of the recently retired *Foch* (R99). The purchase was completed in September 2000 and the ship was commissioned as NAe *São Paulo* (A12) just two months later, arriving in Rio de Janeiro on 17 February 2001. The ship's initial operational period was one of many days at sea with a great number of helicopter and fighter pilots being qualified. In the end, however, a number of serious and fatal mishaps, only natural in a ship of this age, would combine to restrict the availability of the Brazilian Navy's capital ship.

During President Luis Inácio Lula da Silva's second term in office (2007 to 2011) the defence ministry obtained the president's approval for a significant naval construction and acquisitions plan, the Plano de Equipamento e Articulação da Marinha do Brasil (PAEMB, Brazilian Navy's Equipment and Force Distribution Plan). This included two new-built 50-60,000-ton carriers, four landing platform docks (LPDs), six nuclear attack submarines, 15 conventional submarines, 30 escort ships, and other items. However, the severe economic crisis that hit Brazil beginning in 2014 brought this programme to a near-standstill and indefinitely postponed most of these plans.

While Brazil's plans to return the S-2 Tracker to carrier decks may never be realised, the Argentinian Navy trained twice on board the NAe *São Paulo*, during exercises Araex 2003 and 2004.
(Rob Schleiffert)

The Aviação Naval Brasileira (Brazilian Naval Aviation) operates a single squadron of AF-1s.
(Cees-Jan van der Ende)

São Paulo air wing

Operating on a much more modest scale than those of the US Navy, Brazilian naval aviation squadrons' aircraft and personnel deploy on the *São Paulo* as a much simpler Grupo Aéreo Embarcado (Embarked Air Group) and not as part of a US Navy-style pre-existing carrier air wing. Without an independent carrier air wing commanding officer (CO) the several aviation squadron detachments' heads must report directly to the ship's CO for the length of the cruise. Since for the aforementioned reasons the *São Paulo* has mostly not operated on back-to-back long-term (non-training) patrols, the definitive shape and numbers of the air assets to be deployed on its deck and in its hangar are fairly open.

The main aircraft type operating on the *São Paulo* is VF-1 squadron's A-4KU (better known as AF-1 in Brazilian Navy parlance). Twelve AF-1s (nine single-seaters and three two-seat trainers[3]) were set to modernised to a much improved specification by Embraer at its Gavião Peixoto plant. However, work is proceeding at a slow pace. After the decision was made to decommission the *São Paulo*, the Brazilian Navy adjusted the number of AF-1s to be modernised to seven, including in this total the lost modernised aircraft . The upgraded model has a new Elta EL-2032 multifunction radar capable capable of cueing not only short-range infrared-guided air-to-air missiles (AAMs), but also radar-guided beyond-visual-range (BVR) missiles – a capacity that no previous A-4 variant has had. In terms of air-to-ground missions the modernised Skyhawk is able to launch GPS- or laser-guided bombs and is able to have anti-ship missiles integrated in future. Inside the cockpit are two new 5in × 7in tactical displays, a colour multifunction

Brazilian Navy S-70B N-3035 operated by HS-1 squadron. (João Paulo Moralez)

display (CMFD) and hands on throttle and stick (HOTAS) controls. Extra power for these new electronics will be supplied by a completely new generator system. A new on-board oxygen generating system (OBOGS) is being added in place of the original pressurised bottle system. In terms of communication, new Rohde & Schwartz M3AR radios will simplify joint operations with FAB aircraft and ground control stations as well as allowing for future datalink usage. A new radar warning receiver (RWR) set is added together with a third VHF radio for the datalink. The overhauled automatic pilot unit is being integrated with the radio altimeter, TACAN and a new-generation inertial navigation unit and now also receives data from the engine. The J52-P-408 engines are being overhauled in Israel by Israel Aerospace Industries (IAI). Unfortunately, the first aircraft delivered back to the Brazilian Navy was lost on 26 July 2016 following an in-flight collision with another modernised A-4.

Although the IH-6B from HI-1 training squadron does not belong to the carrier wing, it has been a frequent visitor to the carrier.
(Santiago Rivas)

Locally built at Helibras, an Airbus Helicopters subsidiary, the Brazilian Navy operates three variants of the UH-15. Seen here is the utility variant. (Alexandre Galante)

The current plan is for the Skyhawks to eventually be replaced by a new carrier-capable version of the Brazilian Air Force's Saab F-39E/F Gripen (JAS 39E/F in Swedish parlance). The navalised Sea Gripen concept is currently being discussed with the Brazilian Navy's Aeronautics Directorate but actual orders are still some years down the line. The first Brazilian production batch of 36 Gripens will all be directed to the FAB, which has already indicated that it intends to acquire two follow-on batches of the same size. The PAEMB plans indicated a Brazilian Navy need for 48 new supersonic carrier-compatible fighters.

Complementing the Skyhawks and their eventual successors on the *São Paulo*'s replacement were to be two new derivatives of the Grumman Tracker. The first version, to be named KC-2 in Brazilian Navy service (due to its level of simplicity), is a Garrett TPE331 turboprop-equipped Grumman C-1 Trader that will be used for carrier

Seen in September 2002, AF-1 N-1011 from VF-1 squadron is launched from NAe *São Paulo*. (Rob Schleiffert)

UH-12 N-7051, a locally built AS.350 Squirrel, during carrier trials. HS-1 Squadron used the Sikorsky/Agusta Sea King helicopters before converting to the newer MH-16 Seahawks (Cees-Jan van der Ende)

on-board delivery (COD) as well as for air-to-air refuelling in support of the Skyhawks. The second and much more complex version was an airborne early warning (AEW) radar equipped S-2 Tracker. Originally the conversion work was to be completed by Embraer, but the Brazilian manufacturer left the programme due to the lack of funds and the small number of aircraft to be converted. Since 2010 the required S-2/C-1A airframes have been acquired by the Brazilian Navy from US Navy stocks and sent to Marsh Aviation's Mesa, Arizona facilities. Unfortunately, previous US export law violations by Marsh led to delays and eventually the programme's transfer to Elbit's M7 subsidiary in San Antonio, Texas. At the time of writing the AEW variant had been officially dropped from navy plans.

Deliveries of four COD aircraft were initially expected between 2011 and 2012 but this programme is running behind schedule and a crippling lack of funds has delayed deliveries to 2021. Although representing a design that is over 50 years old, the S-2/C-1 family remains the only carrier-capable platform available on the market that can safely operate on a carrier of *São Paulo*'s size. Considering the S-2's original mission, it is perhaps surprising that the Brazilian Navy currently has no plans for fielding a modernised ASW variant of the Tracker.

Under the defence ministry's H-XBR programme, a total of 50 Airbus Helicopters H225M (previously known as Eurocopter EC725) aircraft were contracted to be locally manufactured for all three armed forces by Brazilian subsidiary Helibras. The navy requested three variants of the Super Cougar: the UH-15, a 'vanilla' fleet support cargo and marine troop carrier helicopter; the AH-15B, an anti-surface warfare (ASuW) launch platform for two AM.39 M2B2 Exocet anti-ship missiles, and equipped with a new Brazilian-developed systems console for the operator in the cabin; and the intermediate UH-15A search and rescue (SAR) model, five of which are on order. Due to their size and flightdeck footprint it is expected that these large helicopters could potentially be based on the Brazilian carrier once they become operational. All three models are to be operated by HU-2 squadron.

The most advanced AH-15B model has a nose-mounted navigation radar, a 360° Telephonics AN/APS-143V maritime search radar, a forward-looking infrared (FLIR)/charge coupled device (CCD)/TV/laser rangefinder/thermal vision and digital intelligence gathering system, as well as a laser warning system, missile approach warning system (MAWS), an RWR and chaff/flare launchers on both sides of the airframe. The SAR model is virtually identical to the ASuW version minus the AM.39 missile systems, the Telephonics radar and the operator console.

Another specialist mission aircraft that can be a part of the *São Paulo* air wing is the Sikorsky SH-16 Seahawk. Although designated SH-60 locally, the Brazilian Navy version is in reality a Sikorsky S-70B. These aircraft are flown by HS-1 squadron and are equipped with dipping sonar and AGM-119 Penguin anti-ship missiles. The PAEMB plan calls for a total of 50 Seahawks to be procured under the Multi-Role Helicopter (HME) programme but so far only the initial six have been procured.

Since the 1980s the plane guard task (callsign 'Pedro' during day time and 'Paulo' at night) has been the responsibility of a pair of HU-1's Eurocopter AS350/355 (UH-12/UH-13) Esquilo light multipurpose helicopters. Occasionally seen on the deck of Brazilian carriers are the Bell IH-6B JetRanger helicopters belong to the HI-1 training squadron. They are sometimes used as ad hoc navy VIP transports for short-range ship visits.

HS-1

HU-1

HU-2

VF-1

Brazilian carrier aviation – current units

Unit	Aircraft type	Role	Base	Remarks
HS-1	SH-16 Seahawk	ASW, ASuW	São Pedro d'Aldeia	6/6 S-70B-2 (on order/delivered)
HU-1	UH-12/ UH-13 Esquilo	Utility	São Pedro d'Aldeia	6 UH-12 (AS350B Squirrel) 7 UH-13 (AS355F-2 Twin Squirrel)
HU-2	UH-15/ UH-15A/AH-15B Super Cougar	Utility/ SAR/ASuW	São Pedro d'Aldeia	8/7 UH-15, 3/2 UH-15A, 5/0 UH-15B (H225M)
VEC-1	KC-2 Turbo Trader	COD, in-flight refuelling	São Pedro d'Aldeia	C-1A; 4/0; first aircraft expected to be delivered in first quarter of 2021
VF-1	AF-1 Skyhawk	Fighter	São Pedro d'Aldeia	A-4KU, 23 purchased from Kuwait, 12 to be modernised by Embraer (9 x AF-1, 3 x AF-1A); one modernised AF-1A lost in mid-air collision in 2016

Troubled voyage

On February 2005, as the NAe *São Paulo* departed Rio de Janeiro for a series of AF-1 carrier qualification exercises, a steam duct ruptured inside the kitchen area killing a non-commissioned officer and injuring seven others. This accident marked the beginning of a long period of operational unavailability for the Brazilian carrier. The navy decided to replace a significant portion of the steam ducts that had been corroded by years of service and were found to be paper-thin in various places. The next problem to be dealt with was the need to replace one of the main propeller shafts that warped after sagging under its own weight during the period the ship remained inoperative. After months of negotiating the NAe *São Paulo* was fitted with a spare shaft supplied

from French stocks. To try to make the most of the forced operational pause, this period was used for many small fixes around the ship, while waiting for the imminent restart of training and recertification cruises.

The cockpit of the first upgraded AF-1A.
(João Paulo Moralez)

Upgrade plans

Convinced that more than ever the *São Paulo* needed to be upgraded in order to bridge the gap until the commissioning of any future carrier, the admirals drew and redrew their construction plans as the next ships' in-service date slipped further and further into the 2030s and 2040s. When in 2015 independent engineering consultants vouched for the good state of the ship's hull and structure the navy settled for a DCNS concept of replacing the whole original steam powerplant of the *São Paulo* with a completely new diesel-electric powerplant. Due to its comprehensive nature this was to be an expensive and invasive process to achieve the same configuration that was originally conceived for the future French PA2 aircraft carrier program. With this modernization costing upwards of USD 1 billion the Navy decided to temporarily reduce the manning levels on *São Paulo* to a minimum crew in order to weather the next years' cash-strapped period.

To the Admiralty the definitive 2017 announcement amounted to a very hard choice. In the end it reflected the realisation that when finally the ship returned to service the AF-1 fighters onboard would be functionally obsolete and incapable to operate its intended mission. By not modernizing the *São Paulo* all the money saved could instead be directed to the purchase of a brand new carrier and its modern aircraft. To compensate for this abrupt change of plans the new generation carrier was bumped up to third place in the Brazilian Navy's priority list of industrial programs, now sitting right behind the coveted new (nuclear-powered and conventional) submarines and the

A meeting of old and new: the Brazilian Navy's AIM-9H missiles came from Kuwait together with the Skyhawks. The Brazilian-developed Acauã GPS/Galileo/GLONASS compatible kit for standard Mk 80 series bombs is due to enter production soon.
(Cees-Jan van der Ende)

new indigenous corvettes. Brazilian naval aviation squadrons and its personnel and aircraft are to go about their daily routines unaffected and eventual pilot qualification carrier landings are expected to happen on 'ships of friendly nations'. This seems to be a thinly veiled reference to France's carrier *Charles de Gaulle* as the steel rope bridle configured AF-1s no longer can be launched from the US Navy's nose gear launch bar catapults.

Conclusion

Responding to internal and external 'specialized navy' proponents the Brazilian Navy opted to become a 'balanced navy' instead, a force that has the means to achieve the four basic tasks of sea power: sea denial, sea control, projection of power ashore and also to contribute to [conventional] dissuasion.

The Brazilian National Defense White Book states that 'a naval force composed of different types of ships built around an aircraft carrier, offers mobility, permanence, visibility and versatility allowing for a wide spectrum of missions, from humanitarian to peace keeping to those typical of an international crisis or an armed conflict'. Beyond any current or future funding restrictions, matching a full-fledged carrier navy to the Brazilian political/geopolitical directives is still no simple task. Differently from Brazil the other carrier operators like China, France, Russia, the UK and the US all have military intervention as a long standing normal paradigm in their foreign policies. Brazil in its National Defence Strategy has chosen to present itself as 'a country that will not project power abroad' ... Naval historian Norman Polmar identified five historical roles for carriers: land attack from the sea, sea base for helicopter assault against land, nuclear strike, capital ship in fleet-against-fleet combat and defense of the fleet at sea from enemy aircraft and submarines. Of these only the last two would

As the sun sets on the *São Paulo*'s operational career, the Brazilian Navy's fixed-wing aviation is set to soldier on until a new carrier is procured for it to operate from. (Cees-Jan van der Ende)

be unquestionably cases for Brazilian Navy use. Nuclear weapons are constitutionally off-limits in Brazil and roles one and two would only be fully politically acceptable as either a limited defensive measure relating to the extraction of Brazilian nationals threatened abroad or alternatively under the clear mandate of the UN or another international multinational organisation. Brazilian naval aviation is real but it has so far found it difficult to achieve its full potential for the many reasons described above.

A century later and despite all shortcomings today's Brazilian admirals like their bold predecessors have decided to punch through trying economic times making very hard decisions in order to be able to reach the point in time where the Brazilian government strategic vision will finally evolve to match their own.

1 Of the three battleships ordered by Brazil, two were delivered (*Minas Gerais* and *São Paulo*) and the third, *Rio de Janeiro*, was sold to the Ottoman Navy while still under construction. This ship was eventually taken over by the Royal Navy as HMS *Agincourt* during World War I.
2 Brigadeiros in FAB terminology.
3 In an unorthodox manner, the original Skyhawk single-seaters are known in the Brazilian Navy as AF-1 (no suffix) and twin-seaters as AF-1A. Modernised aircraft are designated AF-1B and AF-1C, respectively.

A hypothetical Brazilian carrier air wing

No. of aircraft	Type	Role and remarks
6–8	AF-1	Air defence
2–3	AF-1A	Air defence
3	UH-15A	SAR
3	UH-15B	ASuW
3	SH-16	ASW
17–22		

A Brazilian carrier battle group

No.	Ship class	Ship name	Fleet	Displacement	Crew
1	*Clemenceau*-class aircraft carrier	NAe *São Paulo* (A12)		24,200	1,920
2	Type-22 *Broadsword 1*-class frigate	*F Greenhalgh* (F46) *F Rademaker* (F49)		4,500 4,500	222 222
2	*Niterói*-class Mk 10 anti-submarine frigate	(F40-F45) (F40-F45)		3,355 3,355	217 217
1	Tanker	NT *Marajó* (G27)		16,000	121
1	Replenishment oiler	NT *Almirante Gastão Motta* (G23)		10,300	121
					3,040

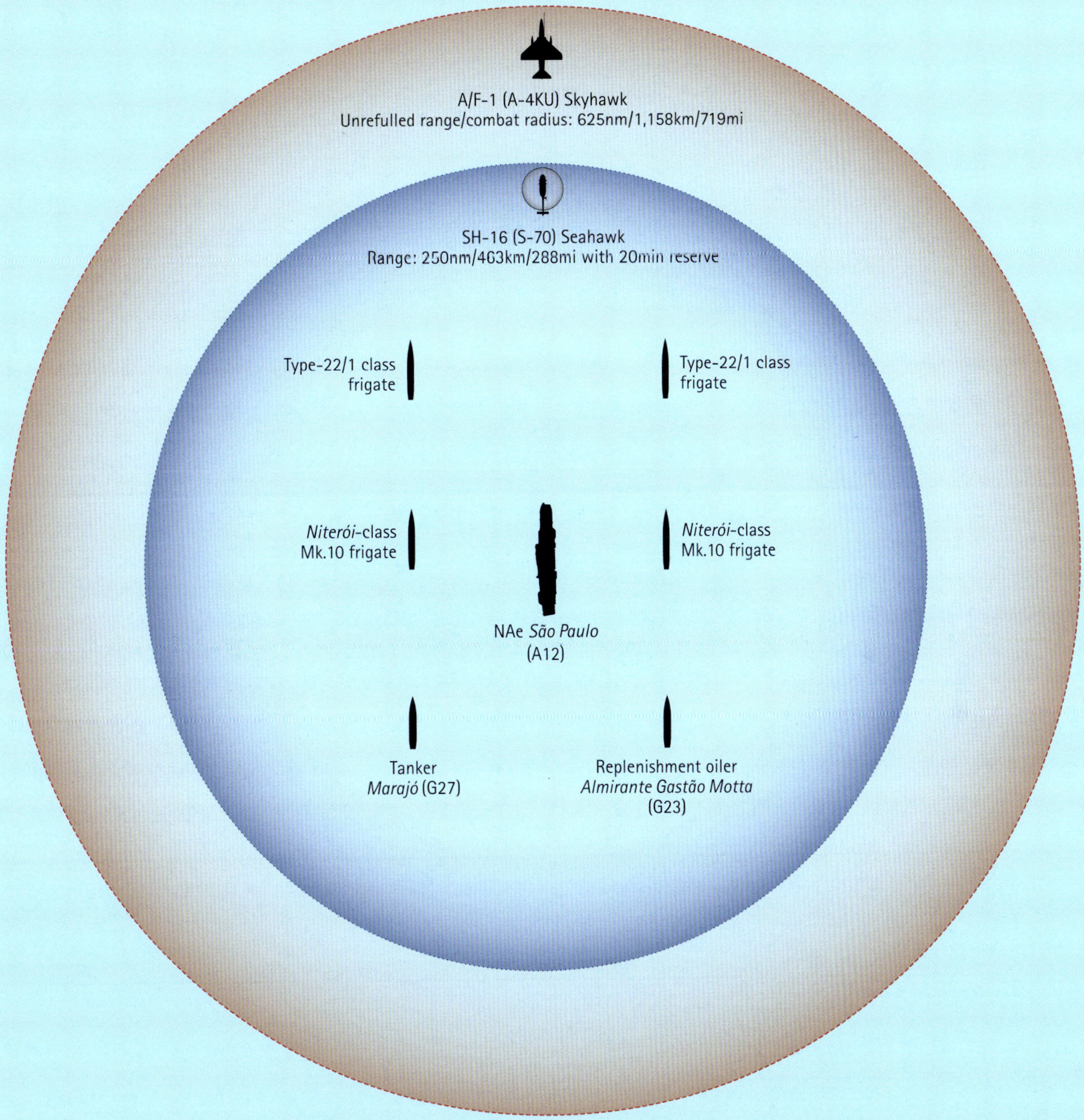

This is a purely schematic presentation of a likely carrier battle group and is not to scale.
In reality, the composition of such a force is dependent on various parameters.

Chapter 2

CHINA

Andreas Rupprecht

PLAN emblem

Although in the Chinese Naval Aviation, often still known by its old name PLANAF, naval aircraft are operated from land bases since some years, the aircraft carrier has only become one of the most recent tools for the Chinese Navy's ambitions for projecting power into its area of interest, but the goal is clear: China is due to establish a decent carrier force and it is not that far-fetched to assume that in a few years it will maintain the world's second largest fleet of carriers.

When the former *Varyag* was commissioned into People's Liberation Army Navy (PLAN) service on 25 September 2012 with the new pennant number as *Liaoning* (CV-16) many observers were still questioning how far the program to achieve operational status – either as a training carrier or a combat platform – might actually have progressed. Now, almost four years later, the People's Liberation Army Navy has officially announced China first aircraft carrier, the *Liaoning* (CV-16), as ready for combat operations. Senior Captain Li Dongyou, the political commissar of the carrier, was quoted by the state-owned *Global Times* newspaper on 14 November 2016 that 'as a military force, we are always combat ready and our combat capacity also needs to be tested by war. At this moment, we are doing our best to promote our strength and use it to prevent war. But we are preparing for actual combat at any time'. Anyway and regardless all claims, the main function is and will be for long to act as a pure training vessel.

PLA Naval Aviation

Roundel of PLA Naval Aviation

A historical review

Even if the public has surely learned in recent years not to underestimate the Chinese Military, its Aviation and Shipbuilding Industry and the news it delivers at a rate no-one would have expected years before, it surely is still a long way to go until a full 'blue-water Navy' will become operational. Anyway these steps are only the most recent results of China's ambitions to gain a carrier capability, which actually have their beginnings more than 25 years ago.

When the former *Varyag* was acquired in early 2002 under the disguise of being transformed into a floating casino nearly all observers highly questioned this story and as such its transformation into the *Liaoning* (CV-16) was followed closely during the following years.

◄ China's first aircraft carrier Type 001 *Liaoning* (CV-16) (via CDF/China Defense Forum)

Seen in April 2010, the former *Varyag* seen during her refit at the shipyard in Dalian. Clearly visible is the more or less completely refurbished island still painted in red especially the huge parts where the new AESA arrays are installed. (via Top.81-Forum)

Since the early 1970s, PLAN was considering the development of a carrier. At that time, General Liu Huaqing was pushing hard for a carrier but in the end it did not take place for a variety of reasons. The original projects were known as 'Project 707' and '891'. They never progressed to a stage where detailed plans were drawn. In general, it seems as if Chinese aircraft carrier development was scheduled in three phases: from 1975 on demonstration on options, from 1985 on technical research and from about 2000 on construction, so that in fact the revised plan to reconstruct the *Varyag* in 2004 came to a generally similar timing. However, the first official considerations by the PLAN in regard to an aircraft carrier date back to 31 March 1987 when the state Commission of Science, Technology and Industry for National Defence approved Admiral Liu Huaqing's plan on an aircraft carrier program in a staged program. Admiral Liu Huaqing's – then the PLAN's C-in-C – is often called the father of China's aircraft carrier project and the creator of the modern PLAN. Under his auspices the PLAN's maritime doctrine was altered dramatically, which included a true blue-water navy capable of projecting power into the western Pacific. However the original plans proved to be too ambitious as the domestic industry at the time could not meet the original schedule. As a result, the plan was drastically scaled back to basic research level and the date for an aircraft carrier entering PLAN service was postponed and eventually put on hold. In the meantime, several efforts were initiated to gain as much knowledge and technology as possible several retired carriers were purchased for either scrap – like the *Majestic*-class aircraft carrier HMAS *Melbourne* from Australia, what provided a first insight into carrier construction – or later two *Kiev*-class carriers (the *Kiev* and *Minsk*) to convert them into game- or theme parks. In the early 1990s it was reported that China was interested in purchasing a carrier from abroad and for the first time rumours about alleged Sino-Ukrainian contacts to buy the unfinished Soviet *Kuznetsov*-class carrier *Varyag* appeared in 1992; however nothing happened at first.

In parallel to the efforts to study, develop and construct a carrier, the Chinese Central Military Commission (CMC) approved a program in May 1987 to prepare the commanders needed for its future aircraft carriers as well as training jet fighter pilots to be future captains. This was established at the Guangzhou Naval Academy.

Life of the *Liaoning* begun as the younger sister ship of the Russian carrier *Admiral Kuznetsov* that was never finished after the fall of the Soviet Union and had fallen into a state of disrepair. In 1992, Ukraine offered to sell the former *Varyag* for about USD 20 million. Consequently, PLAN set up a meeting with officials from various state-owned industrial organisations and shipbuilding teams to evaluate whether the *Varyag* was worth to purchase. In parallel, China was undergoing aircraft carrier research as part of Project 891. Coincidently both the meeting and the project reached came to the same conclusion: the PLAN would needed a CATOBAR carrier equipped with fixed-wing AEW&C aircraft and not a ski-ramp carrier with only helicopter-borne AEW&C. Thus, the PLAN decided not to purchase the *Varyag*. However a bit later, rumours appeared that the ship might be sold otherwise and even Republic of China based companies were interested to procure the *Varyag*. Consequently the central government reverted its original decision and decided to purchase the *Varyag*.

Regardless various concerns, the Ukrainian government sold the empty hull without rudders or engines – which by now has proven wrong – of the *Varyag* – named after the Varangians, as the Greeks named the Vikings, who ruled the medieval state of Rus' between the 9th and 11th centuries – in 1998 for about USD 20 million.

Officially the holding company reported plans to convert it a floating casino and hotel in Macao. Following long negotiations with Turkey – the new owner did not receive permission to pass through the Bosporus, the Straits of Istanbul – but finally in 2001, the *Varyag* was towed to China, passing through the Mediterranean, turned around Africa at the Cape of Good Hope headland, across the Indian Ocean, through the Straits of Malacca, into the China Sea and finally docked – not really surprising not in Macao but – at the Naval Shipyards in Dalian. In the meantime the holding company had disappeared. Here it lumbered on for well over two years under tight security and was undergoing significant works both at the shipyard and an adjacent dry-dock. Following these, the *Varyag* was painted in the standard PLAN navy colours, and in 2010 the PLAN indicated for the first time – leading to many speculations especially in regard to its engines – that the ship would become operational as a training carrier to gain experience in carrier operations while an indigenous carrier would be developed in parallel.

So when in 2002 *Varyag* arrived in China and in September 2003, the PLAN and CSIC officials conducted a condition evaluation of the hull. The analysis came to the conclusion that it was in good shape with only a 'thin' rust layer on top, under microscopic and elemental analysis, the underlying metal sheets were close to brand-new and predictions offered no issues in converting it to an operational platform'. Chief Architect for China's first aircraft carrier became Zhu Yingfu, director of the 701st Research Institute of the 7th Academy of China Shipbuilding Heavy Industrial Group. He is also the chief designer of the Type 052B and 052C destroyers and in 2011 he was elected as a member of the Chinese Academy of Engineering.

When the *Varyag* arrived in Dalian, it was almost only an empty hull plus some old engines. Contrary to rumours in the media that the Varyag was coming to China with a load of design drawings is wrong. There were none delivered and he noted that 'we did

From mid-2016 on the PLAN was expanding the training cruises with the *Liaoning* dramatically, including first steps into the Western Pacific and crossing the first island chain. During that time up to 13 J-15s were spotted on deck. (via Top.81-Forum)

not know at first what to do, because never before exposed to aircraft carrier design, nor is there any reference drawings'. The propulsion system was almost complete with some pipes and ducts unfinished, the electrical system however was desperate condition, mostly due to looting of the cables during its years of neglect. Some of the aviation facilities such as aircraft elevators and turntable were installed. No combat systems were installed. Officially the Varyag was about 60-70 per cent completed, but since the ship staying in Ukraine was exposed to the elements for a long time and a lot of equipment was demolished and damaged later at the yard, it had in fact to be rebuilt entirely again and at best about 40 per cent usable.

Finally on 14 September 2003, the Chinese president Hu Jintao visited the *Varyag* and the decision was made. Between September and October, PLAN and various institutes were discussing the several options on aircraft carrier development in general and concluded a proposal for rebuild of the *Varyag*. Already in November, an official report was submitted to the General Armaments Department and in June 2004, the General Staff Department, General Armaments Department, and COSTIND submitted a report on designing Chinese aircraft carriers to the State Council and CMC. This report was approved in August, and on 13 August the Chinese aircraft carrier project was officially commissioned as 'Project 048' (for 2004/8). Actual work on the future Liaoning began in October 2004. The first task was to draw up overall construction plans for the ship and China also tried to contact the former carrier's design site to provide help, but that request was rejected. Therefore, Ukrainian shipyard experts and former workers were invited to help, but again with only minor results. In the end, the *Varyag* was for us just a like an empty house, and we had to complete it by ourselves according to our needs'. That in return was a considerable difficult task since China had never drawn up such a large naval vessel but also an opportunity, since the former Soviet Union's Navy design ideas and concepts of aircraft carrier – which lays more emphasis on the overall capacity/capability of a single ship as exemplified by the unusual anti-ship-missile positions – was completely different to the US concept, which is more the concept the PLAN will emphasise.' Zhu Yingfu added. The plans were drawn up in little more than 12 months and the technical plans were completed after three years and the analysis of the ship helped a lot to understand the way in which the PLAN could operate the *Liaoning*.

From construction start in October 2004 to the day *Liaoning* was commissioned in 2012, it took eight years and several Chinese sources assume that reconstruction of this ship was barely easier, if at all, than designing a new ship, even if the old 'Projects 707' and '891' never progressed to a stage where detailed plans were ever drawn up.

Between 2010 and summer 2011, the *Varyag* received its sensors and weapons systems and by August 2011 – after initial dock side testing of the engines as well as a first Z-8 landing test on deck – the new carrier appeared ready for the first sea trial. This in fact begun on 9 August 2011 and by September 2012, the ship had completed a total of ten shipyard sea trials since her launch. All speculations ended with the painting of the pennant number '16' on both sides of the bow and on the forward part of her ski-jump in September 2012 and with the renaming as *Liaoning* she was handed over to the PLAN on 23 September 2012. In regard to the next steps, the PLA Chief of the General Staff Cheng Bingde had confirmed in June 2011 that China's plans to construct its own aircraft carrier soon, which is said to be an indigenous design with a conventional power plant and the first of two ships is expected to be built at the Jiangnan Shipyard near Shanghai.

Status

The former *Varyag* was officially handed over to the PLAN on 23 September 2012 and was commissioned two days later on 25 September 2012. During the commissioning ceremony the carrier's name was officially mentioned for the first time as *Liaoning*, in honor of the province in which the ship was rebuild. In Chinese service the carrier call is known as Type 001 and the CV-16 serves as a training carrier from its home port at Qingdao, even if it was declared fully operational in September 2016 also as an operational ship.

China so far has only one aircraft carrier operational and quite interesting the Chinese Navy considers the ship as a true aircraft carrier. For its future plans however there are contradicting reports. Chinese media reported for the first time on 7 June 2011, People's Liberation Army Chief of the General Staff Chen Bingde confirmed that China was constructing its own aircraft carrier. However he stated that no further details would be provided until it was completed. Other reports, some by retired or still active military members like General Luo Yuan were already noting that at least two aircraft carriers were planned to be built at the Jiangnan Shipyard in Shanghai. This has proven wrong, since the actual Type 001A vessel was still under construction at the Dalian Shipyard and – at least until mid-2017 – there are no signs of a carrier currently under construction at Jiangnan. Therefore it can be assumed that the Chinese carrier program has experienced some changes in schedule and capabilities and it seems as if indeed originally the first indigenous carrier was planned to be built at that time at Jiangnan. Following the revised plans, the true carrier Type 002 at Jiangnan was postponed or delayed and it was decided – as confirmed in December 2013 by the powerful China Central Military Commission – at first to commission two *Liaoning*-pattern aircraft carriers by 2020, which were long classified as Type 001A again featuring a ski-jump with the Type 002 to follow when the catapult technology has matured. Only in August 2017, it was revealed that the new carrier is already the Type 002 and so consequently the future CATOBAR-carrier project will most likely be the Type 003.

In consequence since the first Type 002 vessel has left the dry-dock at Dalian in April 2017 or first images appear at Jiangnan, there are currently two possibilities discussed: Following the first option, and these plans also seem to have been revised again, foll-

The aircaft carrier *Liaoning* with its carrier strike group (training) some time in July or August 2016 during intensive training in undisclosed waters. (via http://eng.chinamil.com.cn/)

woing the launch of the first ship of the Type 002 in April 2017, it be followed by again a revised design for long called Type 001B but featuring probably some changes like the deletion of the ski-ramp and the inclusion of catapults as an intermediate step before work on the Type 003 will begin.

Following the second option, which is according to latest the more likely one, the construction of the Type 003 vessel has indeed already begun, but slowed down. This would fit to a report from December 2016, when a brief report about the Jiangnan Shipyard near Shanghai by Professor Jin Yinan – director of the strategic research institute at the PLA's National Defence University – noted that the first true indigenous carrier is already under construction at JNCX. In the end he stated that this carrier is already under construction as a 'flat deck, catapult take off' carrier, which is quite consistent with known rumours, even if he did not specify when the first 'steel was cut'. Given the carrier-construction progress of the Type 002 vessel, which was first spotted with a bit of certainty in February 2015 for the first time as a 'huge ship under construction at Dalian' and that about half a year later in August/September 2015 it was finally clearly identified as a carrier, the spotter communitly for long expected a first clear confirmation of a carrier under construction at Jiangnan at best by mid to late-2017 or early 2018; this however changed again.

In parallel to the carrier construction itself and again a strong indication for that the Type 003 will be a true catapult equipped 'super carrier', both EMALS and steam powered catapults have been constructed at the Huangdicun Naval Air Base for testing. This base is the regular home of the 'Carrier Air Wing', especially for the J-15s and it includes already a facility to train the Naval Aviation pilots on carrier-take-off and landing procedures. The first flight of the improved catapult-capable J-15T occurred in July 2016 and that aircraft was already tested allegedly off the catapult – quite surprisingly from the EMALS at first – in November.

Chinese shipyards with carrier capability

In China there are currently two state-owned enterprises capable to construct carriers at three shipyards, albeit only two are active. The first – where currently the Type 002 was under construction – is the shipyard at Dalian, Liaoning province or in fact the Dalian Shipbuilding Industry Co., Ltd. (DSIC). It was founded in 1898 and it is operated under the China Shipbuilding Industry Company Limited. DSIC, which is the largest shipbuilding company in China is located in Dalian Changxing New Development Zone, at the tip of the Liaodong Peninsula to the Bo Hai Sea. It is part of China Shipbuilding Industry Corporation (CSIC), one of the two state-owned shipbuilding enterprises in China. It was formed in December 2005 by the merger of the Dalian Shipbuilding Industry Company and Dalian New Shipbuilding Industry Company.

The second shipyard – where reportedly the first Type 003 will be build – is the Jiangnan Shipyard (JNCX) in Shanghai is located along the mouth of Yangtze River. It is state-owned since its original founding in 1965 and is now operated as Jiangnan Shipyard (Group) Co. Ltd.. This company is today known as Shanghai Waigaoqiao Shipbuilding Co., founded in 1999 and is a fully owned subsidiary of China CSSC Holding Ltd., a publicly listed company controlled by China State Shipbuilding Corporation (CSSC); the second state-owned shipbuilding enterprises in China parallel to CSIC.

The third possible shipyard is the Hudong-Zhonghua Shipbuilding (Group) Co., Ltd. (HDZH), which is one of the major Chinese shipbuilding enterprises also under the flag of China State Shipbuilding Corporation (CSSC). This company group was formed through the merger of the 1928-founded Hudong Shipbuilding and the 1926-founded Zhonghua Shipyard in 2001 and is now one if not the largest shipbuilding company in China. Hudong-Zhonghua itself is dispersed with its headquarter located at Pudong, Shanghai, and separate shipyards facilities at Pudong, Puxi, Changxing Island and Chongming Island at the Eastern part of Shanghai along the Huangpu River. The main yard facility is the Shanghai Shipyard Co. Ltd., and (see above) Shanghai Jiangnan-Changxing Shipbuilding Co., Ltd., which form a comprehensive industrial conglomerate specialized in building large ships and offshore engineering products. So far Hudong-Zhonghua is rarely mentions in connection with the building of carriers, and so far it produces most of all large LNG-carriers for civilian use but also frigates and landing crafts – like the Type 071 amphibious transport dock (LPD) for the Chinese Navy and it is rumoured to be responsible for the Type 075 landing helicopter dock (LHD), which allegedly is under construction since March 2016.

Aircraft carrier types

Type 001 [*Liaoning* (CV-16)]

Official badge of the People's Liberation Army Navy Ship (PLANS) *Liaoning* (16).

In China, *Liaoning* is officially called Type 001 carrier with the pennant number CV-16 even if it began live as the second hull of the *Kuznetsov*-class carrier (Type 1143.5). Therefore the *Liaoning* is a conventionally powered short take-off but arrested recovery (STOBAR) carrier equipped with a characteristic ski jump. She was laid down by the Nikolayev South Shipyard in 1985 and launched in 1988 as the *Varyag*.

Following her refit as the *Liaoning*, she – unlike her sister ship – no longer carries surface-attack cruise missiles with consequently the anti-ship missile tubes deleted during her refit, reportedly freeing up this additional internal space for hangar or storage use. Therefore the *Liaoning* is equipped only with air defence weapons like the Type 1030 CIWS and the HQ-10 missile system. Concerning her sensor fit, the *Liaoning* has been fitted with a Type 348 active electronically scanned array radar (AESA) installed in four arrays and a Type 381 'Sea Eagle' 3-D radar. Overall – even if not

Another image from mid-2016, showing the *Liaoning* trailed by one of her escorts – here the *Changsha* (DDG-173), a Type 052D guided missile destroyer – in quite unusual rough sea. Visible on deck is one Z-18 transport as well as two Z-18J AEW-helicopters. (via CDF/China Defense Forum)

confirmed – the *Liaoning* has a displacement of 43,000-tonnes (light or empty), about 53,000–55,200-tonnes (standard) and maximum 58,600–67,500-tonnes.

In terms of its operational use, the *Liaoning* is surely different to other countries' carriers, since she – at least by now – is functioning primarily as a training vessel and since she uses the unique ski-ramp. However often criticized with its overall capability hindered by its comparatively inefficient power plant and weak aircraft-launching system, the *Liaoning* anyway represents an important step China's advancing ability to project naval power. The *Liaoning* is by no means a small ship, and surely besides the US super carriers, she is by far the largest and most capable carrier in the South Asian-Pacific. Also the often mentioned limitations to the take-off weight of the J-15 fighters seem to be not as grave, as demonstrated during the *Liaoning*'s November live-firing exercise, when several J-15s were seen with 'heavy' stores including 4 PL-12 + 2 PL-8 AAMs or 2 YJ-83K AShMs + 2 PL-8 and even the buddy-refueling-pod.

Otherwise the *Liaoning's* limited size in comparison to the US carriers belies its limited capabilities and here most of all her steam turbine powerplant limits its top speed. However, even if earlier reports quote the contrary, its propulsion system still consists of the original Russian powerplant that was not removed before hand-over but preserved in grease and later reactivated. Following some Chinese TV-reports, the Chinese made some dramatic modification on the original system most of all to improve reliability and the main change is reportedly a lower operational steam pressure at high speed, which is – by some other accounts – maybe compensated by using larger steam turbine. Consequently the *Liaoning* does not suffer from the same issues the original Soviet power plant had, which – also based on its dated design and poor maintenance – limits the *Kuznetsov's* top-speed as just noted again during their recent deployment to the Mediterranean. During the *Liaoning's* recent cruise through the Western Pacific and the South China Sea she maintained an average speed of 23 knots for 10 hours without the typical *Kuznetsov*-style smoke trail.

Type 002 [probably *Shandong* (CV-17)]

Already right after the *Liaoning's* commissioning, rumours were raising on when the next carrier will be laid down and how it will look like. By now it seems as if 'cutting first steel' for the Type 002 vessel actually took place nearly one year after service entry, on 28 August 2013 and the construction of individual sections started in January 2014. All of this was not visible until the dry-dock in Dalian was empty again. Preparations at Dalian's dry-dock were noted for the first time in February 2015 and the new carrier was reportedly laid down on 10 March. Since then the vessel's construction progress was closely followed and certain milestones were eagerly awaited: For example, the hull itself was finished on August 2016, the deck was closed on 9 September and the island lifted on top of the deck on 25 September and 3 October 2016. Since about the end of 2016 – especially during winter – the ship was externally almost finished and work was shifted to the internal installations. With now the springtime temperatures rising, painting the hull was expected nearly each day and finally by the end of March this important milestone was initiated on 4 April. In parallel to the paint-works and cleaning the deck since the first week of April and the soon to be expected imminent radar installation, rumours were circulation concerning the carrier's launch.

At first sight a rather simplistic but anyway interesting sketch of the Type 002 carrier together with parts of its companioning ships: most of all notable are the new Type 901, which is a 45,000 tons fast combat support ship (FCSS) and the new 13,000 tons Type 055 guided missile destroyer (DDG). Both ships were launched in 2016 as well and will play a major role within each future carrier battle group.
(via CDF/China Defense Forum)

A first official statement in regard to the Type 002's launch was finally given during a press conference on Thursday 30 March, where Brigadier-General Wu Qian, spokesman and deputy director of the Ministry of Defence's Department of Public Information and Public Relations, announced that 'the first indigenous carrier is making progress and is progressing very well. As for the good news you've raised, I think we're not going to wait for long.' This statement was especially tailored to a reporter's question on whether the PLAN's second Chinese aircraft carrier would be launched this year on the Chinese Navy founding day, on 23 April; this date which is very symbolic in China.

In fact launch took place on 26 April 2017 even if the dry-dock was already flooded and a brief ceremony held to commemorate the People Liberation Army Navy's 68th founding anniversary. The 'true' launch was reportedly postponed due to too low tides.

Following the Type 001, the new carrier is officially designated the Type 002 aircraft carrier and is officially the first indigenous carrier class designed and developed for the Chinese Navy. Overall even if externally and surely still in fact a heavily improved *Kuznetsov*-class design, the Chinese engineers were able to incorporate major

For long the first Type 002 ship was known as the Type 001A - aka an improved *Liaoning* design - however its true designation Type 002 was only revealed by surprise in late August 2017.
Here, the ship is seen in late September 2017 after the Type 381 naval 3D search radar was installed.
(via FYJS-Forum)

improvements: Zhu Yingfu explained that most of all the hull interior design is more optimized and abandoned some of the design ideas of the former Soviet Union, while the ship-based electronic equipment also completely new. Through the final construction of the *Liaoning*, China accumulated tremendous experiences so that this second aircraft carrier has vastly improved the ship's operational effectivity, its electromagnetic compatibility, ship safety and combat capability.

Regardless all these improvements, it will remain limited by still keeping the *Kuznetsov*-lineage since it still features a similar sized albeit slightly rearranged flight deck. Even if it has a smaller island it still retains the ski-jump – maybe with a reprofiled angle of 14° – thus limiting the J-15 for STOBAR-launch only. Following official reports, the new carrier is externally complete but overall about 70 per cent complete. All the main systems like propulsion and power supply are already in place and the installation of the other systems will follow soon. By the most reliable predictions it will have a displacement of around 67,000 tonnes and there are some differences, such as for sensors/radar array which are very much different to the *Liaoning*; also the number of J-15s to be carried has reportedly been increased to 36.

Following its launch the work on the carrier continued most of all interaly. Externaly since about early August all the scaffoldings were removed, the flight deck was painted and the Chinese media already reported that the carrier will likely enter mooring trials ahead of schedule, noted Hu Wenming, general director of construction of the aircraft carrier. Overall it will surely be tested extensively and a maiden voyage could occur before September 2018 and commissioning can be expected for late 2019 or early 2020. Quite interesting, it might be designated CV-17 and some sources are already discussing that it will probably be named *Shandong*.

Type 003 (unconfirmed)

Parallel to the carrier construction itself and again a strong indication for that the Type 003 will be a true catapult equipped super carrier, both EMALS and steam powered catapults have been constructed at the Huangdicun Naval Air Base for testing. This base is the regular home of the 'Carrier Air Wing' and especially the J-15s and includes

For long the future configuration China's first CATOBAR carrier was subject to much speculation. Following the latest reports the construction was delayed in order to decide on the catapult. By now it seems as if construction has started in April 2017 for a carrier with about 80,000 tons and three EMALS catapults. (via CDF/China Defense Forum)

Quite surprisingly in August 2017 the Chinese People's Revolutionary Military Museum in Beijing gained another attraction. Even if this model is most likely not a real representative model of a future carrier – some sources state it shown actually not the Type 003, but a future nuclear powered 100,000 tons super-carrier – it clearly demonstrated the PLAN's ambitions: A fully fledged super-carrier together with an integrated carrier-borne AEW (KJ-600), a navalised fifth generation fighter (here a J-20 development) and several UCAVs. (via SDF/Sino Defence Forum)

already a facility to train the Naval Aviation pilots on carrier-take-off and landing procedures including several ski-ramps and arresting gear facilities. The most recent addition to this site however is a dual catapult track for both a steam and an EMALS catapult. The first flight of the improved catapult-capable J-15A occurred in July 2016 and that aircraft was already tested successfully off the catapult – allegedly and quite surprisingly from the EMALS at first – in November 2016.

Following official statements, China already confirmed its intention to build an aircraft carrier larger than the *Liaoning* and most of all able to carry more aircraft. 'The next aircraft carrier we need will be larger and carry more fighters,' stated Song Xue, deputy chief of staff of the Chinese Navy in an interview published by the official state news agency Xinhua and posted on the Chinese defence ministry's website. He even more confirmed that 'China's future carriers will embark not only fighters, but reconnaissance aircraft, anti-submarine aircraft, electronic countermeasures planes, and rotary-wing aircraft' too and such a composite air wing can only be operated effectively off a carrier with catapult assisted take-off but arrested recovery (CATOBAR) capability.

Concerning the Type 003 vessel itself, it is surely too early to conclude but following the most likely scenario it is a further evolution of 002, even if the line between 'evolution' and 'new' (aka 'revolution') can become so blurred it's difficult to discuss it. By the latest rumours the Type 003 will have an increased displacement – often referred is something along the lines of a USN *Forrestal*-class (aka 60,000 tons empty or 80,600 tons operational) – however the two most reliable 'sources' are currently undecided if it will be a bigger departure from the Type 002 as a completely new design with a full displacement of about 80,000 tons. The biggest discrepancy however is related to what kind of catapult will be used, since in recent years, the EM catapult has made so much progress that it is now a serious contender to the steam technology. Allegedly the recent delay is related to this breakthrough, so that the PLAN deems a delay by one year a decent price to pay for an overall more capable catapult. It seems as if the PLAN has decided in favour of the EMALS system. The general consensus seems to be that the Type 003 will most likely have only three catapults. Following the latest reports, construction begin – aka first 'steel cutting' – of the first Type 003 vessel finally occurred at JNCX on 29 June 2017 and even if probably a quite vague estimation, if a similar timeline for the Type 003 can be assumed as seen with the Type 002 vessel, lay down could occur somewhere in the first quarter 2018 and launch somewhere in 2021.

Several J-15 fighter jets are being prepared for another training missing on the flight deck of the aircraft carrier *Liaoning* prior to a training exercise on 1 July 2017. Interesting to note that PLAN closely follows closely USN procedures and colour codes. (via Xinhua/Zeng Tao)

Future plans for the carrier force

This question is often based in the West on the assumption that China's acquisition of an aircraft carrier is driven at first by its desire for international prestige. It is surely correct that in the public opinion an aircraft carrier is widely seen as a symbol of national power and prestige especially since China was the only permanent member of the UN Security Council without an aircraft carrier. However, that cannot be the main reason, as China invests since year tremendous sums of its budget and even more manpower in this program: the main reason simply is that the procurement of a carrier fleet is a consequence of China's rising ambitions both in terms of the role China again wants to play on the international stage, its role as export nation number one and even more in mind of its role as a regional power. A carrier force can therefore only help to better cope with its threat environment that has imposed constraints on China's ability to develop as a sea power.

The main problem for a prediction of a future Chinese carrier force is that any meaningful discussion of the role of carriers in the Chinese Navy turns essentially to the question about the future of the Chinese Navy itself. Consequently any such discussions are founded on considerations that inevitably would include a large amount of speculation or at least 'best informed' extrapolation from known developments, current capabilities and rumoured ambitions.

The first and foremost important question is therefore the question on what type of carrier and what form of carrier-borne naval aviation does the PLAN and the Naval Aviation as its naval air arm plan to use: will the carrier be operated as an air defence platform for fleet air defence similar to the original Soviet Navy or will it be operated as an ASW platform? Will a Chinese carrier form the fleet's centre of a expeditionary force similar to the British or French doctrine or will it – akin to the US Navy – form the core of their fleets? An answer to this question will in return would give very much varying different answer on future fleet size and type of carrier.

The main problem right now is that an answer to this question deeply depends on years if not decades of experience operating carriers operationally and consequently most likely not even the PLAN right now has an answer since only based on these experiences the PLAN is able to develop satisfactory doctrine and therefore requirements for a future carrier force, which in turn will interact with other factors like strategic and political considerations and budget as well. During a conference in July 2012, General Chen Bingde stated that no official decision had been made on how many carriers will be built. However it can be assumed that the role and operational doctrine is more akin to the US' than the Russian Navy.

Following the most reasonable trends in the most recent development of the PLA doctrine a preliminary answer to the first question might be possible. Following their projected development into a true blue water navy, PLAN's baseline is for sure pursuing the ability to hold the first island chain and contest the second island chain in a hypothetical confrontation with the US. This most likely extends up to the Indian Ocean to protect its fleet of merchant vessels along the 'New Maritime Silk Road' up to the eastern coast of Africa. Western experts as well as several Chinese commentators in state media usually suggest that China would need at least three carriers since this vast maritime area alone will probably require at least three, if not four, carriers for effective power projection. If the current *Liaoning* (CV-16) is excluded from this projected Orbat – since it will continue to act as a training carrier not intended to field full combat capability in peace time – it means at least two more carriers after the first Type 002 can be expected, most likely three more. If this includes two Type 002 and two Type 003 carriers or only one Type 002 and two Type 003 is too early to assume. Given the latest predictions it is highly unlikely that the PLAN has a requirement for

Again from mid-2016, showing the *Liaoning* together with parts of its escorts – here the *Haikou* (DDG-171), a Type 052C guided missile destroyer in rather rough seas. In the background, a Type 054A frigate is visible. (via CDF/China Defense Forum)

a fleet that can fight around the globe, but in general it can be predicted that with one carrier always in refit/SLEP or refuelling and one vessel acting as a trainings ship, at least one operational carrier for each of the three fleets should be the PLAN's concept.

As such a carrier fleet of about five to six carriers by 2030/35 could be a sensible estimation for a force that would be useful both as China's own counter-intervention/ anti-access strategy in a high intensity Western Pacific conflict against US and its allies especially if operating in conjunction with land based air power and missiles as well as the rest of the PLAN. The sometimes reported force of 10 carriers in the near future is in the athor's opinion obviously exaggerated since unnecessary and excessive. Andrew S. Erickson assumes that 'Rather than seek to replicate U.S. naval strategy and operations, the PLAN is more likely to develop a limited power-projection capability that enhances China's ability to defend its regional interests; to protect expanding overseas interests; to perform nontraditional security missions such as humanitarian assistance and disaster relief, counterpiracy, noncombatant evacuation, antiterrorism peacekeeping operations, crisis response, and military diplomacy; and to demonstrate international responsibility.' (Andrew S. Erickson, 2012)

Base and assignments

So far the PLAN has only one aircraft carrier operational and since its service introduction on 25 September 2012, *Liaoning* is used as a training ship. Consequently the CV-16 is currently not assigned to any of China's three operational fleets, but by now at least officially under control by the PLAN Headquarters. This was stated by Song Xue, deputy chief of staff of the Chinese Navy and is consistent with previous reports stating that the ship is not intended for operational use, but rather as a training vessel to explore carrier operations and doctrine. That – at least officially – did not change with the recent declaration of being 'combat ready' from November 2016 unless in case of an urgency or national crisis.

While unfolding its wings, J-15 '109' is being prepared for its next flight with another another J-15 taking-off in the background. With now regularly more than 12 fighters operational off the *Liaoning* the Naval Aviation has shown in recent years more intense flight operations than the Russians demonstrated with their Su-33s. (via CDF/China Defense Forum)

In reality – aka operationally (day by day ops) – the *Liaoning* is assigned to the 1st Destroyer Flotilla just south of Qingdao-Xiaokouzi (Tsingtau) (Guzhenkou Bay Surface Fleet Base), close to the 'Guzhenkou-Wan' or 'Xiangzimen'. This region is geographically at the intersection between the North and the East Sea fleets. Since the 1st Flotilla is within the administration of the NSF, the *Liaoning* is at least unofficially also or will be assigned to the Northern Fleet in case of an emergency. Additionally PLA Naval Aviation's first carrier air wing is also based at the Naval Aviation Training Base at Huangdicun – a second base close to Xingcheng, the Naval Aviation Academy's home facility and became operational in May 2013. It is believed all air assets for aircraft carrier *Liaoning* are based here. Parallel to its homeport at Xiangzimen – that is just being expanded to a second carrier-pier – there is already another carrier-capable port with the appropriate infrastructure including a carrier pier available at the naval base at Sanya on Hainan.

Operations

Operationally until late 2016, the *Liaoning* has conducted only short-duration missions mainly in the Bohai and Yellow Seas and all connected to its primary mission of naval aviation training. On 10 August 2011 she set sail for the first time from Dalian Port on her maiden voyage and the so far longest 'distant' deployment led this carrier in late 2013 from its northern home base to the South China Sea to Hainan Island's Sanya naval base. This event was only recently repeated when she also crossed the first chain of islands in the Western Pacific and both events were the so far only examples she was seen sailing with a larger fleet of destroyer, frigate and submarine escorts. At the end of December 2013, the Liaoning carrier group conducted its first exercise in the South China Sea.

However this rhythm of training cruises changed since about mid-2016, when following several similar training exercises up to November 2016, the *Liaoning* and her escort ships conducted her first life-firing exercise in the Bohai Bay including the launch of several AMs and AShMs during simulated anti-aircraft and anti-ship operations. After that she set sail together with her escorting vessels: including 2 Type 052C destroyers – the *Zhengzhou* (151) and *Haikou* (171), 1 Type 052D destroyer – the 173 *Changsha* (173), 2 Type 054 frigates – the *Yantai* (538) and *Linyi* (547), 1 Type 056A anti-submarine corvette – the *Zhuzhou* (594) and 1 Type 903A oil-tanker – the 966 *Gaoyouhu* (966) to cross the first chain of islands in the Western Pacific, to circumvent the Island of Taiwan and finally to joind the South China sea with the Sanya naval base at Hainan on 28 December. The purpose of this first Island chain crossing into the Western Pacific remains unknown, but it is worth noting that Admiral Wu Shengli, Commander in Chief of the PLAN was aboard the carrier *Liaoning* on December 23, the day before the Group crossed and consequently this cruise was more than just a symbolic act.

Another set of exercises were accomplished similar to the cruise in late 2016, when the CV-16 and her carrier training group exercised in the Western Pacific, including passing through the Miyako Strait between the Japanese islands of Miyako-jima and Okinawa and finally visited Hong Kong on 7 July 2017 to celebrate the 20th anniversary of the hand-over to China.

Future deployments

Concerning future deployments or missions the *Liaoning* might perform, it is quite difficult to concern since this depends on several unknown factors. Especially the *Liaoning's* limits inherent of her ski-jump, the current engines but most of all the relative inexperience of its aviators and deck-crews might hinder this ship for sustained high-intensity combat operations even within waters close to the Chinese Mainland, where the *Liaoning* could expect support from land-based aircraft and radars. Consequently given its physical and operational limitations the *Liaoning* might be best suited for regional missions short of high-intensity conflict. This could include missions like humanitarian aid and disaster relief (HADR), training exercises with other nations, showing the flag, and asserting Chinese territorial claims in the South China Sea. Furthermore, the *Liaoning* has considerable utility as a tool of naval diplomacy – providing helicopter lift for HADR missions and engaging in multinational training exercises will signal to other countries that China is a responsible rising power. Such efforts would complement China's growing commitment to multilateral initiatives, such as UN peacekeeping efforts. As the PLAN improves its combined arms capabilities and the *Liaoning's* personnel become proficient in higher-tempo operations, the *Liaoning's* repertoire could expand to include fleet air defense and maritime and land strike further afield from Chinese waters. These missions would require enhanced personnel as well as greatly improved situational awareness, communications, and logistical support far from current Chinese bases—assets that the PLAN may not yet possess in sufficient quantity or quality.

In sum, global combat missions remain outside of the *Liaoning's* reach given its current operational status, and the status and number of the *Liaoning's* potential fleet escorts. Chinese planners may not even have such ambitions in mind. On the other hand, less intensive missions such as noncombatant evacuation, maritime peacekeeping, and maritime antiterrorism provide good training opportunities and will become increasingly feasible for the PLAN in the future. While the *Liaoning's* possible mission set remains unclear, the prestige and attention conferred upon the ship during its construction, subsequent fitting-out, and deployment indicate that Beijing considers the *Liaoning* a symbol of China's great-power status. Regardless of the *Liaoning's* future abilities, the ship commands a degree of political utility as a tool of naval diplomacy through various operations, regional and global.' (Andrew S. Erickson, 2012)

J-15 seen in a typical light CAP load-out armed with – albeit here only with training rounds – PL-8 short-range IR-guided AAMs and two PL-12 active radar homing AAMs. Aircraft '113' is in fact c/n 0204, the fourth batch 02 production aircraft.
(via SDF/Sino Defence Forum)

Carrier aviation aircraft

Fighter/multirole

J-15 unit patch

The so far sole carrier-borne fighter is the SAC J-15, which was chosen as China's first generation carrier-borne multirole fighter developed by both the No. 601 Institute and SAC. It seems as if originally China was heavily interested in a direct purchase of Russian Su-33 fighters in mind of the success of the already operational J-11B and with the help of the Ukraine the J-15 was developed based on the Russian Su-33 airframe and flight control system as well as the J-11B in terms of avionics, radar (Type 1493 PD radar), glass cockpit and weapon systems. Other changes were a greater use of composite materials in certain areas – especially the vertical tails – to reduce weight. At around 2001 one Su-33 prototype (even if most sources say T-10K3, it was in fact T-10K7 c/n 49051003402) was acquired via Ukraine and has been studied extensively. The first J-15 prototype #551 was finished in 2008 and performed its maiden flight on 31 August 2009, powered by two Russian AL-31F turbofan engines. Following a first flight test phase at the CFTE including additional prototypes – (#552 to 556, maybe even #557 – with #554 briefly testing WS-10H engines) these prototypes were undergoing various tests on the simulated flight decks at Xi'an-Yanliang, where a first take-off from a land based ski-jump occurred on 6 May 2010. Carrier trials begun in summer 2012 with practice touch-and-go landings on deck of the Liaoning during her own sea trials and finally on 23 November 2012 two prototypes #552 and 553 landed and took off officially for the first time off the Liaoning.

Additional tests up to September 2013 included take-offs and landing tests with various air-to-air and air-to-surface weapons (including PL-8, PL-12, PL-10 and PL-15 AAMs, KD-88 ASM, YJ-83K AShM and YJ-91 ARM and the a Russian UPAZ-1A buddy refuelling pod) and officially the first Batch 01 serial aircrafts were handed over to the PLA Naval Aviation Carrier Fighter Group in late 2013.

Since late 2014 J-15s are regularly based on-board the *Liaoning* and images from October 2015 indicate that also the first Batch 02 aircraft were operational. Latest photos suggest that the Batch 02 J-15s are air-to surface capable. Altogether so far 24 serial numbers on J-15s have been confirmed with production continuing but reportedly already 3 were lost.

Besides the standard J-15 there were rumours since October 2014 about a CATOBAR-capable version under development by the No. 601 Institute and CSIC 704 Institute. This J-15A – or also known as J-15T – expected to be operated off the Type 003 carrier features a further strengthened forward landing gear featuring a typical catapult gear. The first prototype powered by WS-10H engines took off for the first time on 3 November 2012 and this version was planned to serve not only as a trainer but more as a dedicated multirole-fighter similar to the PLAAF J-16. Another variant is the so far unconfirmed maiden flight of a dedicated EW version on 25 October 2016 called J-15D, which would as an EW-aircraft in the same role as the USN EA-18G. This type reportedly is based on the PLAAF's J-16D. Latest reports however assume, that the trainer-version has been cancelled and the J-15S has been integrated into the J-15D project.

The J-15T prototype #571 seen during catapult trails at the land-based complex. It was first flown in July 2016 and is actually more a technical demonstrator, than a true prototype to test and explore the future catapult capable version J-15A or J-15B, which will also receive a major avionics update including a new AESA-radar.
(via CDF/China Defense Forum)

The second variant of the J-15 is a dedicated twin-seater designated J-15S, which is under development since 2011. This version combines the airframe of the J-15 with the cockpit section of the J-16. The first prototype powered by WS-10H engines took off

The revised second FC-31 prototype during a test flight in May 2017. For long, it was expected that the Naval Aviation's next generation carrier-based stealth fighter would be a version of the SAC FC-31, however recent reports suggest, that neither the PLAAF nor the Naval Aviation are interested in that type, but a final decision has not been yet made. (via CDF/China Defense Forum)

for the first time on 3 November 2012. This version was planned to serve not only as a trainer, but more as a dedicated multirole-fighter similar to PLAAF J-16s.

Another variant is the so far unconfirmed maiden flight of a dedicated EW version on 25 October 2016 called J-15D, which would as an EW aircraft in the same role as the USN EA-18G. This type reportedly is based on the PLAAF's J-16D. Latest reports however assume, that the trainer-version has been cancelled and the J-15S has been integrated into J-15D project.

Future

For long, the next generation carrier-based stealth fighter was rumoured to be a version of the SAC FC-31 currently under development, however recent reports suggest, that both the PLAAF and Naval Aviation are not interested in that type and that either a navalised version of the J-20 or a new design with so far not finalized configuration are on offer. However with the most recent success of the J-20 during 'Red Sword 2016' and in mind that such a naval J-20 is probably difficult to operate off the smaller Type 002 vessels, there might still be a chance for SAC and the FC-31.

Quite interesting, in mid-2017 repeatedly rumours were noted, ranging from an alleged FC-31V3, thru a carrier-based J-20, sometimes a clean-sheet design and also yet an upgraded J-15 as an interim type is mentioned. In general, it seems as if nothing is decided yet, however it also seems as if the Naval Aviation is pressing for a decision. Following the latest rumours the current status can be summarised:

- The Naval Aviation has not made a decision but this requirement will be filled by a 'medium sized heavyweight fighter'
- There are two contenders; one from 601 (alleged an FC-31 version, sometimes called V3) and one from 611 (no further info if a J-20-based design or a new type)
- Therefore both design teams SAC/601 and CAC/611 were said to have received preliminary 'funding' to develop their naval prototypes but none of them already got the final Naval Aviation contract.
- Latest rumour by an apparently quite credible poster is that the Naval Aviation is pressing forward with a decision already by late 2017 since it wants to have a next-gen fighter operational within the next 'few years'.

In consequence it remains interesting on what type the Naval Aviation decides.

A rare image of the JZY-01 naval AEW-technology demonstrator which is known since July 2012. It seems as if it is a structural testbed only and not a real flying prototype. The future carrier-borne AEW type named KJ-600, is believed to be under development at 603/XAC and is projected to operate off the CATOBAR capable carriers. (via CDF/China Defense Forum)

Electronic Warfare/carrier-borne AEW&C

So far the *Liaoning* has to rely on helicopters for AEW duties, but since April 2005 a shipborne AEW&C aircraft is known to be under development at the No. 603 Institute. A first image of a technology demonstrator designated JZY-01 (*JZ*: shipborne, *Y*: AEW&C) – rumoured first in September 2010 to be built by XAC – was unveiled in July 2012 at the CFTE airfield. In common with the E-2 and Yak-44, this testbed based on a heavily modified Y-7/MA-60 airliner airframe features a large circular radar dome mounted on a single mast aft of the wing root, a new tail resembling the four vertical stabiliser arrangement akin to the E-2, a new wing and two WJ-6C turboprop engines (5,100ehp) as used by the Y-9 transport aircraft with 6-blade high-efficient propellers. However, this technology demonstrator appears to function only as an aerodynamic testbed and seems to lack the radar and its sophisticated on-board C^3I

Most likely an interim solution until a dedicated Z-18 SAR will be available, the *Liaoning* operates two Z-8Js and two Z-8JHs onboard for SAR missions.
(via http://eng.chinamil.com.cn)

equipment. Following reports from mid-2016 a new follow-on design, named KJ-600, is believed to be under development at 603/XAC featuring three AESA radar antennas in a triangular configuration similar to the KJ-500 and compatible with catapults.

Rotary wing

Z-8J and Z-8JH

Besides the small Z-9 helicopter, all current helicopters used on the *Liaoning* are based on the 602 Institute/Changhe Aircraft Industrial Corporation (CHAIC). The Z-8, itself is a development of the French SA.321Ja Super Frelon. This helicopter was developed as a land or ship based ASW/SAR helicopter and it has been delivered to PLAN in serveral versions as Z-8J transports, Z-8S naval SAR version and another SAR variant called Z-8JH (serial numbers 95x6) with dedicated medical equipment especially on-board the aircraft carrier *Liaoning*. The naval Z-8 series is to be replaced by the new Z-18 and three dedicated versions are already operational or under OPEVAL.

The Z-18 is an improved medium transport helicopter based on the AC313 design to replace the old Z-8 in PLA service. The standard transport version was the first to enter service with Naval Aviation and two of these helicopters ('380' & '381') and is stationed onboard the aircraft carrier *Liaoning* for crew transportation.
(via CDF/China Defense Forum)

Z-18 White Heron

The first is the standard Z-18 VIP-transport based on the civil AC313 design and featuring a redesigned fuselage with larger internal volume and improved WZ-6C turboshafts (around 1,300kW). For naval use, both the rotor blades and the tail boom can be folded in order to save space on-board the ship and the Z-18 is operational on-board the air-

The Z-18F was the latest member of the Z-18 family to enter flight testing and so far two prototypes or pre-series aircraft were on board during the latest cruises as heavy ASW helicopter. Seen here, this Z-18F is carrying two Yu-7K 324mm light torpedos. (via SDF/Sino Defence Forum)

craft carrier *Liaoning* for crew transportation. Following the latest reports from September 2016 a SAR variant – maybe Z-18S – is under development to replace the Z-8JH.

Besides the standard transport version an AEW variant (Z-18J) and an ASW/anti-ship variant (Z-18F) have been developed for PLAN, but so far all helicopters seen on the *Liaoning* are only prototypes and preseries aircraft.

Z-18J Bat and Z-18F Sea Eagle

The Z-18J AEW helicopter features a retractable radar antenna similar to French AS-532 Horizon battlefield surveillance helicopter located behind a completely redesigned rear fuselage and is thought to be a long-range multi-mode AESA radar developed by the No. 38 Institute. In 2009, a first test-bed was first noted and so far even if this type will be only a stop-gap until a fix-wing AEW&C aircraft enters the service, two prototypes have been build and during the *Liaoning's* recent cruise two operational Z-18Js have been seen.

The next dedicated special-version is the ASW/anti-ship variant designated Z-18F. This type is known since February 2014 and features a large surface search radar under its nose, a new LF dipping sonar through an opening in the bottom of the fuselage and 30 small openings along its rear loading ramp for dropping sonar-buoys. This type also has four pylons on both sides of fuselage for carrying two Yu-7K torpedoes and YJ-9 AShMs. Similar to the Z-18J at least two prototypes have been built and are undergoing currently various tests. As a heavy ASW helicopter, it is expected to complement the *Liaoning's* air wing as two of this type were on board during the latest cruise.

Usually in PLAN service, the Z-9D acts as a shipborne ASW helicopter with anti-ship capabilities, least two Z-9Ds ('370' and '371') have been modified with an additional FLIR turret, a search light and a hoist installed acting in the SAR role onboard the aircraft carrier *Liaoning*.
(via Top.81-Forum)

Z-9

The current standard PLAN naval helicopter is the Z-9 series, itself a licenced development of the AS.565SA developed by the No. 602 Institute and Harbin Aircraft Industrial Group (HAIG). Usually operated as a shipborne ASW helicopter the Z-9C carries two Whitehead A244 or Yu-7K torpedoes and equipped with an indigenous KLC-1 surface search radar and a Type 605 dipping sonar. This however has been either replaced or updated to a new low frequency sonar similar to the US AN/AQS-22 ALFS. An updated version of the Z-9C is the current Z-9D, which is also a dedicated anti-ship and is able to carry up to four YJ-9 AShMs under a pair of detachable stub wings. Additionally the Z-9D features a new KLC-3B fire-control radar. This version is usually based on-board the new Type 056 FFGs and at least two – probably designated Z-9S – are operated off the *Liaoning* in the SAR role.

Future

The future naval medium-weight helicopter requirement to replace the Z-9-series will most likely filled by a naval version of the Z-20. This type of helicopter in the 10t class has been under development at No. 602 Institute, Harbin and Changhe based on the American S-70C design. The Z-20 however features a redesigned cabin of slightly increased volume and a five-bladed main rotor. The first prototype made its first flight on 23 December 2013 and currently there are several prototypes under OPEVAL test for the Army Aviation. Additional variants for naval roles are reportedly planned.

Another option might be a version of the AVIC AC352 – in PLA service as Z-15 – which is a 7-ton class medium-weight utility helicopter jointly developed with Airbus Helicopters as the H175 and HAIG. The AC352 has just performed its first flight on 20 December 2016.

Trainer

As there is actually no true carrier-capable training aircraft available, it can be seen as the still biggest weakness in the Chinese carrier project, the Naval Aviation uses up to date only land-based JL-9 trainers for pilot training to take off and land on the aircraft

Originally the JL-9G was planned to feature a prominent tail hook as seen on first prototype ('423') on the photo above. Since the hook turned out to be causing too much stress to the fuselage, training is limited so far to land-based simulations only without arrested landings. So the JL-9A can only simulate taking-offs from the ski-jump (see image on top) even this is only rarely seen, too.
(via SDF/Sino Defence Forum and Top.81-Forum)

The JL-9G is so far Naval Aviation's sole trainer developed for carrier training. Due to several issues, this training is limited to land-based simulations only. This type is usually assigned to the Naval Aviation Academy, 3rd Training Regiment at Xingcheng, but since 2017 at least four were also seen at the J-15's base at Huangdicun.
(via Top.81-Forum)

carrier deck. (land-based simulation). The type used for this task is a special development of the Guizhou JL-9 designated JL-9G and even if once planned as a dedicated trainer developed as a carrier capable trainer, this type can so far only perform land-based simulations.

In order operate off a carrier it features some extensive modifications like most of all strengthened landing gears and enlarged wings. Additionally enlarged leading edge slaps and leading edge root extensions were installed to reduce the take-off and landing speed and allow a higher AOA. Consequently, the original twin ventral fins were removed and the tail was made taller to offer more stability during the high AOA take-off and landings. Another difference to the standard JL-9-trainer is a DSI intake. The first JL-9G had its maiden flight in 2009 and two prototypes were tested at the CFTE with the first one having its arresting hook installed. However, there must be some structural issues and the hook was soon removed. Consequently, since true carrier-landings would cause too much stress to the fuselage, all so far delivered aircraft are unsuitable for arrested landing. Since November 2013, this type is operational with the 3rd Training Regiment at Xingcheng assigned to the Naval Aviation Academy (Flight Training Institute) and a few were also spotted since late 2016 at Huangdicun, with about a dozen being produced.

For the future it is expected that either GAAC is currently working on a revised true carrier-capable version which would feature a redesigned rear fuselage with an arrester hook installed plus a new, higher thrust engine. The other option would be a dedicated development of the more modern twin-engined JL-10 that has just entered PLAAF and also Naval Aviation service in late 2016. Otherwise the Naval Aviation has to rely on their valuable J-15 fighters or has to wait until the J-15S/D enters service.

Naval Aviation carrier-borne inventory

Overall it is difficult to estimate, since the helicopters are usually assigned to the carrier in times of duty from other regular Naval Aviation units, so that only the number of J-15 are for sure.

The Air Wing assigned to the *Liaoning* – or at least their J-15 fighters – are based Huangdicun (40°30'00'N 120°39'26'E) – also known as Xingcheng-2 – which was constructed as a dedicated carrier-training facility with a ski-jump ramp and hangars for a full J-15 regiment there.

The base is at least officially still under the jurisdiction of Xingcheng, the home base of the Naval Aviation Academy (Flight Training Institute). Also the PLAN remains mysterious/tight-lipped about the true nature of that unit but the text under its unit-badge – which can be translated as 'aircraft carrier-borne aviation troops' or 'Carrier Air Wing' – gives hint that it is probably even a Division-level unit.

Also the Z-18 COD transports and the Z-9D SAR helicopters seem to be assigned solely to the *Liaoning's* Air Wing, however their base remains unknown. All other helicopters so far seen on the *Liaoning* – especially the Z-18J AEW – are only prototypes still under operational evaluation.

Given the still nascent nature of the Chinese aircraft carrier project it is quite understandable, that the number of aircraft programs right now is quite limited. Anyway after less than five years of operating the *Liaoning*, a decent number of specialised types are already available, in the final phase of OPEVAL or in conception for the next carrier generation.

Current units of Chinese aircraft carrier air wing*

Unit	Aircraft type	Role	Base	Remarks
'Carrier Air Wing'	J-15, JL-9A	multirole, training	Huangdicun	Base also known as Xingcheng-2;
'Carrier Air Wing'	Z-9D	SAR	Huangdicun (unknown)	
'Naval Aviation HQ Air Regiment'**	Z-18 Z-18F Z-18J	COD ASW AEW	Huangdicun (unknown)	
2nd Naval Aviation Division (Specialised), 5th Air Regiment	Z-8JH	SAR	Qingdao-Licang	Base also known as Cangkou NAS

Notes:

* Could also be translated as 'Aircraft Carrier Regiment'.
The parent air division or parent headquarters is the PLA Navy Operations Bureau and operationally it is located within the Northern Theatre Command.

** Naval Aviation HQ Air Regiment provides COD, transport, utility, ASW and AEW detachments for North Sea Fleet naval units, including the *Liaoning*.
The parent air division or parent headquarters is the PLAN Operations Bureau and operationally it is located within the Northern Theatre Command.

Often criticised for being limited with its fuel and weapons load carrying capabilities, these limitations seem to be not as grave, as demonstrated during the *Liaoning's* November 2016 livefiring exercise, when several J-15s were seen with 'heavy' stores including 4 PL-12, 2 PL-8 AAMs or 2 YJ-83K AShMs, 2 PL-8 and even the buddy-refuelling-pod.
(via http://eng.chinamil.com.cn/)

Reports concerning the maximum number of aircraft the Liaoning can carry are varying from Chinese sources of a total of 36 fixed-wing aircraft and helicopters to 26 fixed-wing aircraft and 24 helicopters; which seems to be a bit exaggerated. The most reasonable number might be about 24 J-15s or a lower number of fighters complemented by different helicopters.

Current and future estimated CVW structure of PLA Naval Aviation air wings

Aircraft/Helicopter	Current CVW structure *Liaoning* (CV-16)	Future (operational) CVW structure Type 002	Future (operational) CVW structure Type 003
J-15	20-24*	24	36-40
Z-8JH (SAR)	2		
Z-9D (SAR)	2	2	2
Z-18 (COD)	2	2	2
Z-18F (ASW)	2**	6	6
Z-18J (AEW)	4	4	–
Z-18S (SAR)***	–	2	2
Future carrier-borne AEW	–	–	2-4 (when available)
Total	32-36	40	50-56

Notes:
* estimated, a maximum of 13 J-15 was confirmed in December 2016
** only prototypes, not operational so far
*** said to replace the Z-8JH

Latest Chinese carrier battle group (training)

No.	Ship class	Ship name	Fleet	Displacement	Crew
1	Type 001 aircraft carrier	*Liaoning* (16)		57,000	1,500
2	Type 052C air-defence destroyer	*Zhengzhou* (151) *Haikou* (171)	ESF SSF	7,000 7,000	280 280
1	Type 052D guided-missile destroyer	*Changsha* (173)	SSF	9,500	280
2	Type 054 multi-role frigate	Yantai (538) Linyi (547)	NSF NSF	4,000 4,000	165 165
1	Type 056A anti-submarine corvette	*Zhuzhou* (594)	SSF	1,300	78
1-2	Type 093 attack submarine (nuclear)	*???* *???*	??? ???	7,000 7,000	125 125
1	Type 903A replenishment ship	*Gaoyouhu* (996)	ESF	23,000	130
					Around 3,000

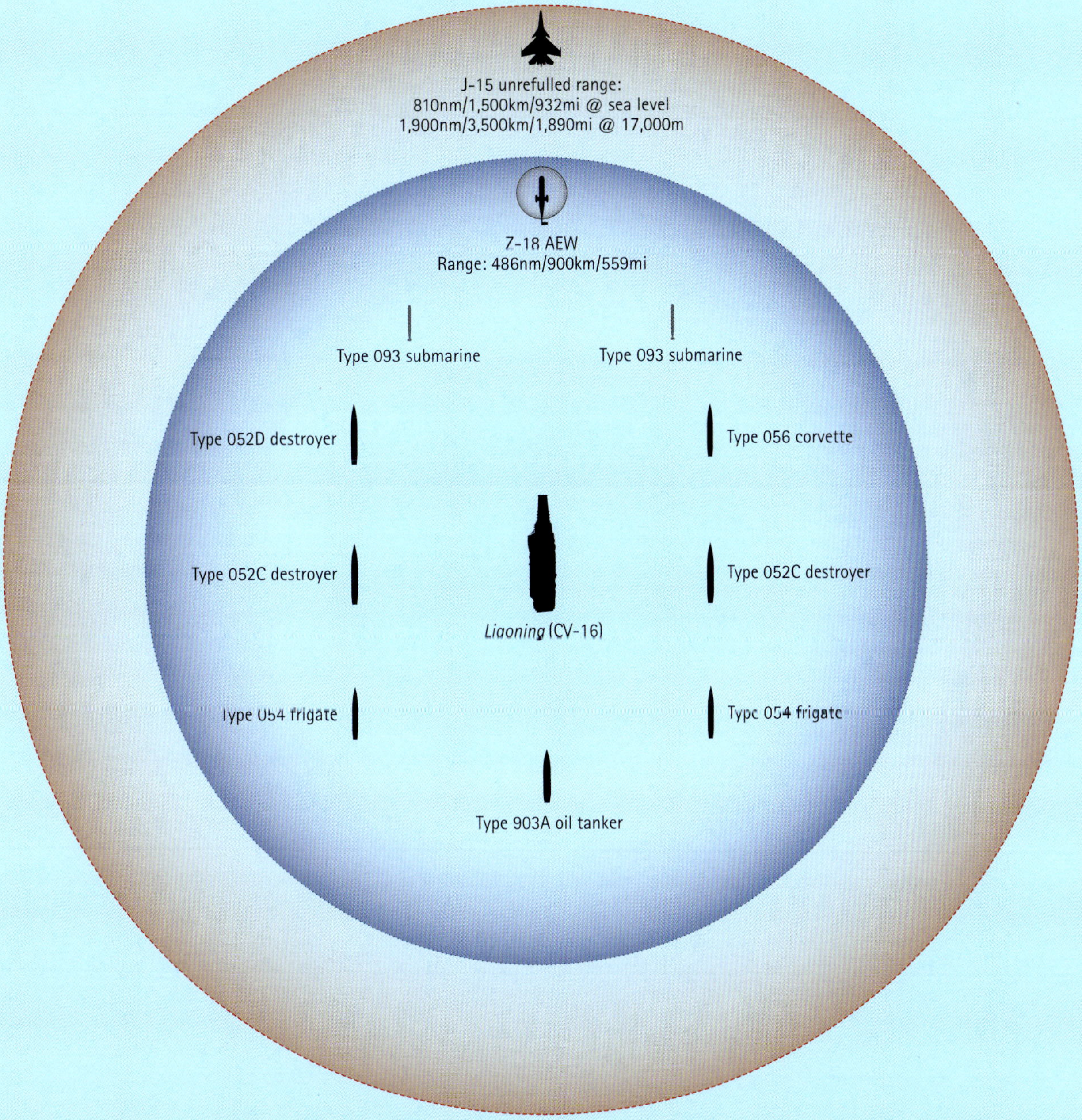

This is a purely schematic presentation of a likely carrier battle group and is not to scale.
In reality, the composition of such a force is dependent on various parameters.

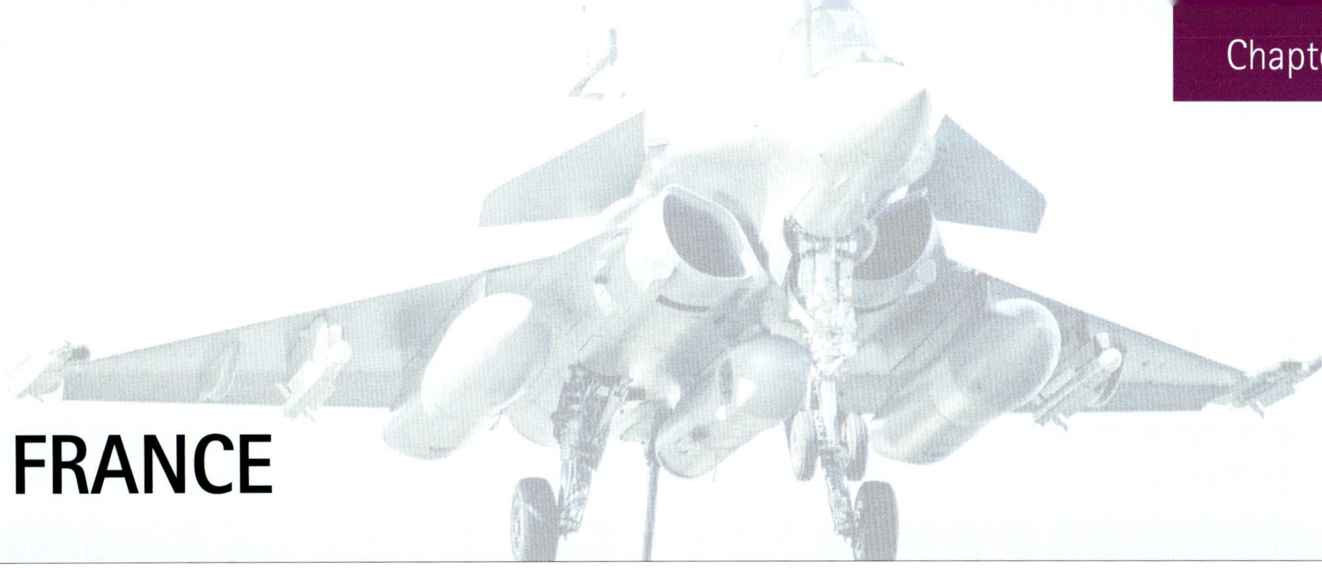

Chapter 3

FRANCE

Henri-Pierre Grolleau

The history of French naval aviation can be traced back to the beginning of the 20th century, when the Service de l'Aviation Maritime was created on 20 March 1912. The first maritime aviation centre was set up in Montpellier in August of that same year, only to be relocated to Fréjus in October. From 1911 to 1913, cruiser *Foudre* was converted into a seaplane transport vessel/floating operating base. When war broke out with Germany, expansion was extremely quick, with countless airship, seaplane and aeroplane bases and units formed over the next few years in continental France, in the French overseas territories and abroad.

Between the wars, the maritime forces declined, but France built its first aircraft-carrier, *Béarn*, from the hull of a Normandie-class battleship. She entered service in 1927 and was used to test operating concepts and refine tactics and doctrines. Two years later, seaplanes-carrier *Commandant Teste* was commissioned into service. She was initially equipped with Caudron G3 and CAMS 55 seaplanes, then Loire 130s and Latécoère 298s. In the late thirties, the French Navy invested in long-range seaplanes operated by reconnaissance Escadrilles. Like a warship, each seaplane was attributed a name and was commanded by an officer. For example, Latécoère 523 No 1 was named *Altaïr*. All French naval development stopped when France was occupied in 1940, and the Marine Nationale was clearly overtaken by British and American naval forces which used aircraft carriers on a massive scale during WWII.

MARINE NATIONALE

Marine Nationale (French Navy)

Aéronautique Navale (French Naval Aviation)

Roundel of French Naval Aviation

From the ashes

In the immediate aftermath of World War II, the French carrier force was reconstructed with help provided by both the Royal Navy and the US Navy. French authorities had sought solutions to quickly bring into service new aircraft-carriers to protect French interests and project forces to the furthest corners of the Globe. Both Britain and the USA had carriers standing idle, and they agreed to hand over a number of vessels to the Marine Nationale. First to transfer was HMS *Bitter*, a US-built escort carrier, renamed *Dixmude* in August 1945. The following year, it was the turn of HMS *Colossus* which became *Arromanches* and proved a successful design, remaining in service until 1974. Next were *La Fayette* and *Bois-Belleau*, respectively ex-USS *Langley* and ex-USS *Belleau Wood*.

◄ *Charles de Gaulle* (R91) (Katsuhiko Tokunaga/D.A.C.T.)

The sole French carrier *Charles de Gaulle* (R91), seen here back in 2010 still with some Super Etendards on board. (Marine Nationale)

To equip these carriers, numerous fighters and attack aircraft – Seafire Mk IIIs and Mk XVs, SBD-5 Dauntlesses, SB2C-5 Helldivers, F6F Hellcats, TBM-3 Avengers, and F4U-7/AU-1 Corsairs – were successively donated to France by the Allies. In 1946, French embarked Aviation was composed of just four units (fighter squadron Flottille 1F, with Seafires, dive-bomber squadrons Flottilles 3F and 4F, both equipped with Dauntlesses, plus training unit Escadrille 54S, with Spitfires, Seafires and Dauntlesses) but it rapidly expanded as France became engaged in a growing number of conflicts.

Combat operations

Indochina, later known as Vietnam, became the first major post-World War II trouble spot for France. Insurgents had been challenging French authorities since the withdrawal of Japanese forces. The situation soon worsened and, from 1947 to 1956, French vessels frequently deployed to the region, conducting thousands of strike and close air support sorties in difficult conditions. *Dixmude* was the first to operate in the area, with Dauntlesses. From 1948, she was followed by *Arromanches*, with an embarked air group composed of Seafire Mk IIIs and SBD-5 Dauntlesses. Due to a high number of Seafire and Dauntless accidents, the carriers did not deploy to the Far East for two years, however. After the delivery of Hellcats and Helldivers, *Arromanches* returned to Indochina in 1951, and again in mid-1952. In April 1953, *La Fayette* arrived in Indochina

A pair of Rafale Ms prepares to take off for a reconnaissance mission. Each carries a Pod Reco NG on the centreline station. (Rich Cooper)

and, from then on, French carriers took turns to maintain combat aircraft in theatre. Combat operations in Indochina reached a climax when the battle of Diên Biên Phu began, in November 1953. Operating from *Arromanches*, Hellcats and Helldivers were heavily committed, and losses were high. Among other French reinforcements, Navy AU-1 Corsairs transferred by the US Navy operated from Hanoï-Bach-Maï air base to try to reverse the situation. In early May 1954, *Bois-Belleau* arrived in Indochinese waters with further reinforcements to relieve *Arromanches*, but, in 7 May 1954, the French garrison in Diên Biên Phu surrendered, and a cease-fire was signed in Geneva on 21 July 1954. Deployments did not immediately come to a complete halt, and *Arromanches*, *Dixmude*, *Bois-Belleau* and *La Fayette* kept on steaming in the Indochinese waters until 1956.

That very same year, Egyptian President Nasser decided to nationalise the Suez Canal. France and Great Britain quickly reacted, and a joint operation was set up to regain control of this strategic area, the Marine Nationale taking an active part in Opération Mousquetaire with *Arromanches* and *La Fayette* carrying Corsairs, and Avengers, plus HUP-2 helicopters for SAR.

The situation had barely settled in Indochina that things started to deteriorate in French Algeria. From 1956, Corsair and Aquilon units participated in fire support missions while shore-based Avenger squadrons launched patrols in an effort to prevent 'rebels' from obtaining weapons and ammunition from friendly vessels. But one of the most significant changes in combat tactics was linked to the introduction of helicopters

Armourers load Rafale Ms with AASMs and GBU-12 laser-guided bombs. (Rich Cooper)

which were intensively used to transport troops, resupply isolated outposts, and provide fire support and medevac. Dedicated naval units were established with S-55/H19 Chickasaws, H21C Shawnees and S-58/HSS-1 Seabats. The Navy soon embarked on a successful programme to fit its helicopters with weapons to keep enemy heads down during airborne assaults: machine-guns, 20mm cannons, and even 250-lbs bombs. In July 1962, Algeria officially became independent, and Aéronavale units progressively left the country.

Home-built carriers

France's shipbuilding industry demonstrated its ability to design and build aircraft carriers on its own when lead of class *Clemenceau* was commissioned in November 1961. The new vessel was soon followed by sister-ship *Foch*, and, over a short span of time, more modern aircraft types were introduced to operate from their decks: Alizé surveillance aircraft, Etendard IVM/P attack/reconnaissance fighters, and F-8E(FN) Crusader interceptors.

The two carriers proved highly successful, serving well into the nineties, and the *Foch* is still in service today with the Brazilian Navy. Their careers were marked by numerous deployments and combat operations: Opérations Saphir 1 and 2, in the Indian Ocean, in 1974-75 and in 1977 to ensure a smooth transition when Djibouti gained independence, Opérations Olifant, off Lebanon, Opération Manta, in the Mediterranean during tensions with Libya, and Opération Prométhée, in the Gulf of Oman, during the Iran-Iraq conflict. When Yugoslavia started to break up, France took a leading role in the peacekeeping effort, and, starting in January 1993, French aircraft-carriers conducted numerous deployments to the Adriatic, their aircraft undertaking hundreds of reconnaissance and electronic intelligence missions. After Bosnia, things started to deteriorate in Kosovo and, when it appeared that force had to be used, the French Government decided to commit a significant number of aircraft, and carrier *Foch* was instructed to participate in the combat operations.

Into modernity

The French Navy currently fields carrier *Charles de Gaulle*, a vessel which encountered a number of teething problems during development and entry into service but has since proved to be a well thought out and reliable operational platform, so reliable, in fact, that over the last few years she has spent more days at sea than any other carrier anywhere in the world. The history of the *Charles de Gaulle* can be traced back to the beginning of the seventies, when the French Navy looked at various options to replace ageing *Arromanches*. After comprehensive studies, it was announced in 1980 that two nuclear-powered carriers would be built to replace both *Clemenceau* and *Foch*. The choice of nuclear propulsion was obvious at a time when France was heavily investing in military and civilian nuclear technologies. It would also allow a reduction in the number of fleet replenishers. Initially named *Richelieu* but soon renamed *Charles de Gaulle*, the first one was ordered in 1986 and first metal was cut at Brest in November 1987. The fall of the Berlin Wall and the ensuing French defence budget cuts had a negative impact on the programme, and completion was considerably delayed, leading to escalating costs. The vessel was not launched until May 1994 and, after a lengthy construction and trials programme, she was accepted into service, in mid-2000. The second vessel was never ordered, leaving the Navy with a partial capability gap.

Advanced design

Although not as big as US carriers, the state-of-the-art *Charles de Gaulle* – the first nuclear-powered surface ship in Western Europe – represents a huge improvement over the venerable *Clemenceau* and *Foch*. Up to 30 aircraft routinely operate from her flight deck, her standard air-group being now composed of two E-2C Hawkeye airborne early warning aircraft, 24 Rafale fighters, three Dauphin plane-guard helicopters and a NH90 antisubmarine/support rotorcraft. Her flight deck is 40 per cent larger than that of her predecessors, her kerosene capacity is increased by 66 per cent, and more than 500 tonnes of aviation ammunition are carried, including an undisclosed number of nuclear missiles. Compared with the *Clemenceau*-class, the *Charles de Gaulle*'s aviation facilities have been substantially expanded and improved. They include two 75m (246ft) C13F steam catapults capable of launching E-2Cs or Rafales at maximum take-off weight. Her hangar is large enough (4600 m², 49,514 sq ft) to accommodate about half of the air group's aircraft. The vessel is fitted with two 21x12m (68.9×39.4 feet)

aircraft lifts abaft the island, two ammunition elevators, and with a state-of-the-art Microwave Landing System which allows landings to be performed in severe weather conditions. For self-defence, she is equipped with two octuple Aster 15 vertical launchers and two Sadral point-defence SAM systems.

Everything was done to ensure she could launch and recover fixed-wing aircraft even in sea states between 5 and 6, quite an achievement for a 42,600-tonne aircraft carrier. The unique SATRAP (Système Automatique de Tranquillisation de la Plate-forme) incorporates two groups of lead weights that move athwartship on rails to reduce roll to an acceptable level for air operations. Additionally, seakeeping behaviour is further enhanced thanks to four pairs of active fin stabilisers. In an effort to increase commonality and keep development and maintenance costs under strict control, the French Navy adopted for the *Charles de Gaulle* the very same nuclear reactors as used in the *Le Triomphant*-class strategic missile submarines. The carrier's first K15 pressurised water reactor achieved criticality in June 1998.

The carrier has been equipped with a complete suite of radar and infrared sensors and of secure communication systems, including Syracuse satellite links. The vessel was provided with a vast intelligence centre and with modern mission planning and command and control facilities. Enough space has been reserved for the embarked maritime headquarters needed to head a complete task force at sea and coordinate combined/amphibious operations, aero-maritime offensive and defensive operations and below the surface actions.

Finally, the *Charles de Gaulle* is fitted with extensive and perfectly laid out Role 1/2 medical facilities to support the whole naval force. To accelerate the movement of litters, these 620m^2 (6,674ft^2) facilities are easily accessed from the flight deck. In fact, everything is organised and optimised for the flow of patients. The most serious cases can then be taken to one of the two operating rooms, and next onto the intensive care ward fitted to the latest standards while the less serious cases are shown into the walking wounded ward for treatment. If outside help and advice from other medical specialists are required, the *Charles de Gaulle*'s doctors have instant access to telemedicine.

The French GAE

The French Groupe Aérien Embarqué (GAE, carrier air group) is the most powerful in Europe. The modernisation of the GAE began with the delivery of the first E-2C Hawkeyes in 1998 and the withdrawal of the F-8P Crusader the following year. The process continued in 2000 when the Marine Nationale said farewell to both the Etendard IVPM reconnaissance fighter and the Alizé embarked maritime surveillance aircraft. On 4 December 2000, Rafales M2 and M3 landed at Base Aéronavale Landivisiau, Brittany, home of the French Navy combat aircraft community, a major event that had been eagerly awaited by pilots and maintainers. Until the arrival of the Rafale, the Aéronavale had no fighter of a kind expected to win in air combat against the latest, potentially hostile types such as the MiG-29 or the Su-27 and its derivatives. This had proved a major problem during Operation Allied Force in Kosovo when the Crusaders had to be sent home, leaving only shore-based fighters to defend the French Task Group. The Rafale filled a vital air-defence capability gap, allowing the task force to operate closer to enemy shores while considerably improving its ability to quickly achieve battlefield air-dominance. The Rafale initially specialised in the air-defence role but eventually replaced the Super Etendard Modernisé (SEM) in the attack, antiship, nuclear deterrence and reconnaissance missions. The faithful SEM was withdrawn from use in July 2016, leaving the Rafale as the only French carrier-borne fast jet.

Enter the Rafale

The origins of the Rafale can be traced back to the early 80s when a requirement was published for a common Air Force/Navy swing role fighter capable of undertaking, from shore bases and aircraft-carriers at sea, the whole spectrum of combat missions until then devoted to more than one type: air-defence/air-superiority, nuclear deterrence, pre-strategic and tactical reconnaissance, antiship strikes, destruction of enemy air-defences, air interdiction, precision strikes, close air support and buddy-buddy refuelling. Development of the new aircraft was uneventful: after the Rafale A demonstrator, two prototypes of the naval variant of the Rafale were built, Rafales M01 and M02. Numerous test campaigns confirmed that the fighter is ideal for carrier operations: it has good engine response, an excellent autothrottle, a very low approach speed, and exceptional handling qualities with remarkable pitch and roll responsiveness.

Everything was done by Dassault Aviation engineers to increase commonality between Air Force and Navy variants and minimise procurement costs. As a result, the Rafale Marine is very close to its Air Force counterpart, changes having been kept to a minimum. The main consequence is that the multi-spar wing cannot be folded. This reduces complexity and weight but means that storage on the carrier will be less easy, and that the number of aircraft carried on the *Charles de Gaulle* will be smaller. Still, up to 30 Rafales can be embarked for surge operations. Among the most obvious modifications compared to the Air Force B and C variants is the massive, longer and stronger nosewheel gear which gives the Rafale M its noticeable nose-up attitude. To ensure total interoperability with US Navy aircraft carriers, the nosewheel leg incorporates a launch-bar coupled with a 'hold-back' system. Other changes include a reinforced main undercarriage, a strengthened airframe, a tail hook, and a carrier-based microwave landing system. A power-operated built-in ladder improves cockpit accessibility and reduces the amount of support equipment needed. Finally, a new fin-top Telemir system, allows the aircraft's inertial navigation system to 'talk' to the carrier's navigation suite and exchange navigation data. The front centreline weapon pylon had to be eliminated because of the oversized nose gear. This will not have any significant impact on the load carrying capability as this pylon cannot be used when a centreline fuel tank is carried. All Rafale variants are powered by SNECMA (now Safran) M88-2 turbofans, each rated at 75 kN (16,861 lb) with afterburner.

Expanding Rafale capabilities

Serial M1, the first production Rafale for the Navy, was delivered in July 1999, and, by early 2017, there were 42 Rafale Ms in service with the Marine Nationale. The Rafale Detachment of the CEPA (Centre d'Expérimentation Pratique de l'Aviation Navale, the

Rafale M28 with a full load of fuel tanks shows at centreline the inflight refuelling pod. (Henri-Pierre Grolleau)

Aéronavale Operational Evaluation Unit) was the first Navy unit to officially operate the new fighter. Its mission was, and still is to check that the Rafale is fully compliant with the French Navy specifications, and to design new tactics, taking full advantage of the considerable capabilities offered by the Rafale weapon system. In December 2000, the Rafale detachment of the CEPA moved from Istres to Landivisiau with Rafales M2 and M3, and, on 18 May 2001, Flottille 12F was recreated at Landivisiau with a complement of four Rafale Ms (M2 to M5). This prestigious unit, which formerly operated the Crusader, specialised in the air-defence role with Standard F1 (for France number 1) Rafales then armed with only MICA EMs (Missiles d'Interception, de Combat et d'Autodéfense Electromagnétique, or radar-guided Interception, Combat and Self-Defence missiles), Magic II short-range missiles and a 30 mm cannon. In 2004, Flottille 12F was declared fully operational with nine Standard F1 Rafale Ms. Over the next few years, the squadron successively received Rafale Standard F2s, then F3s which offered massively expanded capabilities.

A spiral approach has been chosen by the French Armed Forces to reduce risks, and F2 Rafales were the first to be able to carry out air-to-surface attacks. New weapons such as the Scalp stealth cruise missiles, the GBU-12 Paveway II and GBU-22 Paveway III laser-guided bombs, and the AASM (Armement Air-Sol Modulaire, Modular Air-to-ground Armament, also known as Hammer, for Highly Agile, Modular Munition Extended Range) were introduced in this variant. The FSO (Front Sector Optronics), a Link 16 MIDS (Multifunction Information Distribution System) datalink, and air-to-ground modes for the RBE2 radar were also adopted in Standard F2 Rafales. Finally, the MICA IR replaced the long-serving Magic II.

With the advent of the Standard F3, the Rafales were cleared to carry out specialised tasks such as antiship attacks (with AM 39 Exocet Block 2 Mod 2 missile), reconnaissance missions with the dedicated Pod Reco NG (new generation recce pod), and inflight refuelling sorties with a buddy-buddy tanking pod. Standard F3 Rafales also became capable of carrying the Air-Sol Moyenne Portée-Amélioré (ASMP-A, improved air-to-surface medium range) nuclear missile that replaced the earlier ASMP in use on the Super Etendard Modernisé and the Air Force Mirage 2000N. Earlier Standard F1 and F2 Rafales were all brought up to Standard F3, avoiding the problem of having fleets within a fleet and thus easing up maintenance requirements and configuration management.

All Rafales delivered up to October 2012 were equipped with a RBE2 electronic scanning radar fitted with a PESA (Passive Electronically Scanned Array antenna). That very same month, Air Force single-seater C137, the first Rafale fitted with an Active Electronically Scanned Array (AESA), was accepted into Armée de l'Air service, France becoming the first European country to field this technology in a fighter aircraft. The Navy accepted its first AESA-equipped Rafale, M39, in October 2013, initially for operational evaluation by the CEPA at Istres, but the fighter was later flown to Landivisiau for front-line service. AESA radars can generate multiple beams and can shape those beams for width, sweep rate and many other characteristics to track multiple targets with excellent accuracy. At the time of writing, the next standard, F3R, was expected to enter service in 2018, bringing numerous improvements, including the Meteor ramjet-propelled air-to-air missile, the GBU-16 Paveway II laser-guided bomb and the GBU-49 Enhanced Paveway II GPS/laser-guided munition.

Flottille 11F

Three Rafale squadrons

Today, three naval squadrons all co-located in Landivisiau, Flottilles 11F, 12F and 17F, operate Rafales. They each field twelve aircraft, the balance being used as a maintenance/attrition reserve. The three units share exactly the same missions, all their pilots being qualified to carry out the whole spectrum of conventional air-to-air and air-to-surface missions, day and night. Within each Flottille, a classified number of pilots is trained for the nuclear strike mission with the ASMP-A missile. The three units take turns performing front-line and training roles. For example, one year, 11F and 12F will be the duty units ready to deploy on board *Charles de Gaulle* at short notice while 17F will remain at Landivisiau to train younger aircrews. The following year, 11F and 17F will stand ready to deploy while 12F will become the support unit, and so on and so forth. This method of management has proved its worth over the years, helping young aircrews gain experience very rapidly while avoiding the risk of 'burnout' among the most experienced pilots.

Flottille 12F

Since being declared operational in 2004, Navy Rafales have successively, and successfully, participated in the conflicts in Afghanistan, Libya, Iraq and Syria, logging countless close air support, precision strike, air-superiority, destruction of enemy air defences, reconnaissance and in-flight refuelling sorties. Combat experience has shown that the omnirole Rafale offers tactical commanders exceptional operational flexibility,

Flottille 17F

Rafale M12 lands in a heavily loaded configuration with MICA air-to-air missiles, GBU-12 laser-guided bombs and external tanks. (Rich Cooper)

even in a high threat environment, allowing missions to be performed without a dedicated escort. The fighter is now fully mature: its availability hovers at around 85 per cent according to figures provided by the Commander of the French Naval Aviation.

E-2C Hawkeye

Launching Airborne Early Warning assets is the best way to detect incoming strike aircraft armed with sea-skimming antiship missiles as far away as possible from the Task Force. To fulfil that requirement, the French Navy looked at many options, but it was felt that only the E-2C Hawkeye offered the desired level of performance. Accordingly, in November 1994, it was officially announced that the Grumman (now Northrop Grumman) E-2C Group II Hawkeye had been selected. Although five aircraft were needed to maintain a modicum of capability, only two E-2Cs were ordered in April 1995, with another two on option. The first two Hawkeyes were delivered in April and June 1998, respectively. French aircrew members and maintainers were trained in the USA, and the first aircraft arrived at Lann-Bihoué in December 1998, followed by the second one in April 1999. They were initially utilised by the FAGE (Formation Avions de Guet Embarqué, Embarked Aircraft Surveillance Unit) until Flottille 4F was recreated at Lann-Bihoué in March 2000. The option for a third Hawkeye was firmed up in November 1998, but the fourth aircraft never materialised.

Flottille 4F

A Flottille 4F E-2C prepares for a night take-off from the *Charles de Gaulle*. (Rich Cooper)

The Hawkeye has proved very successful in the French Navy, but its operating costs are amongst the highest of any aircraft in service in France. The type's operational records are impeccable, but maintenance requirements are incredibly high. The Hawkeye was barely in service that it was engaged in Afghanistan. The learning curve was steep, but aircrews soon managed to master all the E-2C's advanced systems in a coalition, in difficult conditions. In Libya, Iraq and Syria, the unit demonstrated that it was second to none. In Libya, for example, E-2Cs were sometimes controlling up to 80 fast jets and tankers, coordinating their missions and ensuring that the fighters remained fully topped up, even when there were changes in the refuelling plan. On numerous occasions, the Hawkeyes flew deep inside enemy-held territory to escort a raid and provide a permanent C^2 service.

France is heavily investing in its Hawkeyes to maintain their operational relevance, the aircraft being fitted with more and more advanced systems. For example, French specialists developed in-house the MARC DL (Multi-Asset Recording Computer for Data Links) composed of a tactical display in the cockpit and of a gateway allowing 4F aircrews to share data with other assets on the L11 and L16 networks simultaneously (they were previously restricted to one network at a time). The French Navy is now following with interest the entry into US Navy service of the E-2D Advanced Hawkeye and it is more than likely that the new variant will find its way into the French inventory at some stage.

SA365F Dauphin during plane guard duties, called misssion Pedro in France, off *Charles de Gaulle*.
(Henri-Pierre Grolleau)

'Pedro' helicopters

In October 1951, the first Aéronavale helicopter unit, Escadrille 58S, was formed to train future helicopter pilots. The unit detached some of its rotorcraft (S-51s at first, followed by HUP-2 Retrievers) to aircraft-carriers, and these deployments proved so successful that, in July 1954, a dedicated carrier SAR squadron, Escadrille 23S, was created with HUP-2s. This unit later utilised single-engined Alouette IIIs and twin-engined Dauphins for SAR guard duty until it was supplanted by Flottille 35F which was recreated when Flottille 33F and Escadrille 23S amalgamated in October 1999.

For years, a standard 35F detachment on board *Charles de Gaulle* comprised two SA365F Dauphins and one SA319 Alouette III. This is set to change, however, as the Alouette III deployed at sea on board the carrier for the last time in late 2016, leaving only the SA365F Dauphin for the plane guard duty (called 'mission Pedro' in France). When undertaking SAR guard duties, the Alouette III had several shortcomings anyway: it could not operate at night and its lifting capability was small. The Dauphin is much better adapted for the role as the new type is equipped to a very high standard which allows complex SAR missions to be performed, day and night, even in difficult weather conditions. Its Omera ORB 32.1 radar and its navigation system can handle 147 waypoints, including 40 mobile targets such as ships. The SA365F can maintain height automatically thanks to its advanced autopilot auto-hover mode.

Flottille 35F

A French Navy NH90 Caïman in the hover.
(Henrie-Pierre Grolleau)

NH90 Caïman

The new NH90 Caïman helicopter is the latest addition to the French carrier air group. The first Caïman was delivered to the Marine Nationale in 2010 and the first unit, Flottille 33F, was recreated to operate the type in December 2011. Born out of a collaborative programme between France, Germany, Italy and the Netherlands, the NH90 is produced in two main versions, the TTH90 transport variant for Air Forces and Army Aviations, and the NFH90 naval variant. A total of 27 NH90s, all fitted with state-of-the-art avionics and fly-by-wire controls, have been acquired by the Aéronavale to replace its Super Frelon and Lynx fleets. The Super Frelons had to be withdrawn early due to severe age-related maintenance issues and a pair of EC225 was purchased to fill the gap, the two aircraft being transferred to the Armée de l'Air in July 2016 after a sufficient number of NH90s had been delivered to take over the SAR role from Cherbourg and Lanvéoc-Poulmic on top of their missions at sea. The Lynx will stay in service until 2022 to operate on the few remaining F70-class frigates, the last of which, *Latouche-Tréville*, will decommission that same year. In 2016, a Caïman was integrated into the *Charles de Gaulle*'s carrier air group for the very first time, replacing the French Army Puma detachment which had routinely operated from the carrier since 2001 for the transport/logistics mission. In addition to the transport role, the Caïman is also capable of undertaking aeromaritime surveillance missions ahead of the task force, in the

Flottille 31F

Flottille 33F

Escadron d'Hélicoptères 1/67 'Pyrénées'

same way Alizés performed recce missions from the *Clemenceau* and the *Foch*. With the recent resurgence of the Russian submarine threat, anti-submarine warfare (ASW) has become a priority again and, with its FLASH (Folding Light Acoustic System for Helicopter) dunking sonar and its MU90 torpedoes, the carrier's NH90 is well equipped to reinforce the screen around the task force in support of dedicated ASW assets (frigates and their own Lynx and NH90 rotorcraft and shore-based Atlantique 2 maritime patrol aircraft).

EC725 Caracal

For combat search and rescue (CSAR) missions, the Marine Nationale had flown Super Frelons in the 90s, Flottille 33F then operating the type from carriers *Clemenceau* and *Foch*. In the early 2000s, the mission was taken over by the Armée de l'Air with the introduction of the EC725 (now H225M) Caracal which, in May 2006, became fully operational with Escadron d'Hélicoptères 1/67 'Pyrénées', a joint Air Force/Army/Navy unit based in Cazaux. During the combat operations in Libya, two Caracals and an air force Puma were integrated into the *Charles de Gaulle*'s air group and they were held at constant readiness, providing CSAR coverage to the whole coalition from within a short distance from the Libyan coastline.

Over the last fifteen years, the French Navy has heavily invested to create the most powerful naval aviation in Europe. When the *Charles de Gaulle* is in dry dock for refit and/or upgrade, her carrier air group does not remain idle and her Rafales participate in QRA missions in France, sharing the burden with Armée de l'Air interceptors, and stand ready to deploy abroad and reinforce combat units engaged in the fight against terrorism.

A French Air Force EC725 Caracal combat search and rescue helicopter on the deck of the French carrier. (Rich Cooper)

A Rafale M in a long-range air-to-air configuration with its arrester hook extended. (Dassault)

A single SCALP-EG conventional cruise missile can be carried on the Rafale M's centreline pylon. (Henri-Pierre Grolleau)

Current units of French aircraft carrier air wing

Unit	Aircraft type	Role	Base	Remarks
4F	E-2C Hawkeye	AEW	Lann-Bihoué	3
11F	Rafale M	Fighter	Landivisiau	42 in total in inventory
12F	Rafale M	Fighter	Landivisiau	
17F	Rafale M	Fighter	Landivisiau	
21F	Atlantique 2	ASW, ASuW	Lann-Bihoué	23 in total in inventory
23F	Atlantique 2	ASW, ASuW	Lann-Bihoué	
24F	Falcon 50Mi/Ms	Maritime surveillance, SAR	Lann-Bihoué	8
25F	Falcon 200 Guardian	Maritime surveillance, SAR	Papeete/Nouméa	5
28F	Xingu	Training	Lann-Bihoué	11
31F	NH-90 Caïman	ASW, ASuW	Hyères	19 in total in inventory
33F	NH-90 Caïman	ASW, ASuW	Lanvéoc-Poulmic/ Cherbourg	
34F	Lynx	ASW, ASuW	Lanvéoc-Poulmic	16 remaining in inventory
35F	Alouette III, Dauphin	Support, plane guard, SAR	Hyères/Le Touquet/ La Rochelle/Papeete	19 in total in inventory: 11 of 3 variants in inventory
36F	Panther	ASW, ASuW	Hyères	16
22S	Alouette III	Training	Lanvéoc-Poulmic	
50S	Cap 10M, Cirrus SR20	Training	Lanvéoc-Poulmic	7 and 3
57S	Falcon 10	Training, light support	Landivisiau	6 in inventory

Aéronavale unit designation

Front-line combat squadrons, the Flottilles in French Navy language, and second-line squadrons, the Escadrilles, were/are similarly labelled in the following way:

Unit	Role
1F – 4F	carrier-borne anti-submarine warfare units
11F – 19F	fighter units
21F – 29F	land-based maritime patrol units
31F – 39F	helicopter squadrons
1S – 19S	support and surveillance units
20S – 29S	helicopter units
30S – 39S	transport units
50S – 59S	training units

A typical French carrier air wing

No. of aircraft	Type	Role and remarks
24	Rafale M	One reinforced Flottille; multirole fighter
2	E-2C Hawkeye	AEW
2	NH90 Caïman	ASW, transport, logistics
2	AS365N Dauphin	SAR
30		

Rafale M20 in tanker configuration safely lands on board by catching the correct arrestor cable. (Rich Cooper)

The *Charles de Gaulle*, left, and US Navy guided-missile destroyer USS *Bulkeley* (DDG 84), right, conduct an underway replenishment with the Military Sealift Command fleet replenishment oiler USNS *Arctic* (T-AOE 8).
(French Navy/Frederic Duplouich)

French carrier battle group, Operation Chammal in late 2016

No.	Ship class	Ship name	Fleet	Displacement	Crew
1	Aircraft carrier	*Charles de Gaulle* (R91)		42,500	1,850
1	*Arleigh Burke*-class guided missile destroyer	USS *Ross* (DDG 71), later USS *Mason* (DDG 78)	USA	9,800	323
1	*Horizon*-class anti-air warfare frigate	*Chevalier Paul* (D621)		7,050	236
1	Type F70 *Cassard*-class anti-aircraft frigate	*Cassard* (D614)		4,500	250
1	F122 *Bremen*-class frigate	*Augsburg* (F213)	DEU	3,680	222
1	Type F70 *Georges Leygues*-class anti-submarine frigate	*Jean de Vienne* (D643)		3,500	235
1	*Rubis*-class nuclear attack submarine	(undisclosed)		2,600	70
1	*Durance*-class fleet replenishment oiler	*Marne* (A630)		17,800	159
					3,345

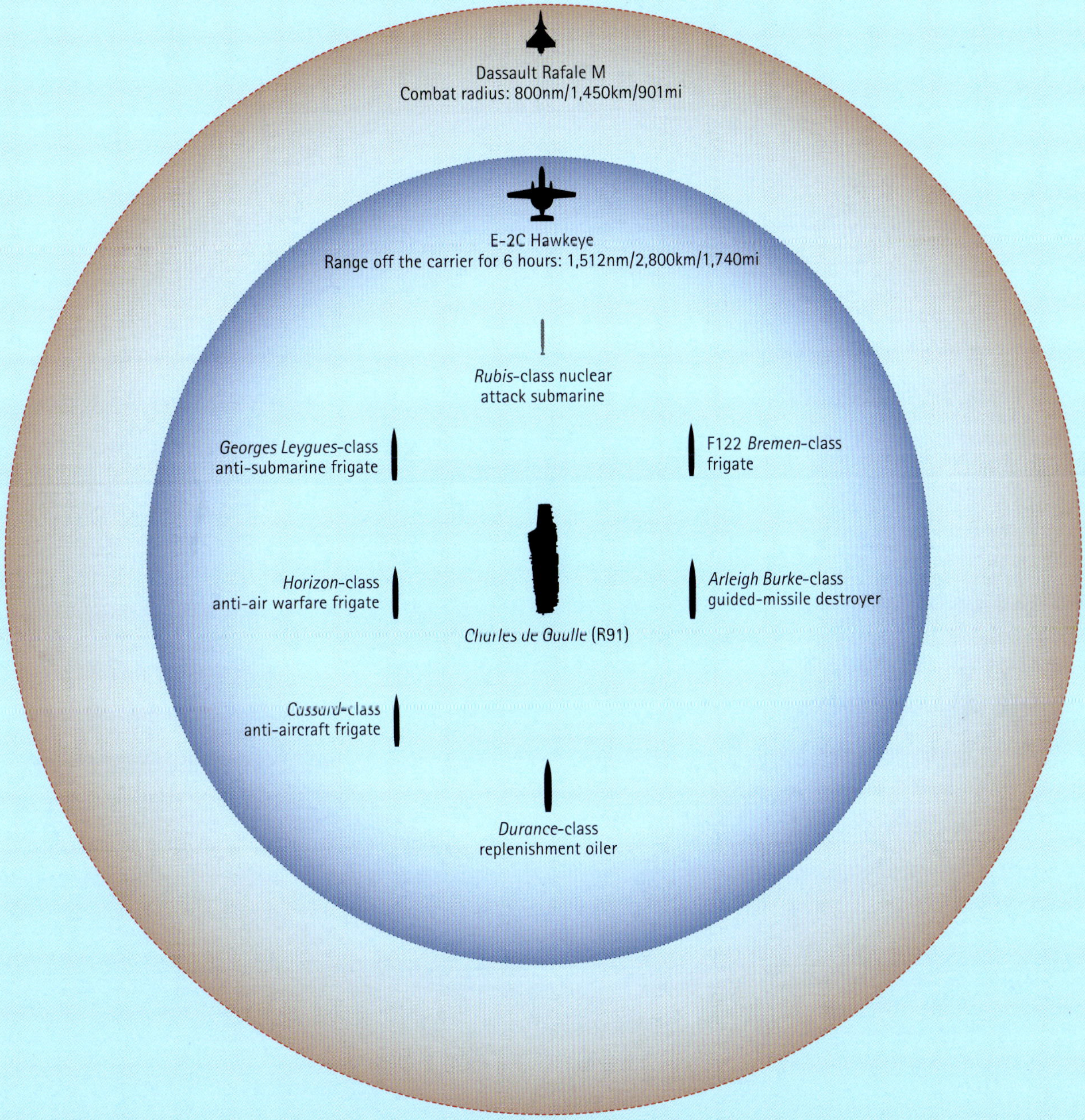

This is a purely schematic presentation of a likely carrier battle group and is not to scale. In reality, the composition of such a force is dependent on various parameters.

Chapter 4

INDIA

Angad Singh

Bhāratīya Nau Senā (Indian Navy)

Roundel of Indian Naval Aviation

Like India's Army and Air Force, the Indian Navy can claim a heritage as a fighting force that predates the country's independence from colonial rule. The East India Company's Marine was formed in 1612, with a handful of warships based out of the state of Gujarat tasked with protecting merchant shipping in the area. Control and utilisation of this force was varied over the next two centuries, but by 1882 it had was renamed the Royal Indian Marine, under which moniker it served in the First World War. In 1934, the Royal Indian Marine was renamed the Royal Indian Navy and went on to serve through WWII and on to India's Independence in 1947. When the Constitution of India came into effect on 26 January 1950, India became a republic and the 'Royal' prefix was dropped.

The lessons of WWII were not lost on the Indians, and naval aviation was planned for from the outset. In 1948, Naval Headquarters proposed a ten-year 'Master Plan' for growth and modernisation that called for the two fleets – Eastern and Western – to initially be built up around a light fleet carrier each. The ambitious blueprint also recommended a large number of shore bases to house training and transport units, Search and Rescue (SAR) flights, Fleet Requirement Units (FRUs) as well as disembarked combat squadrons. But even as the first Indian Navy (IN) naval aviators were out learning their trade in Scotland in 1949, budgetary realities were changing things back home. The Indian Government's austerity measures adopted in the late 1940s nearly put paid to the very idea of Naval Aviation in the country.

In the event, a much more cautious approach was finally settled upon, and the Government agreed in 1951 to the formation of a single Fleet Requirement Unit. Naval Headquarters took the opportunity to establish a fully self sufficient air arm, recruiting and training a skilled cadre of personnel that would eventually go on to support India's fledgling carrier aviation capability a decade later.

The Indian Naval Air Arm's first aircraft type was the Short Sealand amphibian, first of which (INS-101) landed at Cochin in the southern state of Kerala in February 1953. The Service's first air station was the airstrip on Willingdon Island just off Cochin, and was formally commissioned as INS Garuda on 11 May 1953. In 1955, the Service's ten Sealands began to be supplemented with ex-RN Fairey Firefly TT.Mk 1 target towing aircraft. A second batch of Fireflys, 20mm-cannon-equipped TT.Mk 4s, was acquired in 1958 and marked the service entry of India's first armed naval aircraft. Then, in 1959, the FRU was formally commissioned as Indian Naval Air Squadron (INAS) 550, the Navy's first squadron.

◄ India's aircraft carrier INS *Vikramaditya* (R33) (Indian Navy)

However, it was the acquisition of the *Majestic*-class aircraft carrier INS *Vikrant* in 1961 that brought Indian Naval Aviation into its own and established an uninterrupted half-century tradition of carrier aviation in India. The commissioning of *Vikrant* in March 1961 was preceded by the acquisition of Hawker Sea Hawk fighters (forming INAS 300 'White Tigers' in July 1960) and Breguet Alizé ASW aircraft (forming INAS 310 'Cobras' in January 1961). The first arrested landing aboard INS *Vikrant* took place on 18 May 1961, piloted by Lt Radhakrishna Hariram Tahiliani, senior pilot of INAS 300 who would later rise to serve as Navy Chief. Aérospatiale Alouette III helicopters were introduced as a SAR flight aboard *Vikrant* in 1964, before the first unit operating the type was commissioned as INAS 321 'Angels' in March 1969. The Navy operated loaned Indian Air Force Sikorsky S-55s as plane guards until the Alouettes arrived in sufficient number. Over the following decades, the Navy commissioned a number of new squadrons and air stations across India and inducted various types of aircraft, covering all aspects of naval warfare.

Indian carrier aviation's first major upgrade came in the form of BAe Sea Harrier FRS. Mk 51 'jump jets' that commenced operations from *Vikrant* in December 1983, replacing the Sea Hawks as the Navy's fixed-wing fighter of choice. INS *Vikrant* was joined by the *Centaur*-class carrier INS *Viraat* (formerly HMS *Hermes*) in 1987, with the Sea Harrier VTOL fighter operating off the ski-jump equipped deck of the new carrier as *Vikrant* entered refit to receive a ski-jump of her own. The modifications planned for *Vikrant* included removal of her steam catapults, so in May 1987, an Alizé from INAS 310 carried out the type's final launch at sea before the unit was permanently relegated to shore-based operations, serving from land until 1991. The Navy's Alizés were nonetheless valuable participants in Indian peacekeeping efforts in Sri Lanka (Operation Pawan) and the military response to an attempted coup d'état in the Maldives, both in 1988. *Vikrant* herself continued in service with an embarked air wing of Sea Harriers, Sea Kings and Chetaks until she was berthed for the final time in November 1994 and finally decommissioned on 31 January 1997.

Fiscal and operational constraints have prevented the Indian Navy from fully realising its blue water ambitions centred on a multiple-carrier force, but keenly aware that institutional knowledge and experience can rapidly atrophy if left unutilised, the Navy has accorded significant priority to carrier aviation, and has never *not* operated fixed-wing aircraft from carriers at sea since *Vikrant* entered service. This foresight has held the service in good stead with each successive induction of a new carrier or carrier-borne aircraft type.

Indeed, the proficiency of the Naval Air Arm has been borne out over a number of combat actions in the restive subcontinent. In 1961, mere months after *Vikrant* and her aircraft had entered service, the Indian Government launched Operation Vijay ('victory'), a police action to evict the Portuguese from their colonies at Goa, Daman, and Diu. The Navy was instructed to blockade the Portuguese enclaves and *Vikrant* took up station some 50-100 miles off Goa, deploying its Alizés on near-continuous armed reconnaissance missions. In the absence of any hostile moves, naval aircraft were not involved in any engagements, but an Alizé did land at the Dabolim airfield (now INS Hansa, the Navy's premier air station) shortly after it was captured by the Indian Army.

During the 1962 Sino-Indian border conflict, Sea Hawks from INAS 300 were deployed on alert ashore but did not see action on account of both nations opting not to commit their air forces and navies to the hostilities. The 1965 India-Pakistan

With the arrival of INS *Vikramaditya*, India briefly operated a two-ship carrier fleet. In the background INS *Viraat* with its Sea Harriers can be seen.
(Indian Navy)

War broke out at an awkward time for the Navy – while INS *Vikrant* was docked for a scheduled refit. Her air wing was put to use immediately, however, with INAS 300's Sea Hawks deployed to Santa Cruz for the air defence of Bombay, while the Alizés of INAS 310 operated from Jamnagar in the maritime reconnaissance role. Yet again, the Naval Air Arm had no opportunity to fire a shot 'in anger.'

That changed in 1971, during what is often called the Indian Navy's 'finest hour.' Hostilities formally commenced between India and Pakistan on the evening of 3 December, with a series of pre-emptive Pakistani air strikes in north-western India. Even as the Indian Air Force began retaliatory strikes, the Indian Navy entered the conflict in spectacular fashion at dawn on 4 December when eight Sea Hawks armed with 5in rockets or 500lb bombs launched from INS *Vikrant* in the Bay of Bengal to strike and neutralise the Cox's Bazaar airfield in East Pakistan. Later that day, another eight Sea Hawks struck the more heavily defended airfield and harbour at Chittagong. On 6 December, Alizés were tasked with night attacks on Chittagong to prevent repair work under the cover of darkness from undoing the Sea Hawks' day strikes. Tasked to neutralise enemy shore and shipping facilities, prevent Pakistani reinforcements or evacuations, and counter any interference by a third country in the war, *Vikrant*'s Sea Hawks flew and fought by day in clear weather, logging a total of 160 sorties through the two-week conflict, while the Alizés were confined mostly to bombing and mining by night.

In the West, a trio of INAS 310 Alizés carried out anti-submarine patrols from Bombay while Sea Hawks from INAS 551, the training squadron for INAS 300, were on standby at Goa, Cochin and Trivandrum. Action in the Western theatre also saw the Navy's first and only combat loss – a Pakistan Air Force F-104 shot down an Alizé operating from Jamnagar on 10 December.

Today

With the commissioning of INS *Vikramaditya* in November 2013, the Indian Navy was once again a two-carrier force, but it had already been made clear by senior Naval officers earlier that year that the days of INS *Viraat* and her Sea Harriers were numbered. The older carrier and her iconic jump jets soldiered on until 2016, being showcased to the public and the world one last time at the International Fleet Review held off the east coast city of Visakhapatnam in February that year.

After *Viraat* returned to her homeport of Bombay, her Sea Harriers flew to their shore base at INS Hansa, Goa, where they were withdrawn from service a few months later, in May 2016. INAS 300 received new MiG-29KUBs, and assumed the role of training squadron for INAS 303 Black Panthers, which had been commissioned in May 2013 and was by then fully operational as the embarked fighter squadron for INS *Vikramaditya*.

In July 2016, *Viraat* sailed under her own steam for the last time, heading from Bombay to Cochin for her decommissioning refit. The carrier was towed back to Bombay in October, and on 6 March 2017, was decommissioned at a ceremony that celebrated not only 30 years of service under the Indian Naval ensign, but also her 27-year Royal Navy career, with Admiral Sir Philip Jones, First Sea Lord and Chief of Naval Staff of the Royal Navy in attendance along with his Indian counterpart, Chief of Naval Staff Admiral Sunil Lanba.

The Indian Navy returned to a single-carrier force once again, albeit of greatly improved potency with *Vikramaditya* and her MiG-29Ks.

Once the pride of the naval air arm, the Sea Harrier fleet was retired in May 2016. (Angad Singh)

INS *Vikramaditya*

The *Vikramaditya* saga, crucial though it was for the future of Indian carrier aviation, was a tortuous nine-year affair that ran far over budget and caused significant consternation at the uppermost levels of governments of both nations involved.

The carrier has had a chequered past: originally commissioned in December 1987 as *Baku* for the Soviet Navy, she was the last of the *Kiev*-class of heavy aircraft-carrying cruisers designed by the Nevskoye Design Bureau and built at Nikolayev South Shipyard in what is now Ukraine. *Baku* was equipped with twelve P-500 Bazalt (NATO reporting name SS-N-12 Sandbox) cruise missiles in addition to an air wing of 12 Yak-38 VTOL combat aircraft and 12-16 helicopters (Ka-25/27). The angled flight deck extended around two-thirds the length of the ship, and was designed exclusively for VTOL operations, being devoid of a ski-jump or catapults. She was different in many aspects from the preceding *Kiev*-class vessels, being used to trial some of the technologies and weapons that would be used on the larger *Kuznetsov*-class aircraft carriers that were planned to follow, such as the updated surface-to-air missile fit of 192 3K95 Kinzhal (SA-N-9 Gauntlet) SAMs.

After the dissolution of the USSR, *Baku* was renamed *Admiral Flota Sovetskogo Soyuza Gorshkov* in 1991 (commonly shortened simply to *Admiral Gorshkov*), and continued to serve in the Northern Fleet until she was abruptly decommissioned in 1996 and offered for sale. India was immediately interested in the purchase but negotiations were drawn out and an agreement to buy the ship was only reached in January 2004. Under the terms of this initial agreement, the ship itself would be 'free', but the overhaul, upgrade and modifications to convert it into a Short Takeoff But Arrested Recovery (STOBAR) carrier would cost around USD 800 million, with an additional USD 1 billion to be spent on the air wing and on board weapons and systems.

The entirety of the overhaul and modernisation of *Admiral Gorshkov* was undertaken at the Sevmash shipyard in Severodvinsk as Project 11430. This included the removal of the P-500 cruise missile launchers and the four 24-tube 3K95 Kinzhal launchers located on the bow, to make room for a 14.3° ski-jump. Two hydraulic aircraft restraining stands were fitted, allowing fighters to reach full power before making a ski jump-assisted take-off. The 30-tonne capacity 18.8×9.9-metre aircraft elevator beside the ship's superstructure is mostly unchanged, and while there were initially plans to enlarge the aft lift to match, the enclosed nature of the lifts meant that this remained a 20-tonne 18.8×8.6-metre platform. A Proletarsky Zavod manufactured 'Svetlana' aircraft arresting complex, consisting of three 30-metre-wide arresting cables capable of halting a 20-tonne aircraft within the reconfigured landing distance, was fitted on the aft part of the angled deck and new navigation and carrier-landing aids were incorporated to support STOBAR operations, including flight deck lighting systems, a LUNA landing system for MiG-29Ks, and the DAPS landing system for Sea Harriers. While the ship was designed to be able to launch and recover Sea Harriers, the Brtish-made fighters never operated from *Vikramaditya* for any meaningful length of time.

The old flight control centre ('Flyco' in Navy parlance) was converted to a visitors' gallery and replaced with an all-new, elevated and expanded control centre offering a better view of both ends of the flight deck. The new configuration had an overall length of 284 metres and a beam (overall, not at the waterline) of 60 metres, a 198-metre angled deck for recovery of fighters and all helicopter operations, plus two take-off positions – a 'long' 195-metre run, and a 'short' 125-metre run. Although designed to be able to embark a maximum of 36 aircraft, the carrier typically sails with an air wing of about 16 fighters and a mix of helicopters as needed – typically Ka-31s and HAL-built Alouette IIIs (Chetaks). Up to 13 aircraft can be parked on deck without interfering with launch or recovery operations.

The eight boilers were converted to take low-sulphur high-speed diesel instead of heavy furnace fuel oil, and now produce 100 tonnes per hour of steam at a pressure of 64 bar, generating a total turbine output power of 180,000 shp, driving four enormous propellers. Six new Italian-made Wärtsilä 1.5 MW diesel generators were installed, along with a Sperry Bridgemaster navigation radar, a new telephone exchange, new data link and an IFF Mk XI system. A mast aft of the island was built to host communication and ESM antennae. The carrier received an all-new combat management system, LESORUB-E from Russian firm Morinformsystem-Agat, a Rezistor-E TACAN (Tactical Communication and Navigation) system for aircraft control, and Fregat-M2EM and Podberezovik radar sets for air and surface search. Creature comforts were vastly improved, incorporating new reverse osmosis water-purification plants capable of supplying up to 400 tonnes of fresh water per day. York International provided refrigeration and air conditioning, a new galley specific to Indian needs was installed, and interestingly, accommodation included berths for up to 10 female officers (the IN does not currently station women aboard ships or submarines at sea).

For Sevmash, it was important to maintain hull strength and integrity during the modification, particularly because of the large number of openings in the hull (over 500). Old equipment was removed from the ship in drydock, after which the shipyard conducted what was effectively an extensive 'rebuild,' requiring the replacement of over 4,000 tonnes of steel. Whilst a lot of the fresh steel – over 900 tonnes of it – went toward construction of the ski-jump, no effort was spared in refurbishment of the remaining structure: 1,750 of 2,500 compartments were completely rebuilt, and 234 new hull sections fabricated, resulting in a virtually new ship.

In the years following the initial agreement, construction delays and cost escalations strained the deal and threatened derailment. Sevmash and Rosoboronexport had grossly underestimated the scope of work required to bring *Gorshkov* up to modern standards, most (in)famously realising well into the refit that nearly all the cabling in the ship – totalling a mammoth 2,300 km – needed replacement. Additionally, over 300km of new piping was installed, along with all-new electronics, fans, pumps and similar equipment.

A stalemate was reached in 2008, with Russia stating that owing to the severely deteriorated condition of the ship, final delivery cost would be in the region of USD 3 billion. Following months of high-level talks, in March 2009, the final delivery price was agreed upon at USD 2.3 billion, still nearly three times higher than the original contract. Since then, work continued apace, and the aircraft carrier looked on track for a late-2012 delivery date.

In June 2010, a Russian MiG-29K development aircraft was tested for use aboard the *Vikramaditya*, this type being the primary fixed wing fighter to be operated off the carrier by the Indian Navy. A total of 45 MiG-29K/KUBs are now operational with the Navy, deliveries having run from December 2009 to February 2017. Project 11430 dock trials began in March 2011, with focus on the main power generation units and Indian-made equipment that had been integrated over the course of the refit. Indian Navy per-

Flight operations on board of INS *Vikramaditya* during a demonstration for the Prime Minister in December 2015. (Indian Navy)

sonnel began training on *Vikramaditya* in April 2011. A year later, it was announced that all internal systems were functioning, and the ship was entirely self-contained. Measurement of the ship's magnetic field and centre of gravity were performed before sea trials were undertaken.

Vikramaditya sailed for the first time under own power on 10 June 2012, after almost 17 years spent inactive. The ship departed for the crucial 120-day pre-delivery trials from Severodvinsk in June itself, with projected handover on 4 December 2012, celebrated as 'Navy Day' in India. However, the programme was struck a widely-publicised blow during this final set of trials – during full-power testing in September 2012, seven of the ship's eight boilers failed and had to be shut down.

Russian contractors insinuated that the failure was a result of India's insistence to replace the asbestos insulation around the boilers. Asbestos is a known carcinogen, and India had sought to replace the material based on health and safety concerns. Post-trials discussions between India and Russia examined the asbestos issue in great detail, and the two sides eventually agreed to re-install the asbestos insulation with a non-carcinogenic outer layer that would protect the asbestos from any environmental degradation.

The delivery date was pushed back by a year, and the ship returned to Severodvinsk. In July 2013, following boiler repairs and other work conducted over the 9-odd months since the decision to defer delivery, *Vikramaditya* headed into the White Sea where speed and manoeuvring trials were conducted, along with testing of the electronic warfare (EW) systems. All systems were put under full load and during this phase of trials, the carrier achieved a speed of 29.2 knots. After the White Sea trials in July, the ship proceeded to the Barents Sea, for the second stage of trials, beginning in early August. This involved flight operations of MiG-29K/KUBs from the ship, including night flying. Over 2,500 people were on board *Vikramaditya* during the Barents Sea trials, including specialists from all subcontractors involved in the project, along with some 1,000 Indian Navy personnel. There were 88 arrested landings, all piloted

by Russians, and the carrier controlled a total of 778 flights. EW capability was also demonstrated to the satisfaction of the Indian side. *Vikramaditya* then returned to the White Sea for a second round of manoeuvring trials, recording a 29.5 knots maximum forward speed and a full reverse speed of 15.9 knots. On 20 September 2013, the trials were declared successfully completed and *Vikramaditya* docked at Severodvinsk, where it was finally commissioned into the Indian Navy on 16 November 2013, with Cmde Suraj Berry as commissioning CO and Capt Janak Bevli as Captain (Air).

The carrier then headed for India, even as the designated fighter squadron to be embarked, INAS 303 Black Panthers, began working up at the Shore Based Test Facility (SBTF) at their home base of INS Hansa in Goa. The SBTF approximates the take-off and landing portions of an aircraft carrier – in this case the STOBAR configured INS *Vikramaditya*. It features a ski-jump and restraining stands identical to those on the carrier, and an arresting gear complex, albeit with two cables instead of three. In addition to being used by the MiG-29K units at Goa, the SBTF is also used for developmental test flying for the naval variant of the HAL Tejas.

INS *Vikramaditya* reached Indian waters in early January 2014, taking part in a few basic exercises with ships of the Western Fleet before heading to her home port of INS Kadamba at Karwar, a few hundred miles south of Goa. By February, she had 'trapped' her first INAS 303 MiG-29K, and in May 2014 was declared 'fully operational,' taking part in a Western Fleet exercise off Goa.

Since then, the ship has undergone periodic maintenance within India and has already received a few upgrades and modifications, carried out in-country. These include new Rohde & Schwarz ESM equipment and, crucially, self-protection updates in the form of three 8-cell IAI Barak-1 point-defence missile launchers fitted on the island, above the old Flyco, and two AK-630 Close-In Weapon System (CIWS) turrets with associated electro-optical directors mounted on either side of the fantail. The defensive weaponry was removed from the frigate INS *Godavari*, which was decommissioned in 2015. Fire control is via an Elta EL/M-2221 STGR (Search Track & Guidance/Gunnery Radar) located on the aft mast, with SATCOM equipment relocated from the mast to the island superstructure.

In 2016, INS *Vikramaditya* was dry docked in India for the first time, completing a 43-day scheduled refit at Cochin Shipyard from September to November, before heading back to its home port and then out to the Arabian Sea.

The Future

While technology has marched inexorably on since the 1950s, little has changed in the Indian Navy's plan to field a multiple-carrier force. The nature of the neighbourhood and India's expanding regional and global aspirations mean that the Navy would prefer to have separate assets available for home waters and distant deployments. Well before INS *Vikramaditya* began its planned 40-year service life, the Navy had decided that the Russian vessel would be its last imported carrier. In 1999, the Cabinet Committee on Security approved construction of an Indigenous Aircraft Carrier (IAC) under 'Project 71' at Cochin Shipyard in Kerala. In 2003, the specifications for the vessel were broadly frozen at 40,000 tonnes displacement, 262-metre length and 60-metre beam.

To be named *Vikrant*, after India's first carrier, the IAC is broadly similar to *Vikramaditya*, in that it is a STOBAR carrier designed around a similar air wing, but given that it has been designed from the ground up as a dedicated aircraft carrier, not converted from a different design, there are a number of key differences. Propulsion is to be provided by General Electric LM2500 gas turbines instead of steam boilers, providing a similar 7,000 nautical mile range and 45-day endurance as *Vikramaditya*, but with much greater reliability and safety. The hangar and deck are more optimised on the IAC, being free of many of the constraints of the *Vikramaditya* conversion and benefiting greatly from the involvement of Italy's Fincantieri as consultants on design, integration and validation. The aviation complex will be more or less identical to *Vikramaditya*, with the same Svetlana arresting system, landing and navigation aids, but the aircraft lifts on IAC-1 will be sized differently and placed on the starboard edge of the deck, one on either side of the superstructure. The island itself is a much cleaner design overall, and will integrate four active electronically scanned radar arrays, the selected hardware being the IAI Elta EL/M-2248 MF-STAR, capable of search and track of air as well as surface contacts. Unlike *Vikramaditya*, the IAC's principal SAM system will be the much longer-ranged IAI Barak-8, in addition to AK-630 CIWS.

As with any new ship design, Project 71 has had to contend with delays and cost overruns, with the projected date of commissioning first slipping from 2014 to 2018, and now even further, beyond 2020. Given that the vessel will enter service at a time when nearly half the airframe life of the combined MiG-29K fleet will be consumed, the Navy is already planning for a future air wing to be shared between *Vikrant* and the next indigenous carrier, dubbed IAC-2. In January 2017, the service released a Request For Information (RFI) for 'approximately 57 multi-role carrier borne fighters', with the specifications indicating intention to operate these from the STOBAR *Vikrant* as well IAC-2, which will likely have a catapult-launch system (CATOBAR).

IAC-2 itself is projected to be a much larger vessel, in the region of 65,000 tonnes, and the Indian Navy has set up a Joint Working Group (JWG) with the US Navy to enable possible collaboration on the programme in the areas of aircraft, launch and recovery systems, propulsion, and design. The programme, however, is still in its early stages – finalisation of the configuration, detailed design and first steel cutting remain some time away, with commissioning of this carrier expected no earlier than the mid-2030s.

Carrier Operations Today

As the flagship of the Indian Navy, INS *Vikramaditya*'s role extends from operational to regional diplomacy. Despite its location in a region where geopolitical tensions are often high, *Vikramaditya* has not been involved in any combat actions since she was commissioned, instead taking part in exercises large and small across the Indian Ocean Region (IOR), and 'flying the flag' for India and the Navy as and when required. Since she was declared operational in May 2014, the carrier has progressively extended and validated new capabilities and integrated with the Western Fleet. In 2016, she was the centrepiece of the International Fleet Review, a mammoth multinational event held at the east coast city of Visakhaptnam, where over 70 warships and submarines assembled for a pageant of military might. En route to the eastern seaboard, she made a port

An Indian Navy Ka-28 prepares to land on the flight deck of the *Ticonderoga*-class guided-missile cruiser USS *Bunker Hill* (CG 52) in support of Malabar 2012 exercise. (US Navy/MC3 John Grandin)

call at Colombo, with the specific aim of bolstering India-Sri Lanka relations at the military as well as political levels.

Following her refit in late 2016, she took part in the Navy's annual Theatre Level Readiness and Operational Exercise (TROPEX) from 24 January to 23 February 2017. TROPEX is usually conducted in conjunction with the Army and Air Force, and is the Navy's largest annual exercise. The 2017 edition saw over 45 vessels from the Western and Eastern fleets deploy to Arabian Sea, where they simulated an out of area contingency operation with the Army and Air Force, including special forces from all three services. The exercise specifically included a Large Force Engagement (LFE) by the combined fleet against threats simulated by the Air Force, comprising maritime strike Jaguars, A-50/Phalcon AEW&C, and Su-30MKIs, all supported by Il-78MKI tankers. Attacks were designed to be particularly challenging for the carrier and defending fleet, being launched from multiple directions, but official Ministry of Defence statements noted that all threats were 'neutralised … using the Beyond Visual Range (BVR) capabilities' of the carrier's MiG-29Ks, operating in coordination with other fleet units.

Unlike western arrested recovery carriers, *Vikramaditya* lacks an emergency barricade system to recover aircraft in case of cable issues on deck or equipment failures on aircraft that might preclude normal arrested landings. Combined with the relatively unproven 'go around' (bolter) performance of the MiG-29K, this is a notable peacetime operational limitation, often requiring the carrier to operate within distance of a shore-based diversion airfield. Given the long range of the MiG-29K and the type's 'buddy-refueling' capabilities, however, diversion distances even on a single engine are quite large. This nonetheless remains an area of concern, and the Navy has issued an RFI for barricade systems for both Vikramaditya and IAC-1, which share the Russian Svetlana aircraft arresting complex.

Fly Navy

The only aviation units 'formally' attached to the carrier at present are its fighter squadron, INAS 303 'Black Panthers' and a flight of HAL Chetaks from INAS 321 'Angels' for SAR and utility purposes. Even if INS *Vikramaditya*'s air wing appears small, the carrier is designed to be able to operate virtually any rotary-wing asset of the Indian Navy, to varying degrees. The aviation facilities on board can host Kamov Ka-31 AEW helicopters and Ka-28 ASW helicopters as part of the integral air wing if necessary, while Westland Sea Kings (Mk 42B and 42C) can operate from the flight deck, but are not designed to be hangared or supported on board for extended periods.

In any case, a mix of Ka-28s, Ka-31s, and Sea Kings are usually embarked on *Vikramaditya*'s escort vessels when she is underway, so the roles required of these rotorcraft in the context of a carrier deployment are always fulfilled.

Equally important to the effective fielding of the Navy's carrier aviation capability are the training units, INAS 551 'Phantoms' operating BAE Hawks out of INS *Dega* in Visakhapatnam, and INAS 300 'White Tigers,' the Navy's first fighter squadron, now conducting conversion training for the MiG-29K at INS Hansa in Goa.

Future carrier aviation programmes are also underway, as part of a general push to bolster naval aviation. Chief among these are new rotorcraft acquisitions, one programme to replace the ageing Chetaks in the utility and SAR roles, and another to induct medium-weight multirole helicopters to supplant the Ka-28 and Sea King fleets. While the Navy's operational needs are making these acquisition programmes increasingly urgent, the Indian Government is seeking to leverage the large quantities of helicopters required and convince helicopter makers to set up manufacturing, assembly, and maintenance facilities in India, as part of a broader push to expand the country's industrial capabilities. As such, the initial tender for 16 multirole helicopters has been held up indefinitely since the selection of the Sikorsky S-70B (the exact variant and specification was not disclosed) in December 2014. A long-awaited re-organisation of the MoD's procurement policies currently underway should provide a clearer path for the Navy, and indeed broader military procurement, from 2017 onward.

A much more distant programme, and one that is likely to impact the indigenous carrier *Vikrant* and IAC-2 more than INS *Vikramaditya*, is the 'Multi-Role Carrier Borne Fighter' (MRCBF). As noted earlier, an RFI for 57 MRCBF was issued in January 2017, a month after the Navy Chief, Admiral Sunil Lanba, dismissed the idea of inducting the Naval variant of the Tejas Light Combat Aircraft (LCA). The Naval LCA (N-LCA) programme has resulted in a maritime version of the IAF's Tejas, developed by DRDO's Aeronautical Development Agency (ADA) and built by Hinudstan Aeronautics Limited (HAL). The N-LCA uses the same GE F404 afterburning turbofan engine, but incorporates a strengthened undercarriage and fuselage, a tailhook for carrier landings, leading-edge vortex controllers (LEVCONs) at the wing roots for additional lift and control authority at low speeds, and extensive usage of new corrosion-resistant materials for sea-based operation. The LCA, even in its land-based variants, has been plagued with well-documented weight and power issues, and in maritime garb, where strengthened landing gear, airframe and tailhook add further weight penalties, the Navy has judged that the fighter lacks performance that is essential for a naval aircraft, not just in terms of combat utility but also safety.

In light of these issues, plans were already underway since 2010 to re-engine both variants of the LCA with GE F414 engines, but when the IAF ordered 120 F404-engined LCAs, effectively abandoning the new engine programme, the Navy was forced to reconsider its own indigenous fighter plans in light of the reduced funding and time available for fielding a new carrier fighter. However, even as Admiral Lanba nixed the operational future of the N-LCA, he stressed that the service would continue to support the development of a home-grown carrier fighter as it evaluated foreign options for the MRCBF requirement.

The decision to evaluate alternatives also appears rooted in an unstated acceptance that the MiG-29K-and-*Vikramaditya* combination, while certainly more potent than anything fielded before, is essentially a technological cul-de-sac. Acquiring more such aircraft, with 25-year/6,000-hour service lives for carriers projected to enter service from the mid-2020s onward is seen as a retrograde step when more capable (or at least CATOBAR-compatible) aircraft could be sought instead. It is for this reason that the MRCBF RFI specifically demands information regarding the ability of any proposed aircraft to operate off the STOBAR IAC-1 (*Vikrant*) with its ski-jump and Svetlana arresting system, as well as the planned CATOBAR IAC-2 which could use C-13 series steam catapults or electro-magnetic catapults (EMALS) for launch and Mark 7 Mod3 or Advanced Arresting Gear (AAG) for recovery.

Beyond the launch and recovery parameters, the RFI indicates that the MRCBF is to be day/night and all-weather capable, employed for Air Defence (AD), Air to Surface Operations, Buddy Refuelling, Reconnaissance, and Electronic Warfare (EW). The document is generally exploratory in nature, seeking details of available fighters worldwide, in order to frame appropriate qualitative requirements to be issued with the eventual RFP. The RFI also indicates that technology transfer and licence production of the fighters in India is preferred, and that aircraft deliveries are expected to commence within three years of contract signature, and be completed after a further three years (a rate of three fighters every two months).

Depending on political sanction and funding for IAC-2, other decisions on carrier aviation – such as AEW assets and logistics aircraft – will be considered in the distant future, but that is well beyond the scope of this work.

Current units of Indian aircraft carrier aviation (August 2017)

Unit	Aircraft type	Role	Base	Remarks
INAS 300 'White Tigers'	MiG-29K, KUB	Training	INS Hansa, Goa	12
INAS 303 'Black Panthers'	MiG-29K, KUB	Multirole fighter	INS Hansa, Goa	32
INAS 312 'Angels'	HAL Chetak	SAR, utility	INS Hansa, Goa	>30 in IN
INAS 330 'Harpoons'	Sea King Mk 42B	ASW, ASuW	INS Shikra, Mumbai	18
INAS 333 'Eagles'	Ka-28	ASW	INS Dega, Visakhapatnam	10
INAS 339 'Falcons'	Ka-31	AEW	INS Hansa, Goa	14

Carrier Aviation Units

INAS 303 'Black Panthers'

INAS 303 'Black Panthers'

The Black Panthers first began operating as an 'Intensive Flying Training Unit' (IFTU) with the arrival of the first MiG-29Ks in December 2009. The unit's first 10 pilots, including the CO, qualified on the MiG-29K in Russia before setting up the IFTU, but the first batch of newcomers arrived fully 'carrier qualified' from the US Navy (on T-45s) under a training agreement between the Indian and American Governments. In a significant departure from the past, the IFTU included Wg Cdr Manish Nigde from the IAF, a Fighter Combat Leader 'on loan' to the Navy to assist with formulating tactics and standard operating procedures for full exploitation of the fighter in combat.

The formidable supersonic fighters have more in common with the MiG 29M/M2 than the IAF MiG-29Bs that are more familiar around the subcontinent, prominent differences being an all new mould-line with a common canopy for twin- and single-seat variants, enhanced low-speed lift devices, an all-important arrestor hook and increased use of radar absorbent material (RAM). Under the skin the differences are even more pronounced, with a digital fly-by-wire (FBW) flight control system (FCS), an all-glass cockpit with a ShKAI wide-angle monochrome head-up display (HUD) and MFI-10-7 liquid-crystal multifunction displays (MFDs). Additionally, the MiG-29K/KUB flight and navigation system is based on an 'open architecture' principle built around the MIL-

Indian MiG-29K IN819 during Exercise Malabar 2017, training with US Navy Carrier Strike Group 11 (CSG 11). (US Navy)

STD-1553B standard data bus enabling integration of weapons and sensors from a variety of sources, mirroring the architecture of many Indian fighters, including the Sukhoi Su-30MKI, Mirage 2000I/TI, and DARIN-standard Jaguars. Additional fuel tanks have been accommodated in the fuselage and leading edge extensions, increasing total fuel capacity by some fifty per cent compared to early variants of the land-based MiG-29, and the fighter is cleared for a centreline Zvezda PAZ-MK 'buddy refuelling' pod, allowing it to act as a range-extension or recovery tanker. The MiG-29K's Klimov RD-33MK afterburning turbofans produce 88 kN of thrust at full power, nearly 7 kN more than their land-based counterparts, and are digitally controlled and designed for greater reliability and ease of maintenance.

The main sensor is the Phazotron Zhuk-ME, X-band pulse-Doppler radar, with an aerial target detection range of 150 km. It can initiate track beginning at 130 km range, against a target with radar cross-section of five square metres and can Track-While-Scan (TWS) 20 targets and simultaneously engage four targets. Passive detection equipment consists of an OLS-UE Infra-Red Search and Track (IRST) sensor and laser range-finder, which incorporates look-down capability. The aircraft also feature a host of non-Russian avionics, including Sagem's Sigma-95 Inertial Navigation System/Global Positioning System (INS/GPS), Thales TopSight helmet mounted sighting system, IAI Elta EL/M-8222 ECM pod, and a host of Indian comms equipment.

The IFTU was formally commissioned as a squadron at INS Hansa, Goa, on 11 May 2013, under the command of Captain Ajay Daniel Theophilus. In the tradition of numbering frontline Navy squadrons in the 300s, the Black Panthers were assigned 303, in reference to the .303 calibre rifle cartridge developed in the late 1800s. The .303 was an accurate and devastating cartridge, setting the standard for firearm design over the better part of a century. It was therefore deemed fitting that the game-changing capabilities of the MiG-29K be acknowledged with a nod to the venerable rifle cartridge. The squadron insignia, in keeping with its name, depicts a snarling black panther against blue waves and an azure sky.

INAS 303 initially functioned as a nucleus for MiG-29K operations in preparation for *Vikramaditya*'s arrival, conducting training of new pilots fresh from either the USA or the co-located training unit, INAS 551 'Phantoms.' Once an initial cadre of pilots was 'day ops' on the carrier by mid-2014, the unit gradually worked up to a more frontline operational posture. Today the unit is the 'sword arm' of the carrier and indeed the Navy, relied upon for air defence, surface strike at sea or ashore, as well as reconnaissance. Principal armament includes RVV-AE BVR missiles, R-73 close-combat missiles, and variants of the Kh-35 anti-ship missile alongside standard air-to-ground munitions such as unguided rockets. The MiG-29K is also fitted with a 30-mm Gryazev-Shipunov GSh-301 single-barrel gun, with 150 rounds of ammunition.

Once INAS 300 took over conversion training for the MiG-29K, INAS 303 transitioned completely to a frontline combat unit, and now trains and operates exclusively in this role.

INAS 321 'Angels'

INAS 321 'Angels'

The Indian Navy was an enthusiastic early adopter of the Aérospatiale Alouette III, licence-built in India as the HAL Chetak. The Navy began inducting Chetaks in the mid-1960s, utilising them for SAR, liaison/communications, utility, and as 'Multi-role Anti-submarine Torpedo Carrying Helicopters' (MATCH), equipped with two Whitehead A244S torpedoes. By the end of the decade, the Navy had enough Chetaks on strength to justify a new unit, and INAS 321 'Angels' was commissioned at INS Hansa on 15 March 1969. The squadron's appellation was a reference to the Chetak's primary SAR role. Since then, every Naval Air Station has had a locally-based INAS 321 Flight, even though the squadron is nominally headquartered in Goa. 'Floating airfields' are treated no differently, and all carriers have a permanent INAS 321 Flight for SAR duties, with a secondary utility role.

An Indian Navy HAL Chetak from the locally-based INAS 321 Flight departing INS Dega on a training sortie. (Angad Singh)

INAS 300 'White Tigers'

INAS 300 'White Tigers'

The White Tigers were commissioned on 7 July 1960 at RNAS Brawdy in the United Kingdom. The squadron was initially equipped with the Sea Hawk, converting to the Sea Harrier FRS. Mk 51 in 1983. For over half a century, INAS 300 was the Navy's sole fixed-wing combat squadron, being joined by INAS 303 only in 2013.

During the unit's Sea Harrier days, the Navy's fighter pilot training pipeline used to see Naval Aviators earn their wings at the Air Force Academy at Dundigal and completing the IAF's three-stage training syllabus before arriving at INAS 551 'Phantoms' to learn Navy-specific flying on HAL Kiran jet trainers. They would then head across the ramp to INAS 552 'Braves' to convert to the Sea Harrier and earn their Deck Landing Qualification (DLQ), transitioning to operational flying from the carrier with INAS 300.

However, once INAS 303 had worked up to a suitable level of operational proficiency from INS *Vikramaditya*, the Navy decided a similar training pipeline would be required for the MiG-29K. With the retirement of the Sea Harriers in May 2016, the conversion training role was passed on to INAS 300. The White Tigers began their transition to STOBAR fighters in May itself, drawing senior pilots and instructors from INAS 303 and trainees from INAS 551, now operating BAE Hawk Mk 132s out of INS *Dega* on the east coast.

INAS 300 will now convert Naval Aviators from the Hawk to the MiG-29K, see them through their first solos on the type, all the way through to their carrier qualifications on *Vikramaditya*. When pilots are 'day ops' on the carrier – qualified to conduct daytime/fair weather air defence operations from deck – they will move to INAS 303 and begin operational flying, picking up more qualifications (night, strike and so on) along the way.

It is planned for INAS 300 to eventually form the nucleus of the air wing for the new INS *Vikrant*, and when the White Tigers switch back to frontline status, a new MiG-29K training unit, with the correct numbering convention (500-series) will be established.

MiG-29KUB IN678 taxiing in to the INAS 300 ramp at INS Hansa while folding its wings. (Angad Singh)

INAS 333 'Eagles'

INAS 333 'Eagles'

INAS 333 was commissioned at Goa on 11 December 1980, operating Kamov Ka-25 ASW helicopters that had been inducted with the five *Kashin*-class guided-missile destroyers ordered in the 1970s. The Eagles added far more capable Kamov Ka-28s in 1989, but these helicopters were soon shifted to INAS 339 'Falcons,' replacing the Sea Kings there in 1993.

In 2000, the Eagles were re-based at INS Dega, and in 2009 the unit retired its Ka-25s and received all of INAS 339's Ka-28s as replacement. The Eagles typically deploy on the Navy's Soviet- or Russian-origin warships, but INS *Vikramaditya* is designed to be able to hangar and support these helicopters, with Russian Ka-27 being used extensively in the SAR and utility roles during the carrier's pre-delivery trials. Indian Navy Ka-28s have a sensor package comprising an Osminog (Octopus) surface search radar, VGS-3 dunking sonar, and a range of sonobuoys, and can carry up to two torpedoes or an undisclosed number of depth charges in a ventral weapons bay.

Ka-28 IN583 parked at the type's home base, INS Dega. (Angad Singh)

An INAS 339 Ka-31 in flight with radar array stowed. (Angad Singh)

INAS 339 'Falcons'

INAS 339 was raised on 23 November 1990 at INS *Kunjali* in Bombay, operating Westland Sea Kings. The squadron transitioned to Ka-28s from March 1993, moving to INS Hansa that same year. In 2003, the Falcons received Ka-31 AEW helicopters that had accompanied the newly-acquired *Talwar*-class from Russia. These helicopters operated alongside Ka-28s at INAS 333 for some time, before being sent to INAS 333 at Visakhapatnam as noted earlier.

INAS 339 'Falcons'

The Ka-31 is fitted with a NIIRT E-801M Oko (Eye) airborne radar, with the 6 × 1 metre planar array mounted beneath the fuselage. The 200-kg array is stowed flush to the fuselage for take-off and landing, only unfolding once the helicopter is above a certain speed and altitude. Once deployed, the radar can conduct a 360-degreee mechanical scan every ten seconds, and is able to simultaneously track up to 40 airborne or surface threats. Detection ranges for fighter-sized targets are well in excess of 100 km, while warships can be detected out to the radar's horizon. Capable of operating between 200-300 km from a parent ship, the Ka-31 significantly extends the air-and-sea picture of a fleet. Target co-ordinates, speed and heading can be transmitted via encrypted data-link to a ship or shore-based command post. Although typically based on the frigates that they were delivered with, the IN now operates 14 Ka-31s, freeing up several to fly from other capital ships, including *Vikramaditya*.

A Sea King Mk 42B in flight displaying some of the tools of its trade – search radar atop the fuselage, SAR winch above the starboard door, Elbit electro optical turret under the cockpit window, and ESM arrays on the nose.
(Angad Singh)

INAS 330 'Harpoons'

INAS 330 was commissioned on 17 April 1971, operating Westland Sea King Mk 42s from INS *Hansa*. The first Sea King landed on INS *Vikrant* in July that year, and the unit was swiftly made part of the carrier's air wing. Later marks of the Sea King continued to serve aboard *Vikrant*, and then *Viraat*, before the arrival of INS *Vikramaditya* ended regular carrier deployments for the squadron. However, the Sea King's ASW performance and carrying capacity in the utility/transport role mean that the type does often operate from *Vikramaditya*'s flight deck – with the caveat that it is not able to be stationed on the ship 'overnight.'

The Sea King variant in service with the unit today is the ASW Mk 42B, equipped with a MEL (later Thales) Super Searcher radar and Thomson Sintra (later Thales) HS-12 dunking sonar. The Mk 42B can employ the BAe Sea Eagle anti-ship missile, along with a range of torpedoes, depth charges and sonobuoys, making it one of the most potent helicopters in the Navy.

INAS 330 'Harpoons'

A pair of INAS 303 MiG-29Ks dispensing flares over Visakhapatnam during the International Fleet Review 2016. (Angad Singh)

An Indian carrier air wing (based on recent deployments)

No. of aircraft	Type	Role and remarks
18	MiG-29K and KUB	Multirole fighter
2–3	Chetak	SAR
2–4	Ka-28	ASW
2–4	Ka-31	AEW
1–2	Sea King Mk 42B	ASW
25–31		

An impression from the MiG-29K simulator. (Angad Singh)

As is the case with most carrier-operating navies, the Indian Navy does not operate a fixed Carrier Battle Group (CBG) or similar formation. The carrier sails with escorts as determined by the flotilla's tasking and expected threat environment. Naval tactical publications detail a series of escort dispositions ('screens') for three principal threat environments – Air Defence (AD), Anti-Submarine Warfare (ASW), and multi-threat, the last involving surface and submarine escorts capable of prosecuting threats at sea, on land, in the air and underwater.

Using single-shot kill probabilities of available SAM systems, an optimum air defence coverage area around the carrier is worked out and two, three or four AD ships are positioned to create a defensive screen against air and missile threats. Similarly, depending on bathythermal conditions for a given day and AOR, the sonar ranges available from escorting ASW or multi-role vessels are worked out, and ASW escorts are allotted positions to maintain a 'sonar front' which hostile submarines will not be able to penetrate undetected. A final surface vessel is often placed next to the carrier as a last-ditch air defence asset, as well as for 'plane guard' (SAR) duties if required.

In the air, early warning radar and sonar 'pickets' (Ka-31 AEW and Ka-28 ASW helicopters) are deployed well ahead of the flotilla. These helicopters could be organic to the carrier or hosted aboard any of the surface escorts to extend their range ahead of the flagship. If available and within range, shore based long-range patrol aircraft also provide early warning to the carrier group. Similarly, a nuclear attack submarine can also integrate into the battle group, sailing well ahead of the formation in the 'hunter-killer' role. In the IOR, however, the Indian Navy's carrier group can rely on speed to elude subsurface threats. The absence of hostile nuclear attack submarines in the region – at least at present – means that the flotilla can outpace any underwater threat simply by maintaining reasonably high transit speeds of 16–18 knots, creating Limiting Lines Of Approach (LLOA) that all but ensure the carrier cannot be successfully targeted by a diesel-electric submarine (typically limited to 10 knots at 'silent' speeds).

A theoretical Indian carrier battle group

No.	Ship class	Ship name	Fleet	Displacement	Crew
1	*Kiev*-class aircraft carrier	INS *Vikramaditya* (R33)	Western	45,400	1,610
2–3	*Kolkata*-class stealth guided missile destroyers	INS *Kolkata* (D63) INS *Kochi* (D64) INS *Chennai* (D65)	Western Western Western	7,400 7,400 7,400	390 390 390
3-4	*Talwar*-class guided missile frigates		Western Western Western Western	4,000 4,000 4,000 4,000	260 260 260 260
1	*Akula*-class nuclear attack submarine	INS *Chakra* (S71)	Eastern	8,140	80
1	*Aditya*-class fleet tanker or *Deepak*-class fleet tanker	INS *Aditya* (A59) or INS *Deepak* (A50)	Western Western	24,600 or 27,500	200 or 200
					4,100

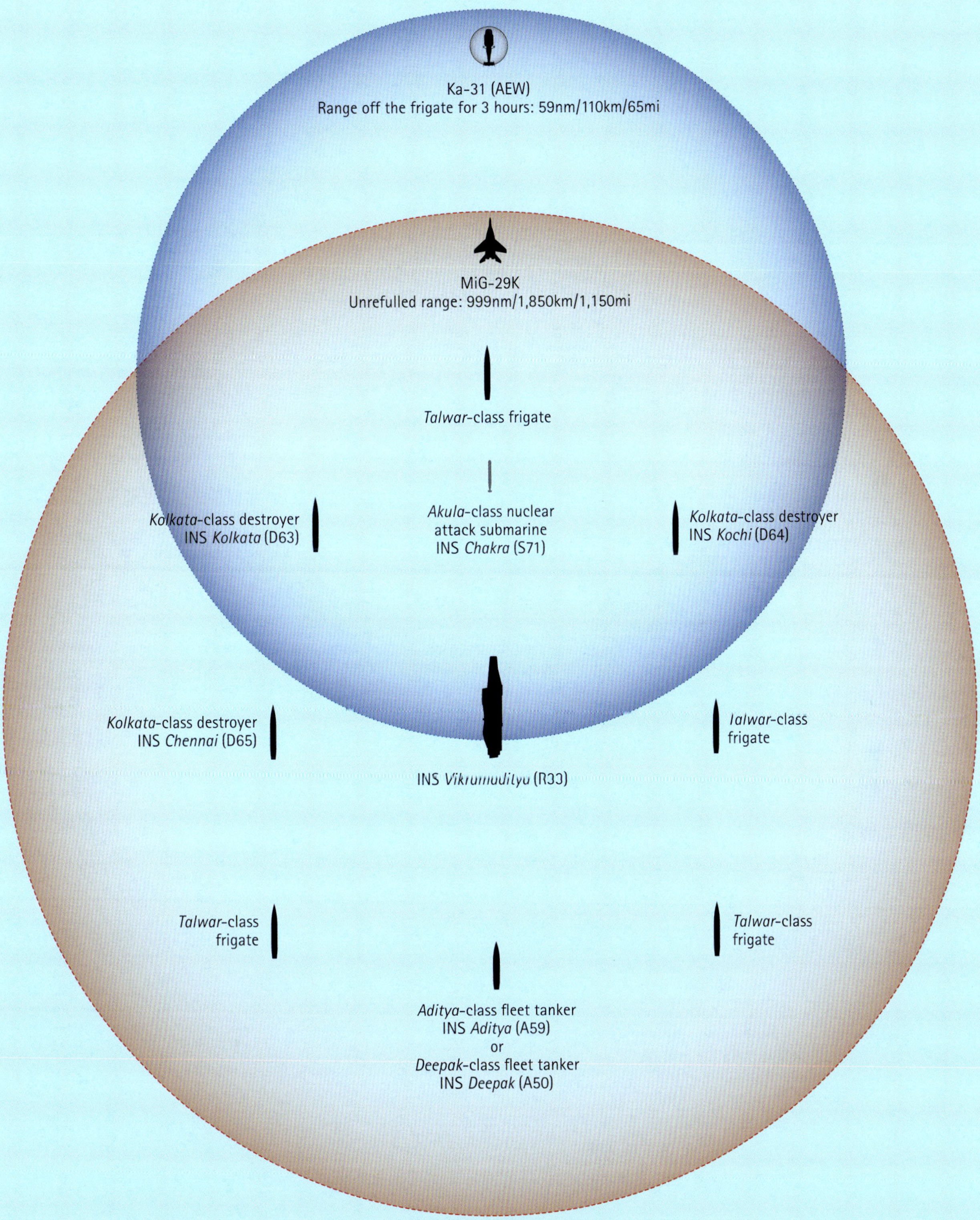

This is a purely schematic presentation of a likely carrier battle group and is not to scale.
In reality, the composition of such a force is dependent on various parameters.

Chapter 5

ITALY

Riccardo Niccoli

Marina Militare (Italian Navy)

Roundel of Italian Naval Aviation

The origins of the Italian naval aviation officially dates back to 1913, as on 27 June of that year, the Chief of Staff of the Regia Marina (Italian Royal Navy) established the Servizio di Aviazione della Marina (navy aviation service). As a matter of fact, air activities had already begun some years before, with the use of balloons, airships and seaplanes. The first Italian pilot to gain a flying licence was just a navy officer, Lt Mario Calderara, who qualified on 10 May 1910. In 1911, naval aviators, flying in Army airplanes, participated also to the first air operations at war in history, during the Italian-Turkish war in Libya.

In 1914, the Regia Marina operated two seaplanes stations, at Venice and at La Spezia, equipped with 14 aircraft (Borel, Brèguet, Curtiss, Albatros, Farman and Guidoni models), plus three airship stations at Ferrara, Jesi and Pontedera. In 1915, the Royal Italian Navy introduced into service the Regia Nave Appoggio Idrovolanti *Europa*, a ship dedicated to support seaplanes.

In May 1915, when Italy entered World War I, the Regia Marina had only 38 pilots, 396 technicians and 15 seaplanes. However, during the war, also the Italian naval aviation recorded huge developments, and at the end, in November 1918, it was able to deploy 791 pilots, about 10,000 technicians, 552 seaplanes, and 86 airplanes, having reached peaks of 1,100 seaplanes and 130 airplanes.

During the war, the Regia Marina had already understood the strategic possibilities offered by aircraft carriers, and in 1921, at the Naval Conference in Washington, Italy was grant the possibility to have a displacement allowing to deploy two carriers. Thus, in 1923 it was introduced into service the Regia Nave Appoggio Aerei *Giuseppe Miraglia* (*Giuseppe Miraglia* aircraft support royal ship), a seaplanes carrier that could be considered the first real Italian aircraft carrier. However, only few weeks later, on 28 March 1923, Italy introduced a law destined to establish the Regia Aeronautica (Royal Italian Air Force), being the new armed force the only allowed to operate aircraft. Thus, about 850 seaplanes and aircraft, plus five airports and 42 seaplanes stations passed under the air force control.

During World War II all air operations were controlled by the air force, and only in 1941 it was decided to build two aircraft carriers, through modifications of two passengers ships, *Roma* and *Augustus*, which received the new names of *Aquila* and *Sparviero*. They never entered service.

After the war, the new Marina Militare (Italian Navy) decided to re-establish its naval aviation, thanks also to the support of the US Navy. In 1950 it was re-opened the

◄ Italy's current aircraft carrier *Cavour* (550). (Italian Navy/Marina Militare Italiana)

Italian aircraft carrier *Giuseppe Garibaldi* (551) in 2005 when it has been Italy's prime carrier. (Luigino Caliaro)

Ufficio per l'Ispettore della Marina (naval aviation inspectorate), and plans were made to receive from the USA a light aircraft carrier (CVL) through the MDAP assistance program. Training of aircrews started again, sending a first group of personnel to NAS Corpus Christ in Texas, in order to gain pilot and technician qualifications. Also, a first batch of 24 Curtiss S2C-5 Helldiver from US Navy surplus had to be delivered. In 1952, the first two Helldivers arrived in Italy, but a new law was under way (approved in 1956), destined to give the Aeronautica Militare (Italian Air Force) control over all the military air activities, and on all the fixed-wing aircraft with a weight above 1,500 kg. The naval aviation was again stopped, and the Helldivers were assigned to the air force, while no CVL was ever delivered.

However, the law didn't include helicopters, and in 1953 after some trials, the navy acquired the first three AB.47G. The 1° Gruppo Elicotteri (GRUPELICOT 1, of 1st helicopter squadron) was established at Augusta on 1 August 1956. Since then, the Marina Militare enlarged its helicopter fleet, acquiring in the years other and more modern types: AB.47J, SH-34G/J, AB.204, SH-3D, and AB.212. Up to five helicopter squadrons were activated, on three MARISTAELI (naval helicopter stations).

The ships

The first modern aircraft carrier of the Italian Navy was finally ordered in 1977. In order to overcome the problems coming from the law, it was formally labelled as an 'incrociatore portareomobili' (helicopter carrier cruiser), but having in mind the possibility that in the future also the Navy could be authorized to operated fixed-wing aircraft heavier than 1,500 kg. The new ship, baptised *Giuseppe Garibaldi*, was laid down in the shipyard of Fincantieri on 20 February 1978, and was launched on 4 June

Today's flagship of the Italian Navy, *Cavour* (550). (Italian Navy/Marina Militare Italiana)

1983. Acceptance trials were commenced on 15 January 1985, and the unit entered the fleet on 30 September 1985. Finally, in 1989, the Italian Parliament approved Law 36, introduced on 1 February 1989, which permitted the Marina to equip itself with embarked fixed-wing aircraft. The *Garibaldi* was thus capable of being designated as an 'aircraft carrying cruiser', in fact performing the functions of light aircraft carrier. The ship was classified by NATO as a CVHA, identifying it as a unit capable of operat ing with aircraft and helicopters.

From a technical point of view, the *Garibaldi* (pennant number C551) has a standard displacement of 13,850 tonnes at full weight. The crew comprises 780 personnel, while the ship's overall length is 180 metres. The topside is the now classic continuous flying deck, with the island on the starboard side, enabling the maximum availability of space for flying operations The principal characteristic of the hull is the large hangar located immediately below the flight deck. The hangar has a height equivalent to two decks (6,35m), a maximum length of 110m, an average width of 15m, and covers an overall surface area of 1,600 square metres. The hangar can accommodate all the aircraft of the Marina, and even the large CH-47 helicopters of the Esercito Italiano (Italian Army).

The flight deck is linked to the hangar by two elevators both located at the starboard side, one in front of and one behind the island: each elevator measures 18 × 10 metres and can carry up to 15 tonnes. At the bow is a ski-jump featuring an exit angle of 6.5°, facilitating the operation of STOVL aircraft. The island is a three-bridge structure, the rear section of which incorporates the engine exhaust stack, and supports above it a large part of the on-board electronics.

The ship is powered by a COGAG configuration, two modules installed in two different locations, each formed by two LM-2500 gas turbines linked to a shaft driving a fixed pitch propeller. Maximum continuous power is 82,000hp (60,400kW), which cor-

A nice air-to-air shot of AV-8B+ '1-15', from the GRUPAER. (Luigino Caliaro)

responds to a speed of around 29.5 knots. Cruising speed is 20 knots, and at that speed a range of over 7,000 nautical miles (12,964 km) is available.

At the heart of the operational functions of the vessel lie the electronics and weapons systems. The *Garibaldi* possesses a particularly wide range of systems, and the unit usually functioned as the command ship of a Gruppo Navale d'Altura (high seas task force). As for communications, the vessel is equipped with a complex of receivers and transmitters in single side band (SSB) for long range communications, of telephone, radio telewriter, in code, and as scrambled data, transmitters and receivers for optical communications, marine radios for maritime and international radio traffic, and receivers for the encrypted satellite-transmitted data from the SICRAL system. The surveillance electronics and jamming systems are interfaced with the weapons systems and with the operational personnel in the Combat Operations Center (COC) through an automated system of command and control based around computerised consoles; the system is capable of simultaneously tracking up to 200 surface and airborne targets. The command and control system can additionally communicate with similar systems on board other units of the task force, enabling the production and presentation of the complete tactical situation.

Until 2011, the *Garibaldi* was the flagship of the Italian Navy, but in that year it was replaced in that role by the new *Cavour* carrier. After 30 years of service, in 2013-2014 the *Garibaldi* underwent large overhaul and upgrading works, in order to let the ship operate in the new role of helicopter command and control carrier for amphibious operations.

The first main cruise of the *Garibaldi* occurred in 1991, when it sailed to the United States, in order to take delivery of the first two Harriers for Italy, the two TAV-8B trainers. In 1992-94 it was deployed twice to Somalia, to support the Italian armed forces activity within the UN operations in the area, while in 1994 headed again to the USA, to accommodate the first three AV-8B+ fighter-bombers, with technical stops at Baltimora, Boston and New York. In 1995 it was again in the Somalia waters, to provide the retirement of the Italian contingent, while in 1997 it took part to Operation Alba Neo, non-combatant evacuation of civilians from Albania. In 1999, during the Kosovo War, it took part in Operation Allied Force, in which its AV-8B+ performed several missions, also of air-to-ground attack. Following the terrorist attacks on 11 September 2001, the *Garibaldi* led an Italian naval group that took part from November 2001 to March 2002 to Operation Enduring Freedom, loitering in the Arabian Sea.

In 2006 the *Garibaldi* led Operation Leonte, destined to deliver a peacekeeping force in Lebanon. In 2011, it took part to NATO Operation Unified Protector, and finally, in June 2016 it became flagship of Operation Sophia, guided by EUNAVFOR Med, replacing the *Cavour* carrier in this role.

The current flagship of the Italian Navy is the *Cavour (C550)*, an aircraft carrier much more larger and capable than the *Garibaldi*. It was ordered on 20 November 2000, to the Fincantieri, and was launched on 20 July 2004. After having being completed in March 2008, it entered service with the fleet on 10 June 2009.

The *Cavour* has a displacement of 21,160 tonnes (empty), and 27,900 tonnes at full load, so nearly three times the *Garibaldi*. The typical crew is composed by about 1,200 personnel, divided into: 451 ship crew, 203 air group crew, 140 high command crew, 416 Rgt. San Marco fusiliers (Italian marines). The ship's overall length is 244m, with a maximum width of 34.50m (at the flying deck). At full weight the immersion depth is 7.5m. The flying deck is 220m long, and is equipped with a 12° ski-jump; it hosts seven landing spots, and two elevators with a 30 tonnes capacity to transfer aircraft from the hangar. The hull has been designed according to the latest standards, to optimize efficiency.

The propulsion system is of COGAG type, formed by four General Electric/Avio LM-2500 turbines, delivering a maximum power of about 118,000hp (88,000kW), plus six Diesel-generators Wartsila CW12V2000 for energy production, plus two axles groups delivering 2,200kW, for a total of 17,600kW. The maximum speed of the *Cavour* is 29 knots, with a maximum range of 7,000nm at 16 knots. The endurance is about 18 days, and the fuel tanks have a capacity of 2.5 million litres of F76 naval fuel.

The *Cavour* has been designed since the beginning for a dual use. In its traditional role, it is a flagship, able to operate as high and complex command post, to support amphibious operations, and to deploy an air wing for offensive and defensive air operations, but it can also be employed for civil protection and humanitarian relief missions, thanks to the capability to embark vehicles and materials, to host an hospital, and to accommodate extra military and civil personnel.

The main weapon of the *Cavour* is of course its air component. The ship can embark a maximum of 36 aircraft. Usually it hosts a mix of AV-8B+ fighter-bombers and H-101/H-90 helicopters. A typical configuration includes ten Harriers, plus 12 helicopters. The hangar can accommodate up to 12 helicopters, or a mix of eight aircraft, and four helicopters. On the flying deck it is possible to park up to 24 aircraft.

The first operational mission assigned to the *Cavour* was a relief mission, Operation White Crane, in which Italy provided help to the Haiti population, after a catastrophic earthquake, in 2010. The following year, the ship was deployed in Southern Mediterranean, to take part to Operation Unified Protector, the NATO air war against

Gruppo Aerei Imbarcati

1° Gruppo Elicotteri

2° Gruppo Elicotteri

3° Gruppo Elicotteri

4° Gruppo Elicotteri

5° Gruppo Elicotteri

Libya. From November 2013 to April 2014, the *Cavour* led the 30° Gruppo Navale in a 'show the flag' mission around Africa, destined to increase cooperation, and also to advertise the Italian defence industries. From June 2015 to May 2016, it was the flagship of mission Operazione Sophia, of the EUNAVFOR Mediterranean, destined to help and control the immigration fluxes from Africa to Europe.

The Italian Navy operates also three all-deck amphibious assault ships (LPD), the *San Giusto* (*San Giusto*-class), and the *San Giorgio*, and *San Marco* (*San Giorgio*-class). These ships are featured by ro-ro solutions for embarking and disbarking of vehicles. They have a bow door, all-long flying deck, lateral island, and a flooding dock at the stern, in which three landing craft LCM can operate. These ships are about 8,000 tonnes of displacement, with a length of about 135m (443ft), and a width of 20-25m (66-82ft). Each ship can accommodate about 350 soldiers and 30 vehicles of all kinds. They also accommodate helicopters, usually two of H-212 or H-90 type, plus two of H-101 type.

The air component

The air component is the principal 'raison d'etre' behind the vessel, and forms, as in all carriers, the principal weapons system. The Italian naval aviation is operationally controlled by the Comando delle Forze Aeree (COMFORAER, or air forces command), activated in 2000, while under the administrative and bureaucratic point of view it depends to the 6° Reparto of the Stato Maggiore Marina (Navy general staff). The commander of the two bodies is the same person, a Commodore who is also a pilot.

Tip of the spear of the Italian naval aviation is the Boeing AV-8B+ Harrier II, a version of the AV-8B which was developed by the US Marines together with the navies of Italy and Spain. The service began to receive its first fixed wing jets on 31 May 1991, when two TAV-8B Harrier II trainers were accepted at MCAS Cherry Point; at the same time, a new squadron was activated, the Gruppo Aerei Imbarcati (GRUPAER, or aircraft squadron), with base at MARISTAER (naval air station) Grottaglie, near the Navy's main base at Taranto. The 16 operational AV-8B+ were, however, delivered between 1994 and 1997. The first three units were built by McDonnell-Douglas at St.Louis, and remained in the USA for some months, to let the crews familiarise with the new aircraft. The remaining 13 aircraft were assembled in Italy by Alenia, and the first (MM.7212) was delivered on 11 October 1995, while the last on 25 November 1997. During 25 years of service, two single seaters have been lost in flying accidents.

The Italian Harriers are featured by their main sensor, the AN/APG-65 Doppler multi-mode radar, which give the aircraft a real air-to-air and air-to-ground all weather multi-role capability. Standard equipment includes Rolls-Royce Pegasus F402-RR-408 engines, AN/ALR-67 radar warning, AN/ALQ-164 ECM jamming system, chaff and flare dispenser. To be noted that, for logistical reasons, in 1994 the two TAV-8B were re-engined with the -408 engines. Armament of the Italian Harriers included since the beginning free-fall Mk 81, Mk 82 and Mk 83 slick and retarded bombs, Mk 20 Rockeye cluster bombs, TV and IR-guided AGM-65 Maverick missiles, various LAU rocket pods, and the five-barrel GAU-12 25mm gun with 300 rounds. Later, in 2003-2006, the aircraft were qualified to use also the AN/AAQ-28 Litening II targeting pod, and Precision Guided Munitions, such as GBU-12, GBU-16, and more recently GBU-32, GBU-38, and

GBU-54. Air-to-air armament includes AIM-9L Sidewinder and AIM-120B AMRAAM missiles. The Harriers have in-flight refuelling capability, but to train in this activity they have to wait for the availability of Italian Air Force (KC-767A or KC-130J), or foreign tankers. Starting in 2012, the Italian Harriers are undergoing a modernization program linked to that of the US Marines; works are carried out by the Fleet Readiness Center East at MCAS Cherry Point. The GRUPAER primary role is to provide air defence to the Italian fleet operation areas, while the secondary role is close air support (CAS) in favour of the Brigata Marina 'San Marco', the Italian Marines unit, of brigade size.

The Harriers started carrier operations in 1994, and their first operational use came very soon, in early 1995, with participation to UN Operation Somalia 3/United Shield. The baptism of fire occurred in May 1999, during the NATO operations in Kosovo, flying directly from the *Garibaldi* carrier in bombing missions. Following the terroristic attacks of 11 September 2001, also Italy took part to Operation Enduring Freedom, and the *Garibaldi* carrier group was deployed to the Arabian Gulf, to launch the Harriers over Afghanistan for armed reconnaissance and Close Air Support missions. From November 2001 to March 2002, the Italian Harriers carried out some 288 missions over Afghanistan, flying more than 860 hours. Another international mission was Operation Leonte, in 2006, when the Italian forces were deployed to Lebanon as peacekeeping contingent. In that case, the Harrier flew about 200 hours, in armed reconnaissance and patrol missions. The GRUPAER was again called to took part to a crisis in 2011, during NATO Operation Unified Protector, the air war over Libya. In this case, the eight Harriers on board of the *Garibaldi* carrier logged some 1,040 flying hours, dividend into 12 air defence, 85 attack, and 176 reconnaissance and surveillance missions, delivering some 160 missiles and bombs against targets on the ground.

The biggest helicopter in service is the Leonardo (AgustaWestland) AW101, which according to the Italian Mission Design Series has three different designations,

Two H-101 taken while landing on the carrier *Giuseppe Garibaldi* (551). On the deck there is a EH-101A model, while approaching is a UH-101A. (Remo Guidi)

SH-90A '3-05' from GRUPELICOT 5 taken in hovering during ASW training activity. (Luigino Caliaro)

depending on the versions. The type has been acquired in 22 samples, the first of which flew in December 1999, and was delivered to the operational unit in March 2001. In total, the Service received ten samples of SH-101A, destined to maritime patrol (MP), anti-submarine (ASW), and anti-surface vessels warfare (ASuW); four samples of EH-101A (equipped with a search radar for Airborne Early Warning role), and eight UH-101A (for airborne assault, support to amphibious and special forces operations). The type is assigned to the 1° and 3° Gruppo Elicotteri, on the bases at Luni and Catania. The SH-101 has a completely integrated mission suite, formed by Helras dipping sonar, MM/APS-784 radar, FLIR, Link 11 data-link, ESM suite, and self-defence suite. It can be armed with four MU-90 and Mk 46 torpedoes, or two Marte Mk 2/S antishipping missiles. The UH-101 is featured by a rear ramp, a sophisticated SIAP self-defence system, ballistic protection for the crew and the cargo area, SATCOM communications systems. It can accommodate up to 35 soldiers, and can be armed with three 7.62mm MG42/59 machine guns. Finally, the EH-101 is featured by a HEW-784 pulse Doppler long range radar, which is monitored by two operators, and can be used as platform for command and control of air operations. The H-101 have been widely operated by the navy in all the international missions, starting in 2006, with Operation Leonte. In 2011, three UH-101 were deployed to the ISAF mission in Afghanistan, to form the Task Group Shark, charged to perform transport, surveillance and MEDEVAC missions.

The other modern helicopter in service is the NHIndustries SH-90A, whose first sample for the Italian Navy has been delivered in June 2011 to the 5° Gruppo Elicotteri at Luni naval helicopter station. Today, it is operational also with the 4° Gruppo Elicot-

UH-212B '7-20' from GRUPELICOT 4 taken in-flight at sea. This is the version dedicated to heliborne assault. (Andreas Zeitler)

teri. The Service has an overall order for 56 samples of this type, 46 in SH-90 configuration, for anti-submarine and ASuW missions, while ten will be in UH-90 configuration, with a rear ramp, and destined to heliborne assault. The first UH-90 has been delivered in December 2016 to the 5° Gruppo Elicotteri. Also the SH-90 is a quite advanced helicopter, equipped with Fly-by-Wire controls, ENR search radar, Helras sonar, sonobuoys, FLIR, Link 11 data-link, and full electronic warfare (ESM/ECM) suite. It can be armed with MU-90 and Mk 46 torpedoes, Marte Mk 2/S missiles, 7.62mm Gatling M134D miniguns at the doors.

While the old Sikorsky/Agusta SH-3D have been completely retired by July 2013, the other 'legacy' helicopter of the Navy, the Agusta-Bell AB.212ASW, acquired in 68 samples and introduced into service in 1976, still is operational. It was assigned to three squadrons (2°, 4° and 5°) in ASW, heli-assault and ECM/ESM roles. The SH-212 is equipped with an MM/APS-705 search radar, and with an AN/AQS-13B dipping sonar, and can be armed with two Mk 46 torpedoes. Being under replacement with the SH-90, the 212 is still operated in less than 20 samples, assigned to 2° and 4° Gruppo Elicotteri. Most of them are of the SH-212A version, for ASW, and SAR missions, plus six in UH-212B version, for heliborne assault.

The latter have no ASW equipment, and can carry up to seven soldiers; they are equipped with RWR, Kevlar ballistic protections, and armed with two side doors 7.62mm machine-guns, or with two rocket pods. To be noted that heliborne assault is performed by the Reparto Eliassalto of the 4° Gruppo Elicotteri, which in the past used a mix of SH-3D/NLA and UH-212, while today the squadron operates UH-212 (AB.212EA), waiting for the delivery of the first UH-90. In recent years, the UH-212 has been deployed also to Afghanistan, to take part to the ISAF mission with transport, reconnaissance and MEDEVAC missions.

All these helicopters can be embarked on the carriers, according to the mission assigned to the ship, and to the naval group. However, the Italian Navy hosted on its carriers also other helicopters, from the Army. The first occasion occurred in 1994–95, during the UN operations in Somalia, when AH-129 Mangusta and CH-47 Chinook were carried and operated on the *Garibaldi*. Recently, Navy-Army joint trials have been carried out on the *Cavour*, in order to certify the deployment of Army helicopters on the carrier in case of overseas operations.

Current units of Italian carrier air wing

Unit	Aircraft type	Role	Base	Remarks
Gruppo Aerei Imbarcati	AV-8B+, TAV-8B		MARISTAER Grottaglie	Air defence, CAS
1° Gruppo Elicotteri	SH/EH/UH-101A		MARISTAELI Luni	ASW, ASuW, AEW
2° Gruppo Elicotteri	SH/UH-212		MARISTAELI Catania	OCU, ASW, utility
3° Gruppo Elicotteri	SH/EH/UH-101A		MARISTAELI Catania	OCU, ASW, ASuW
4° Gruppo Elicotteri	SH/UH-212*, SH-90		MARISTAER Grottaglie	ASW, ASuW, assault
5° Gruppo Elicotteri	SH/UH-90		MARISTAELI Luni	ASW, ASuW, assault

* AB.212 is being replaced by SH-90A

The sole surviving TAV-8B '1-01' trainer during carrier qualifications on board of *Cavour*. The second example has been already retired. (Luigi Sani)

Future

The future of the Italian naval aviation is dominated by the introduction into service of the Lockheed-Martin F-35B Lightning II, the new STOVL combat aircraft. In origin, the Italian Navy had to receive 22 samples of this type, but after a spending review in 2012, the Italian MoD decided to cut this number to 15 aircraft. Three of them will be based in the USA, at the International Training Centre for the type, with the US Marines, while the remaining 12 will be located in Italy, at the Italian Air Force base at Amendola, home of the 32° Stormo, the first Italian Wing with the Lightning II, which will operate two more squadrons: one with F-35A, and another with F-35B (of the air force). All the Italian F-35 will be assembled at the FACO factory at Cameri, where the first F-35A have been completed, and flew in 2015. The first F-35B is included in the 2017 assembly program. In the plans, a first operational capability on the F-35B should be attained by 2023, while the phase-out of the Harriers (linked to the US Marines fleet) is expected by 2024–2025. The *Cavour* carrier has been designed having in mind the possibility to operate the Lightning II, so only a limited number of modifications had to be introduced, when specific data have been made releasable.

Another important step in the future of the Italian naval aviation is the introduction of Unmanned Aerial Systems (UAS), to be integrated into the shipboard operations. Test and evaluations started in 2010, first with the Scan Eagle system (the same used by the US Navy), and later with the Camcopter S-100, a rotary-wing UAS.

The first Italian F-35B (MM.7451) had its maiden flight from Cameri air base (home of the FACO factory) on 24 October 2017. It was still lacking any unit markings. (Riccardo Niccoli)

An Italian carrier group during Exercise Amphex 2012, in November 2012. Two FREMM frigates lead the flotilla, followed by both aircraft carriers, *Cavour* and *Giuseppe Garibaldi*, and a series of escort and support ships. (Italian Navy/Marina Militare Italiana)

An Italian carrier air wing

No. of aircraft	Type	Role and remarks
10	AV-8B+ Harrier II	Air defence
6	EH/SH/UH-101	Multirole helicopters
6	SH/UH-90	Multirole helicopters
22		A maximum of 36 aircraft can be deployed

A typical Italian carrier battle group

No.	Ship class	Ship name	Fleet	Displacement	Crew
1	Aircraft carrier	*Cavour* (C550)		30,000	1,202
2	*Andrea Doria*-class air-defence destroyers (*Horizon*-class)	*Andrea Doria* (D553) *Caio Duilio* (D554)		7,050 7,050	230 230
3-4	*Bergamini*-class frigates (FREMM)	(F59x) (F59x) (F59x)		6,700 6,700 6,700	199 199 199
1	*Todaro*-class submarine (Type 212-class)	*(S52x)*		1,524	27
1	*Etna*-class replenishment oiler	*Etna* (A5326)		13,400	162
					Around 2,450

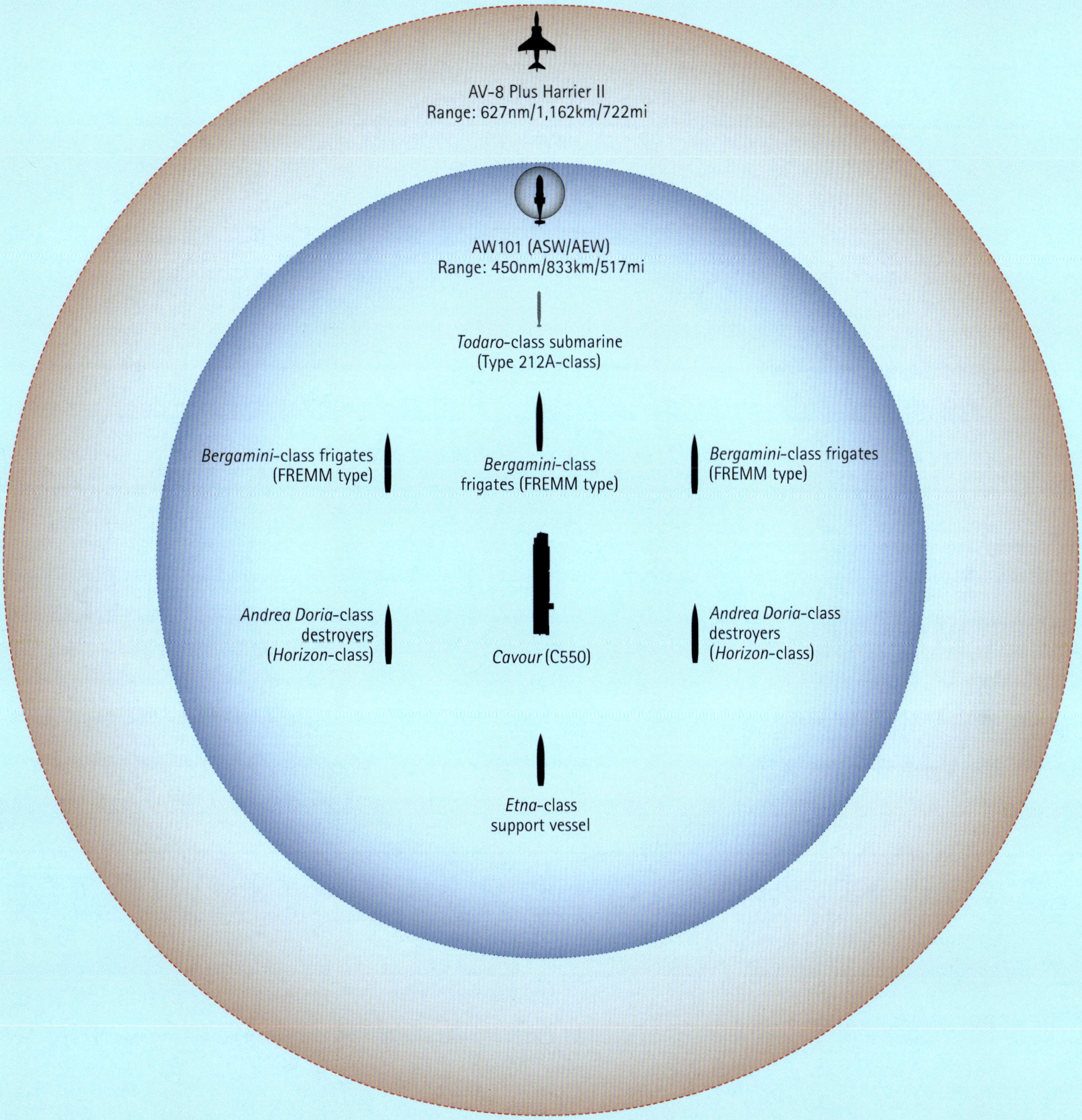

This is a purely schematic presentation of a likely carrier battle group and is not to scale.
In reality, the composition of such a force is dependent on various parameters.

063

Chapter 6

RUSSIA

Piotr Butowski

Voyenno-Morskoy Flot Rossiyskoy Federatsii (Russian Navy)

Aviatsiya Voenno-Morskovo Flota (Russian Naval Aviation)

Roundel of Russian Naval Aviation

After the World War II the USSR began having interests in remote regions of the world and since that time aircraft carriers have been necessary for the Russians. Commanding officers of the Soviet Navy Nikolai Kuznetsov (1939–1947 and 1951–1955) and Sergey Gorshkov (1956–1985) incessantly appealed for aircraft carriers. Immediately after the war they planned construction of six heavy aircraft carrier for the Pacific Fleet and three heavy and six light carriers for the Northern Fleet, but Joseph Stalin, land commander, objected it. After Stalin's death, on 23 March 1955 the first in the history of the USSR official government resolution about construction of two Project 85 aircraft carriers, each with 40 Tiger (MiG-19) jet fighters was issued. However, the subsequent Soviet leader Nikita Khrushchev had his idee fixee – missiles – and considered large warships anachronism. Work on the aircraft carrier was cancelled and air cover of the ship group was to be provided exclusively by anti-aircraft missiles.

The first warships adapted for accommodation of large numbers of aircraft in the USSR were helicopter carriers of the Project 1123 *Moskva* (commissioned in 1967) and *Leningrad* (1969), each carrying 14 Ka-25 ASW helicopters. The construction of the third ship was abandoned and the uncompleted hull was scrapped. This change of plans was caused by the demonstration of the experimental vertical take-off and landing aircraft Yak-36 during an air show at Domodedovo in July 1967. The aircraft made great impression on state and armed forces leaders. On 2 September 1968 government decision started work on the new Project 1143, twice larger than the 1123, which was to accommodate Yak-36M (later renamed Yak-38) aircraft. The first prototype of Yak-38 VTOL fighter flew on 15 January 1971 and on 18 November 1972 Mikhail Deksbakh made the first vertical landing of the Yak-38 on the deck of *Moskva* helicopter carrier on the roadstead of Feodosia, Crimea. It was the first landing of a fixed-wing aircraft aboard a ship in the USSR.

All Soviet aircraft-carrying warships were designed by Nevskoe Design Bureau in Leningrad (St. Petersburg) and built by Mykolaiv shipyard in Ukraine.

The first ship 1143 *Kiev* was launched on 26 December 1972 and in August 1976 arrived at its permanent base near Murmansk. Immediately after *Kiev*, assigned to the Northern Fleet, the sister ship *Minsk* was built intended for the Pacific Fleet and based in Vladivostok. The air groups of *Kiev* and *Minsk* comprised a mix of 20 Yak-38 jets and Ka-25 ASW helicopters, and additional two Ka-25PS rescue helicopters. The third ship 1143.3 *Novorossiysk* (assigned to the Pacific Fleet in 1983) and fourth 1143.4 *Baku* (in 1988 to Northern Fleet) carried 30 Yak-38 or Ka-27 aircraft.

◄ Russia's sole anti-submarine cruiser with aircraft armament *Admiral Kuznetsov* (063). (US Department of Defense)

The aircraft carried by the 1143 ships were tasked with protecting the ship group from the air. But the Yak-38 could not perform these tasks since its small load capacity did not allow installation of the radar and beyond-visual range air-to-air guided missiles. The subsequent carrier-based VTOL fighter Yak-41, first flown on 9 March 1987 remained only in two prototypes.

In 1982 in the Mykolaiv shipyard the ship 1143.5 *Riga*, later renamed to *Leonid Brezhnev* (1982-1987), then changed to *Tbilisi* (1987-1990) and eventually on 4 October 1990 to *Admiral of the Fleet of the Soviet Union Kuznetsov*, was ceremonially laid down. Although the number of the project is continuation of the *Kiev* class, in fact it is a totally different ship, with 50 per cent greater displacement, and the entire area of the deck intended for aircraft operations. On 1 November 1989 the Su-27K (piloted by Viktor Pugachev) landed aboard the ship in the Black Sea, followed by a MiG-29K and Su-25UTG; for the first time in Russia conventional aircraft landed aboard a ship. In face of the USSR disintegration, in December 1991 the Russians redeployed the ship from the Black Sea to Murmansk, where it joined the Russian Northern Fleet.

Disintegration

The Soviet Union lived to its final days with two 1123 *Moskva*-class helicopter carriers, four 1143 *Kiev*-class ships and one 1143.5 *Admiral Kuznetsov*. Two subsequent ships were under construction: *Riga*, a sister ship for *Kuznetsov*, intended for the Pacific Fleet, and larger *Ulyanovsk* with 75,000 tonnes displacement, nuclear propulsion, 60-70 aircraft and two catapults.

During 1989–1991 the collapse of the USSR began. The Russians renamed *Tbilisi* to *Admiral Kuznetsov*, *Baku* to *Admiral Gorshkov* and *Riga* to *Varyag*: they did not want their biggest warships to be named after capitals of now foreign countries. The Russians had ceased to fund the completion of *Varyag* and *Ulyanovsk* in Mykolaiv shipyard, and the Ukrainians did not need these ships, so *Varyag* was sold to China, where she currently serves as *Liaoning* and *Ulyanovsk* was dismantled in the dock.

In 1991, the *Leningrad* was decommissioned due to the lack of money for overhaul; *Moskva* met the same fate in 1995. The Russians also failed to retain any *Kiev*-class ship in service: *Kiev* and *Minsk* were sold to China, where the former serves as a luxury hotel and the latter as a part of a military theme park. *Novorossiysk* was scrapped. Only the newest *Admiral Gorshkov* still serves under Indian flag, modernized and named INS *Vikramaditya*. Russia is left with a single aircraft carrier – *Admiral of the Fleet of the Soviet Union Kuznetsov*.

Currently there is no program of construction of another aircraft carrier being implemented in Russia and – taking into account the difficult economic situation of the country – it is doubtful that Russia builds a new ship of this class within the foreseeable future.

Russia has no aircraft carriers

According to official nomenclature Russia has never had an aircraft carrier and still has none. Ships of 1123 *Moskva*-class were classified as anti-submarine cruisers with

A pair of Su-33s is prepared for launch from the deck of the *Admiral Kuznetsov* during its maiden combat cruise that took place between October 2016 and February 2017.
(Northern Fleet Press Office via Georg Mader)

aircraft armament and the ships of Project 1143, from *Kiev* to *Kuznetsov*, are heavy aircraft-carrying cruisers (tyazholyi avianesushchiy kreyser, TAKR).

Many commenters think that the Russians had named their ships 'aircraft-carrying crusers' to omit stipulations of the 1936 Montreux Convention that prohibits passage of aircraft carriers through the Turkish Straits. In my opinion this was a secondary cause. The most important is the fact that the primary offensive weapons of Project 1143 ships were Bazalt and Granit heavy surface-to-surface cruise missiles and the aircraft were intended primarily for defence. The Montreux Convention states that aircraft carriers are ships 'designed or adapted *primarily* [the author's emphasis] for the purpose of carrying and operating aircraft at sea'.

The main task of *Admiral Kuznetsov* is to provide cover for Russian ballistic missile-armed submarines approaching positions for attack. The current deployment to Syria, where the aircraft flying from *Kuznetsov* attack ground targets is an exception, not a standard task of this ship.

Ideological reasons also should not be underestimated. As early as February 1992 in conversation with the then – and last – Commander-in-Chief of the Soviet Navy, Admiral of the Fleet Vladimir Chernavin, 'I used carelessly the term 'aircraft carrier' referring to *Admiral Kuznetsov*, for which I was scolded, because 'only the imperialists have aircraft carriers. The aircraft carrier is an attack ship and our ships are aircraft-carrying cruisers, performing primarily defensive tasks'. In Soviet Union there had been a propaganda campaign against aircraft carriers emphasizing (true and made-up) disadvantages of aircraft carriers, their enormous cost and vulnerability.

Admiral Kuznetsov heavy aircraft-carrying cruiser

The *Admiral Kuznetsov* has the flight deck occupying entire area of the deck and ending with the ski-ramp angled at 14.7°. It has three launch positions with holdback fittings and raised jet blast deflectors. Two are situated at the foot of the ski-jump and provide the take-off roll of 105 m (344ft) length. The third position (take-off roll of 195m, 640ft) is situated on the port side, approximately in the middle of the landing strip. The recovery strip ends with four arrester wires, stretched across the deck at 12m (39ft) intervals and are braked hydraulically. Beneath the deck there is the hangar, 183m (600ft) in length and 29m (95ft) in width. Two elevators, each with load capacity of 40 tonnes hoist the aircraft from the hangar onto the deck.

The ship has no catapult, which limits the speed of use of the air group, because recovering fighters block the take-off strip. Moreover, using the ski-ramp the fighters have the maximum take-off weight limited at the cost of fuel or weapons load. The Russians have not adopted the catapult because in the north, which is the main operational area of *Admiral Kuznetsov* it is hard to achieve satisfactory reliability of steam catapults. The ship's four steam turbines, each with two boilers, are fuelled with black oil, which produces thick smoke billowing from the funnel. The advantage of black oil is its low cost.

The offensive armament of the ship comprises 12 flush-mounted P-700 Granit (SS-N-19 Shipwreck) surface-to-surface cruise missiles with range in excess of 500 km, carrying HE or nuclear warhead. The anti-aircraft armament consists of 24 Kinzhal (SA-N-9 Gauntlet) missile launchers, eight Kortik (CADS-N-1) SAM/gun systems and six AK-630M 30 mm guns while the anti-submarine armament consists of two RBU-12000 (Udav-1) anti-submarine mortars.

Su-33 '64 Red' wears the eagle insignia of the first squadron of the 279th OKIAP. (Sergey Kuznetsov)

Missions

Admiral Kuznetsov is permanently based in Murmansk, at the pier of 35th Ship Repair Plant.

On 23 December 1995 Kuznetsov set off for her first operational deployment in the Mediterranean Sea, leading a group of 12 ships. In February 1996 she visited Tartus naval base in Syria. Aboard were 13 Su-33 fighters, two Su-25UTG trainers and 11 Ka-27 helicopters. Carrier-based aircraft flew about 400 sorties during that cruise and the helicopters – 700. The ship returned to Murmansk on 25 March 1996.

Kuznetsov made her second cruise to the Mediterranean only after 12 years, from December 2007 to February 2008 and further deployments to the Mediterranean were between December 2008 and March 2009, December 2011 and February 2012, December 2013 and May 2014. During these deployments she carried 8-10 Su-33 fighters, 1-2 Su-25UTG trainer aircraft and Ka-27 helicopters.

Syrian expedition 2016–2017

The sixth deployment of *Admiral Kuznetsov* to the Mediterranean became her combat debut.

In September 2015 the Russians commenced military intervention in Syria and deployed their air contingent to Humaymim air base, 15km from Lattakia. Along with it they planned a cruise of the *Admiral Kuznetsov* to Syria. The ship had then just undergone a three-month overhaul in a dock of the 35th repair plant in Murmansk, after which she set off for the Barents Sea where Su-33 pilots commenced flight training. However, it was decided to carry out further repair of the ship and adaptation to the needs of new fighters and helicopters. Between January and June, 2016, the boilers, steam turbines and electric generators were repaired. Cellars for air ammunition were

MiG-29KR '41 Blue' prepares to launch from the carrier during its combat deployment in the eastern Mediterranean.
A Ka-27PS is on plane guard duty.
(Northern Fleet Press Office via Georg Mader)

converted to fit new weapons; additional systems necessary to operate new aircraft types, including MiG-29KR, were established.

In June and by mid-July 2016, three MiG-29KRs and two MiG-29KUBR two-seaters of the 100th OKIAP as well as four Su-33s and three Su-25UTGs from 279th OKIAP trained at Saki base on Crimea on Nitka facility. On 2 July 2016, an Su-33 and an Su-25UTG landed on board the carrier for the first time after the ship's overhaul; first MiG-29KR arrived on 8 August.

Su-33 with SVP-24-33 system

Along with it quick upgrade of the Su-33 fighters, for which the Russians could not decide for years, has been implemented. It concerned the navigation system, which has partially been replaced by the SVP-24-33 system, developed by the Gefest & T Company from Zhukovsky, originally for Su-24M tactical bomber. The SVP-24 (Spetsializirovannaya Vychislitelnaya Podsistema, special computation subsystem) is a low-cost and effective device that enhances the accuracy of the navigation thanks to new computer and radio navigation system coupled with a satellite receiver. Gefest & T claims that the accuracy of navigation is increased by a factor of two to three. Another advantage of the new system is the ability to use unguided weapons during complex manoeuvring (previously the fighter could only employ unguided weapons in straight-line flight only).

The SVP-24-33 systems were installed in the summer of 2016 on at least eight Su-33s (tail numbers 60, 67, 71, 77, 78, 84, 85 and 88) in Gefest & T workshops at Zhukovsky. Note that even after this upgrade the Su-33s remain air-superiority fighters for carrier defence.

The cruise

On 15 October 2016, the *Admiral Kuznetsov* left Murmansk for Mediterranean Sea assisted by nuclear battlecruiser *Pyotr Velikiy* and several smaller ships. On 26 October the group passed the Strait of Gibraltar and entered Mediterranean Sea and on 8 November reached the destination point off Syrian coast.

A tractor equipped with a turbojet is used to clear the deck of the carrier of any FOD prior to flying operations. (Archives Georg Mader)

Rather small air group was boarded on the *Admiral Kuznetsov*, comprising at least nine Su-33 fighters (tail numbers 62, 66, 67, 71, 76, 78, 84, 85 and 88 were observed; as it is easy to count, five had been retrofitted with the SVP-24-33 system), Ka-27 (one, '06' was seen), Ka-27PS (three, '52', '55' and '57' were seen) and two Ka-29 ('23' and '75') helicopters. New aircraft types aboard the carrier, making their operational debut are three MiG-29KR ('41', '47' and '49') and one MiG-29KUBR ('52') fighters, Ka-52K attack helicopters (one was seen on the deck, without the number, but perhaps there was another one under the deck) and Ka-31R radar-picket helicopter (one, '90' was seen on the deck).

On 15 November 2016 the Su-33 fighters from *Admiral Kuznetsov* attacked targets in Syria with free-fall bombs. Reportedly, four Su-33 fighters took part in the mission, each with two 500kg (1,102lb) iron bombs. It was the first combat use of aircraft from *Admiral Kuznetsov*. It is hard to expect it to be of great operational significance.

The *Admiral Kuznetsov's* deployment has no practical significance for the operation in Syria, because with the permanent base at Humaymim the Russians can conduct the strike missions more effectively, simpler and cheaper using the ground-based aircraft they have already deployed to Syria. Because of small number of multirole fighters and lack of combat experienced pilots, any strike missions from the Admiral Kuznetsov are limited. The main objective of the deployment to Syria – apart from propaganda – is building first skills in conducting strike operations from a carrier.

On 6 January 2017, the Russian Ministry of Defence recalled the *Admiral Kuznetsov*. It has returned to Murmansk on 9 February 2017. The commander of the Russian contingent in Syria, General Colonel Andrey Kartapolov, reported that 'during the two months of the military operation, the Navy aviation pilots conducted 420 combat sorties, 117 of which were conducted at night'. He did not specify, how many of these missions were performed from board of the ship. For some time, the Su-33 and MiG-29K fighters were deployed to Humaymim air base near Latakia. Reportedly, over a half of the naval aircraft's missions were performed from this air base. The ship-based aviation made also more than 750 search and rescue, transport, surveillance and other support flights, Kartapolov added.

Two fighters lost

On the evening of 13 November 2016 a MiG-29KR crashed into the Mediterranean Sea. On that day three fighters took part in a training flight. The first one landed aboard the *Admiral Kuznetsov* without problems, but the second one damaged the arresting wires on the landing. The Russians did not want to send the third aircraft to ashore airfield, because then they would have had to admit the failure. They hoped they would manage to replace the wires – but they didn't. After having ran out of fuel the aircraft sank near the ship; the pilot ejected safely and was recovered by Ka-27PS helicopter.

Another aircraft, this time the Su-33 '67' sank in the Mediterranean Sea on 3 December 2016. Again an arresting wire broke on landing; the aircraft failed to stop on the deck and fell into the sea. The pilot ejected himself safely. Russian media, referring to the sources in the Main Staff of the Navy and in the air industry claim that the Su-33 was lost because of a pilot's error. The pilot exceeded the tolerance from the landing axis that created excessive load and tore off the arresting wire. The deviation of the landing axis made 4.7m, while the allowed value is 4.2m. It was supposed initially that a production spoilage could be the cause of the wire break. However, this version is rejected by the manufacturer, Proletarsky Zavod in St. Petersburg making the arresting gears. Exactly in the same way the Russians lost another Su-33 eleven years earlier, on 5 September 2005 in Atlantic Ocean.

Carrier air wing

The design line-up of the air group aboard *Admiral Kuznetsov* comprises 50 fixed-wing aircraft and helicopters, including 26 Su-33 or MiG-29K fighters, 18 Ka-27 ASW helicopters or Ka-29 (or, since recently, Ka-52K) attack helicopters, four Ka-31 radar-picket helicopters and two Ka-27PS rescue helicopters. In fact, there were never so

A view over the flight deck of *Admiral Kuznetsov*, showing armed Su-33 from both squadrons and several Ka-27s. (Northern Fleet Press Office via Georg Mader)

many aircraft aboard. The present Russian Ministry of Defence's media information specifies the air group as consisting of 12 fighters and 24 helicopters. The air group is not permanent and is formed before each deployment.

Carrier-borne aircraft

According to the original plans the main aircraft armament of *Admiral Kuznetsov* was to consist of Yak-41 short take-off/vertical landing (STOVL) fighters. Conventional fighters Su-27K and MiG-29K, taking off from the ski jump were to be additional armament. However, later the accents changed: the Yak-41 did not enter service while Su-27s and MiG-29s take-off trials from ground ski-ramp confirmed their fitness for carrier-borne service.

The Mikoyan MiG-29K ship-based medium multirole fighter was originally developed against an order of India that acquired 45 fighters for the INS *Vikramaditya* aircraft carrier; first fighters were delivered to India in December 2009. In February 2012, the Russian Navy also ordered a batch of 20 MiG-29KR (R for Russia) fighters and four MiG-29KUBR trainers; all of them were delivered in 2014-2015 and formed 100th OKIAP regiment in Yeysk. This is the first multirole fighter for *Admiral Kuznetsov* that is armed with four subsonic Kh-35 or supersonic Kh-31A anti-ship missiles as well as four KAB-500Kr TV-guided bombs. Air-to-air weapons are up to six medium-range R-77-1 or up to eight close-air combat R-73 missiles; the fighter has a single 30 mm cannon.

Two Ka-52Ks – dedicated maritime versions of the land-based Ka-52 attack helicopter – were tested on board the *Admiral Kuznetsov* from late 2016 until early 2017. (Kamov via Alexander Mladenov)

The veteran Sukhoi Su-33 is an air-superiority and air-defence fighter. 26 Su-33s (plus 9 test Su-27K aircraft) were made by Komsomolsk-on-Amur factory and delivered in 1993–1996. Before the recent deployment to Syria some aircraft were subjects of upgrades consisting in fitting SVP-24-33 navigations.

The Su-25UTG is an old shipborne trainer converted from Su-25 attack aircraft, with weapon system removed, and instrument landing system and arrester hook added. It is used at an initial stage of the carrier's pilots training.

Kamov Ka-27 is presently the only operational anti-submarine helicopter in Russia, operated as both ship- and shore-based aircraft. It is now a subject of the Ka-27M upgrade with Boomerang radar and other new mission sensors and weapons; first Ka-27Ms returned to the service after upgrade in December 2016. The Ka-27PS is its search and rescue version.

The Kamov Ka-29 is an assault helicopter made of Ka-27 with new fuselage for 12 troops and Shturm-V anti-tank missile system borrowed from Mi-24 Army Aviation's helicopter.

The Kamov Ka-31 radar picket helicopter is another derivative of Ka-27 with the fuselage modified to fit E-801 surveillance radar with rectangular 6 m (20 ft) long rotating antenna beneath. Since 2003, 23 helicopters were sold to India and China. The Russian Navy placed the first order for two Ka-31R versions on 20 November 2008; they were delivered in 2012.

New program that started for the needs of *Mistral*-class landing helicopter docks is the Kamov Ka-52K helicopter. Compared to original Army Aviation's version, the Ka-52K has shorter folding wings and folding rotors' blades; the landing gear is

The Ka-27PS is the standard search and rescue helicopter embarked on board the *Admiral Kuznetsov*. (Sergey Kuznetsov)

strengthened. The radar and electro-optical targeting system are to be adapted for the needs of naval tasks but for now they remain unchanged. Anti-ship weapons are to be added including Kh-35UV anti-ship missiles. The Russians had planned the purchase of 32 Ka-52K helicopters for two *Mistral*-class ships. But after the French refusal they cancelled this order. Only four helicopters of the pre-production batch were produced, two of which were delivered to the Navy.

More about the Russian ship-borne aircraft read in *Russia's Warplanes, Volume 1 & 2.*

Carrier aviation units

279th OKIAP (Otdelnyi Korabelnyi Istrebitelnyi Aviatsionnyi Polk, Independent Ship-borne Fighter Aviation Regiment) was formed at Saki air base, Crimea, in December 1973 as 279th OKShAP (Sh for Shturmovoy, attack). In March 1975 the regiment received its first Yak-38 STOL aircraft. In the summer of 1976 the ship *Kiev* with 279th OKShAP transited to Murmansk and joined the Northern Fleet. The aviation regiment was deployed to Severomorsk-3 air base, where it has been stationed until present. The 279th OKShAP was the aviation complement of the aircraft-carrying cruisers *Kiev* and *Baku* (*Admiral Gorshkov*); a similar regiment, 311th OKShAP was formed as a part of the Pacific Fleet to be the aviation complement of the cruisers *Minsk* and *Novorossiysk*, with station Knyevichi air base near Vladivostok. In early 1990s the Russians

The Ka-31 radar picket helicopter was tested on board the Admiral Kuzentsov early in its development phase, but the Russian Navy only received the first two Ka-31R versions in 2012. (Stanislav Bazhenov)

decommissioned their four *Kiev*-class aircraft-carrying cruisers along with Yak-38 aircraft. The 311th OKShAP ceased to exist and in March 1993 the 279th OKShAP received new aircraft – Su-33 (Su-27K) carrier-borne fighters and became a fighter regiment.

The regiment has two squadrons of Su-33 fighters; aircraft with numbers 60 through 76 and eagle emblem on the tailfin belong to the first squadron and aircraft with numbers 77 through 88 with tiger emblem to the second squadron. Altogether there are 14 Su-33s in service as of the end 2016. The third squadron has five Su-25UTGs, several Su-27UB trainers and two Su-30SM two-seat fighters that arrived in 2016. In future, the third squadron is to be fully completed with Su-30SMs. The full name of the unit is 279th Smolensk OKIAP awarded with Red Banner and named after Double Hero of the Soviet Union Boris Safonov. The commanding officer since January 2015 is Col Pavel Podguzov.

100th OKIAP was formed on 1 December 2015 at Yeysk on Black Sea coast especially for new MiG-29KR/KUBR fighters. In 2017 the regiment was redeployed to Severomorsk-3, together with 279th OKIAP. The commanding officer of 100th OKIAP is Col Vladimir Kokurin.

The regiment refers to tradition of the former 100th IIAP (Issledovatelskiy Instruktorskiy Aviatsionnyi Polk, Research and Training Aviation Regiment), which was formed on 10 March 1986 in Novofyodorovka (Saki) in Crimea, tasked with training pilots of MiG-29K and Su-27K (Su-33) carrier-borne fighters for the *Admiral Kuznetsov*, then under construction. The first commanding officer of the regiment was Lt Col Timur Apakidze. Initially the regiment had Su-27 aircraft (standard, not K variants)

Another type associated with the *Admiral Kuznetsov* since its early years of service is the Ka-29. The combat transport helicopter returned to the carrier during the Syrian campaign, in a CSAR capacity. (Northern Fleet Press Office via Georg Mader)

and then also MiG-29, L-39C and Su-25. During 1990–1991 regiment's pilots took part in state evaluations of new Su-27K and MiG-29K carrier-borne fighters. After the disintegration of the USSR the regiment was absorbed into the Ukrainian armed forces. In December 1991 a group of 16 pilots and about 40 technicians, who did not want to stay in Ukraine, moved to Severomorsk-3 with the aircraft and the ship Admiral Kuznetsov and were incorporated into the present 279th OKIAP. The 100th regiment was disbanded in Ukraine in 1996.

7050th AvB (Aviatsionnaya Baza, Air Base) in Severomorsk-1 (20 km, 12 miles north-west of Severomorsk-3) groups helicopters for *Admiral Kuznetsov*; the base has more than 30 Ka-27s, as well as single initial Ka-31R and Ka-52K helicopters. Apart from them in the base there are also Il-38 ASW aircraft, transport aircraft and Forpost UAVs. The air group at Kipelovo, subordinated to the 7050th AvB has Tu-142 aircraft. The full name of the unit is 7050th Kirkeness Aviation Base awarded with Red Banner.

In the past the helicopters belonged to the 830th Independent Shipborne ASW helicopter regiment (OKPLVP), formed in Murmansk in 1954 with Mi-4M ASW helicopters (until 1958 as a squadron). In 1960 the regiment moved to Severomorsk-2 air base (5 km, 3 miles from Severomorsk-1) and in 1998 to Severomorsk-1. In 2009 the regiment was merged with other units into the 7050th base.

Current units of Russian carrier air wing

Unit	Aircraft type	Role	Base	Remarks
100th OKIAP	MiK-29KR, KUBR		Severomorsk-3	22 in service
279th OKIAP	Su-33, Su-30SM, Su-27UB, Su-25UTG		Severomorsk-3	14/2/?/5 in service
7050th AvB	Ka-27, Ka-27PS, Ka-29 Ka-31R, Ka-52K		Severomorsk-1	Over 30 some in service 2/2 in service

A well-weathered Su-25UTG '11 Red', the carrier trainer version, from the 279th OKIAP's 3rd squadron. (Stanislav Bazhenov)

Training facilities in Saki and Yeysk

In 1980 in Novofyodorovka near the town of Saki in the Crimea started construction of a research facility, named colloquially Nitka (Nazemnyi Ispytatelnyi Trenirovochnyi Komplex, Ground-based Research Training Complex; nitka is thread in Russian), being a runway with a ski-ramp and an arresting gear imitating the deck of future Admiral Kuznetsov aircraft carrier. On 21 August 1982 an experimental MiG-29 made the first take-off from the ski-ramp and Su-27 began trials a week later. Basing on the results of the trials the final form the ship's ski ramp was designed. The Nitka is presently suitable to limited use only; since 1999 only Su-25UTG trainers, which are lighter than fighters, take off from the ski-ramp.

In 2012, started construction of a similar facility in Yeysk, at the 859th Combat Training and Flight Crew Training Centre of Naval Aviation. It is expected to be ready for use in 2017.

A Russian carrier air wing

No. of aircraft	Type	Role and remarks
9–10	Su-33	Air defence
4	MiG-29KR and KUBR	Multirole fighter
4	Ka-27 and Ka-27PS	ASW and SAR
2	Ka-29	Assault and CSAR
1–2	Ka-31	AEW
1	Ka-52K	Attack
21–23		

IThe Russian warships *Petr Velikiy* (centre) and the *Admiral Kuznetsov* (background) are shadowed by the Royal Navy's HMS *St Albans* (foreground) and three Royal Air Force Typhoon fighters as they transit the English Channel in early 2017. (Royal Navy/L(Pho) Dave Jenkins)

The complete Russian carrier battle group during 2016/17 cruise to Syria

No.	Ship class	Ship name	Fleet	Displacement	Crew
1	Project 11435 *Kuznetsov*-class aircraft cruiser	*Admiral Kuznetsov* (063)	NF	43,000	1,690
1	Project 11442 *Kirov*-class nuclear heavy guided missile cruiser	*Pyotr Velikiy* (099)	NF	24,300	710
2	Project 1155 *Udaloy I*-class anti-submarine warfare destroyer	*Severomorsk* (619) *Vice Admiral Kulakov* (626)	NF NF	6,930 6,930	300 300
1	Project 61 *Kashin*-class missile destroyer	*Smetlivy* (870)	BSF	4,390	300
1	Project 11356P/M *Admiral Grigorovich*-class frigate	*Admiral Grigorochiv* (494)	BSF	4,035	200
1	Project R-5757 *Nikolai Chiker*-class sea-going rescue tug	*Nikolai Chiker*	NF	7,542	71
1	Project 1452 *Ingul*-class sea-going rescue tug	*Altay*	NF	4,072	87
1	Project 22870	*Professor Nikolay Muru*	BSF	1,670	62
1	Project 733S *Okhtenskiy*-class sea-going rescue tug	SB-5	BSF	890	31
2	Project 1559V *Boris Chilikin*-class fleet replenishment oiler	*Sergey Osipov* *Ivan Bubnov*	NF BSF	22,460 22,460	80 80
1	Type Dubna oiler	*Dubna*		12,891	62
1	Project REF-675 *Kaliningradneft*-class oiler	*Kama*		8,913	32
					4,005

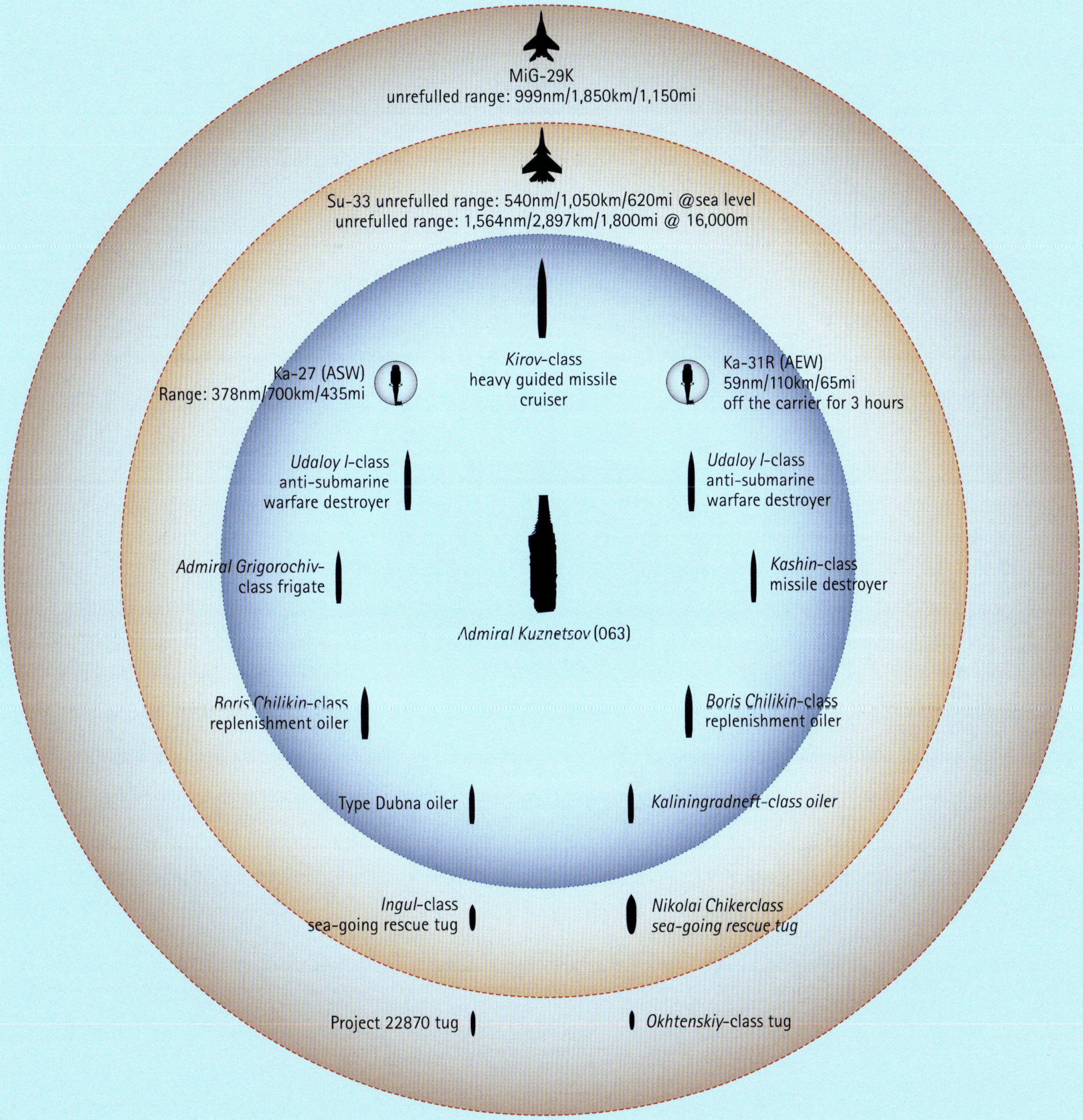

This is a purely schematic presentation of a likely carrier battle group and is not to scale.
In reality, the composition of such a force is dependent on various parameters.

Chapter 7

SPAIN

Salvador Mafé Huertas

Armada Española (Spanish Navy)

Spanish Naval Air Arm

Roundel of Spanish Naval Air Arm

◄ The Spanish multi-purpose amphibious assault ship *Juan Carlos I* under way in the Mediterranean. (NATO/Christian Valverde)

Although a fact often overlooked, Spain has wide and extensive naval experience and has traditionally placed great importance on possession of a vessel with aviation capability. This fact hold true today, although the future of the fixed-wing carrier-borne aviation component is uncertain.

Spain was a pioneer in the use of aviation at sea, as seen in its operation of the carrier *Dédalo*, a warship that resulted from the conversion of the former German merchant vessel *Neuenfels* that had belonged to the Hansa shipping company. This was a very important vessel for the Armada Española (Spanish Navy). It participated in the War of Morocco and provided good service until it was decommissioned in 1936, coinciding with the beginning of the Spanish Civil War.

After the civil war was over there followed a period of political and economic isolation. However, agreements signed with the United States led to the Spanish Navy's aspiration to operate a true aircraft carrier. The United States sold to Spain the light aircraft carrier USS *Cabot*, of around 16,000 tonnes displacement. In Spain, she was named *Dédalo* and was first employed as a helicopter carrier with the incipient Spanish Navy's fleet air arm, and then, with the arrival of the AV 8B Harrier II, she became the first aircraft carrier in the world to operate this type of aircraft. The *Dédalo* was decommissioned in 1988.

The Spanish Navy, now with much important naval experience, wanted to operate a modern aircraft carrier and planned to undertake the construction of a small and economical ship, based on the idea of the Sea Control Ship (SCS). This was a design abandoned by the US Navy for a small, low-cost and easy-to-manufacture carrier that would be able to escort convoys along oceanic routes. The result was the first aircraft carrier built by Spain. It was launched in 1982 and named *Principe de Asturias*. This ship, with around 18,000 tonned displacement, operated Harriers from the outset. Unlike comparable British aircraft carriers, since its manufacture it was equipped with a suitable launching ramp ('ski jump') of 12°. The 'Principe', as she was known in the navy, proved to be a good vessel with excellent operational capabilities, superior to those of contemporary ships such as Italy's carrier *Giuseppe Garibaldi*. Very stable and seaworthy, perhaps its only limitation was its lack of self-defence capability.

The *Principe de Asturias* gave good service and allowed the navy to develop an important surface force, small in number but with high operational capabilities. Its premature retirement after a service life of only 25 years is somewhat difficult to understand. At the time, its withdrawal was justified on economic grounds. However,

An Armada Española carrier group with the previous carrier *Principe de Asturias* (front) and the current *Juan Carlos I*. (Salvador Mafé Huertas)

it poses a major challenge to the capacity of the Spanish Navy, despite the entry into service of a new carrier, *Juan Carlos I*. Although the *Principe de Asturias* participated prominently in numerous manoeuvres and national and international exercises, the truth is that she did not get have the chance to take part in any real combat operations, unlike the Italian *Garibaldi*, for example. This lack of political ambition to use the navy's main warship deprived the navy of an experience that would have undoubtedly been very important.

The construction of the aircraft carrier *Principe de Asturias* served to catapult Spanish naval industry into a prominent position. After the construction of a custom-built aircraft carrier for Thailand (HTMS *Chakri Naruebet*) and a number of other highly successful ships, such as the *Galicia*-class amphibious assault ships, the Norwegian *Nansen*-class frigates and the F-100 frigates, Spain had become a benchmark for military shipbuilding. This was followed by other ambitious and ultimately highly successful programmes, such as the construction of a new type of multipurpose vessel – the future *Juan Carlos I*.

Juan Carlos I is a large vessel that exceeds 27,000 tonnes. Although officially termed a Strategic Projection Ship (Buque de Proyección Estratégica, BPE), she can be categorised as an aircraft carrier on account of her considerable capabilities in this regard. *Juan Carlos I* is the result of combining two or three different warship types in a single hull. This is the virtue and also the weakness of the BPE, being simultaneously

An EAV-8B+ Harrier II from the Flotilla de Aeronaves with long-range fuel tanks, gun pod and Maverick anti-ship missile. (Salvador Marín González)

an aircraft carrier with an equivalent (or even superior) aviation capacity to that of the *Prince of Asturias*, as well as an amphibious assault ship with its floodable well deck, and a strategic transport.

As an aircraft carrier it is very capable in terms of air operations and in future could deploy the F-35 without problems (it was designed to accommodate this aircraft from the outset). It can also embark large aircraft, including CH-47 Chinook helicopters or the MV-22 Osprey tiltrotor (the latter repeatedly demostrated by carrier qualifications by US Marine Corps crews from Morón air base, Spain, which is home to the Special Purpose Marine Air-Ground Task Force-Crisis Response-Africa (SP-MAGTF-CR-AF).

But the BPE's weakness lies precisely in this versatility, since while it fulfills one function it can not attend to another. Thus, when it is necessary to use the BPE as a transport, it cannot be used as an aircraft carrier. Switching from one role to another is a sometimes lengthy process, requiring the training of an appropriate crew, which could lead to the warship missing its operational window. As a ship, the BPE features an innovative and highly versatile propulsion system based on adjustable pods, which provides an extraordinary level of manouevrability. The *Juan Carlos I* also includes modern and efficient electronic systems, 3D radar, an efficient combat system. Overall the BPE has proven to be a very successful and functional design, winning export orders from Australia (as the *Canberra*-class LPH). One element that requires improvement is its defensive armament, which urgently requires an upgrade.

In the current scenario, the future of Spain's naval air capacity appears somewhat bleak. The early retirement of the *Principe of Asturias* leaves the fleet air arm of the Spanish Navy in a precarious situation. After some halfhearted attempts to keep the vessel 'hibernated' and even some rumours suggesting its sale, the truth is that it the 'Principe' has been discharged and is awaiting scrapping. The AV-8Bs remain in service, but even taking into account the maximum potential of the platform their days are numbered. The Harrier II cannot continue in service beyond 2025. Spain has to make some important decisions and if the Harrier is not replaced by the F-35, the air defence role will have to be left to the fleet's AEGIS-equipped F-100 frigates (undoubtedly very effective). At the same time, retirement of the Harrier without replacement would see the Spanish Navy lose much of its offensive capacity. The *Juan Carlos I* would become a mere helicopter platform for support of amphibious or humanitarian operations.

The case of Spain is certainly in contrast to those of other countries in a similar situation. Italy, for example, has a comparable economy and a similar requirement to replace the Harrrier II. And yet, Italy has made a firm decision to maintain its fixed-wing carrier-borne capability. Rome sees this as vital for the defence of a modern sea-going country. As such, it is the Italian Navy and not the Spanish that is currently equipping itself with platforms that allow deployment of forces to practically any part of the world and with plans to maintain a naval force that is reduced in size but nonetheless capable.

Seen deploying countermeasures and carrying a dummy Penguin anti-ship missile, this SH-60B Block 2 Seahawk belongs to the 10ª Escuadrilla. These helicopters usually operate from the frigates, but sometimes form part of the *Juan Carlos I* air group. (Salvador Mafé Huertas)

A Special-Purpose Marine Air-Ground Task Force Crisis Response-Africa (SPMAGTF-CR-AF) MV-22B Osprey during carrier qualifications aboard *Juan Carlos I*.
(Salvador Mafé Huertas)

Carrier qualifications

In recent years the Spanish Army Aviation (Fuerzas Aeromóviles del Ejército de Tierra, FAMET) has undergone a major process of change. This has been motivated in the first instance by the incorporation of the Tigre (Spanish military designation HA.28) attack helicopter. On the other hand, change has been due to the constant need to adapt to new missions developed by the Spanish armed forces. The future induction to service of the NH90 helicopter also involves significant challenges. Adjustments have had to be made before their arrival, and all this under a very difficult economic climate with stringent budget constraints.

The new LHD *Juan Carlos I* (L61) was commissioned in 2010. Due to her special characteristics, this warship is destined to become a centrepiece with which to conduct future deployments by the Spanish armed forces in general. Recent operations have focused on the continued navalisation of FAMET's helicopters and crews.

With eight landing spots for Harriers and helicopters over flight deck that is 201.9m (662.4ft) long and 32m (105ft) wide flight deck, the *Juan Carlos I* has the capacity to operate Chinook-size helicopters from some of these spots, as well as the Osprey.

Given the size of the ship and its considerable logistical capabilities, its hangar can accommodate other materiel and equipment, for a total of 10 helicopters the size of the Chinook, or up to a total of 30 helicopters of Cougar/NH90 size.

A joint training plan was launched with an initial practice phase in late 2011 and early 2012 under the direction of the Spanish Navy's Centre for Operational Combat

3ª Escuadrilla

5ª Escuadrilla

6ª Escuadrilla

9ª Escuadrilla

10ª Escuadrilla

Readiness (CEVACO). A series of studies were completed in which data was collected on the compatibilities between the new ship and FAMET helicopters, the types of support required for the operations of these aircraft, protocols for moving aircraft on board the vessel, and plans for maintenance and hangarage. The initial phase of this joint plan was developed for the certification of the Tigre, Cougar and Chinook. The helicopters were loaded onto the ship using the ship's crane, requiring only the dismantling of the rotor blades. After this was done, a second test phase saw the helicopters shipped via the access ramps to the hangars from the dock and then manipulated by specialists within the ship. This served to establish the action protocols in addition to checking compatibility with the deck elevators.

After this static phase there followed a second in which a series of take-offs and landings on the vessel were undertaken while docked at Rota Naval Station. These implemented action protocols for 'cold' and 'hot' refuelling, security procedures on deck, mobility, tie-down, and all other manoeuvres required during the execution of air operations with army helicopters on a large flight deck.

After this initial phase the subsequent work focused on training the crews, who had to be certified to operate from the ship.

At Rota the crews received a series of lectures taught by instructors from the Escuela de Dotaciones Aeronavales (EDAN, Aeronautical Training School). They were trained in procedures for conducting naval air operations with helicopters on the ship, flight safety, signalling, movement on deck, flight deck personnel identification by jacket colours, communications, phraseology, etc.

Accompanying the lecture phase and as a fundamental part of the training received by the FAMET crews, in October 2012 they had to pass a course of survival and movement in the water. The navy's Water Survival Centre provided hands-on survival training including evacuation from a ditched helicopter, using the crew training pool better known as 'the Dunker'.

The FAMET's Chinooks lack rotor brakes so they could not be certified to operate from a ship under way. With this limitation the Chinook could only be certified for transfer and subsequent projection from a stationary vessel.

Given the limitations of the Chinook, the practical phase during navigation could be performed only with the Tiger and Cougar. Based at Rota Naval Air Station, these types flew directly to the carrier, which was sailing 60 miles (97km) off shore, for a total of eight landings per pilot over three days. These comprised the initial qualifications, before night-time qualifications were performed during 2013 using night-vision goggles (NVGs). Next it will be the turn of the new NH90s.

Current units of the Spanish air wing

Unit	Aircraft type	Role	Base	Number
3ª Escuadrilla	AB.212+	Assault/ISR/logistics	Naval Station Rota	2
5ª Escudrilla	SH-3D Sea King	Logistics/assault	Naval Station Rota	4
6ª Escuadrilla	Hughes 369HM	Training/reconnaissance	Naval Station Rota	2
9ª Escudarilla	EAV-8B+ Harrier II	Fighter	Naval Station Rota	6–8
10ª Escuadrilla	SH-60B Seahawk	ASW/ASuW	Naval Station Rota	2–4

One of the seven upgraded AB.212+ helicopters belonging to the 3ª Escuadrilla. (Marco Dijkshoorn)

Joint collaboration

During 2016 the Spanish Army and, more specifically, components of three helicopter battalions of the FAMET, carried out several naval training exercises in collaboration with their French neighbours. These saw the Spanish helicopters make numerous take-offs and landings on the French Navy's amphibious assault ship *Dixmude*.

Under the framework of a bilateral collaboration agreement, these manoeuvres took advantage of the transit of the *Dixmude* along the Spanish coast. The FAMET carried out several periods of naval training that served to qualify the Spanish crews for operations from the French Navy's *Mistral*-class strategic projection vessels. The collaboration is intended to provide improved interoperability for the Spanish armed forces with its allies and partners. Such exercises are undoubtedly also carried out with a view to future joint military operations that could be presented to NATO.

Given the instability in areas of common interest to Spain and France allies, and France's participation in military operations in Africa, it is not far-fetched to consider that Spain might participate in joint missions with its neighbour. One such collaboration that has already been proposed could see Spain's deployment of a group of heavy helicopters, which would undoubtedly enhance and improve France's tactical and logistical capabilities. These shortcomings have been manifested on several occasions and French military officials reportedly see the Chinook as a fundamental tool for today's unconventional and asymmetric military operations.

An EAV-8B Harrier II Plus launching from the 12° ski-jump on the *Juan Carlos I*. (Salvador Mafé Huertas)

Tigers, Cougars and Chinooks participated in these joint training exercises that were carried out off the south coast of Spain and elsewhere in the Mediterranean.

The missions utilised the different take-off spots found on the French vessel and allowed the Spanish crews to familiarise themselves with operations along the entire 199m (652.8ft) deck. At the same time, they served to standardise the necessary procedures, signals and voice communications for the approach, take-off and launch of the aircraft in order to comply with all safety protocols.

In the case of the Chinook, its characteristics and size mean that it should always operate from the most suitable position on the deck. With smaller dimensions than the *Juan Carlos I*, the *Mistral*-class amphibious assault ship only has the capacity to receive Chinook-type helicopters at its number one landing spot. After these joint exercises, the Spanish crews are undoubtedly familiar with operations from the French Navy's assault ships.

Exercises of this kind continue to reinforce the collaboration and agreements that Spain maintains with its northern neighbours in the area of defence. These exercises consolidate the support provided by the Spanish aircraft deployed in Dakar and Liebreville to French troops in their operations in the Sahel and the Central African Republic.

The SH-3D Sea King is the old, but reliable workhorse, being operated by 5ª Escuadrilla. (US Navy/MC2 George Bell)

Hughes 369HM HS.13-10 of 6ª Escuadrilla flies over Naval Station Rota, in the background *Juan Carlos I* can be seen. (Patrick Rogiues)

A typical Spanish carrier air wing

No. of aircraft	Type	Role and remarks
6	EAV-8B+ Harrier II	Air defence
4	SH-3D Sea King	Assault and logistics
2–3	AB.212+	Assault, ISR and logistics
12–13		

A Spanish carrier battle group

No.	Ship class	Ship name	Fleet	Displacement	Crew
1	BPE multipurpose vessel	*Juan Carlos I*		26,000	433
1	*Álvaro de Bazán*-class anti-air defence frigate			6,000	250
1	*Santa María*-class guided missile frigate			2,851	176
1	*Agosta*-class fast-attack submarine			1,760	41
1	Replenishment oiler	*Patiño* (A14) or *Cantabria* (A15)		17,045 or 19,500	148 or 122
					Around 1,048

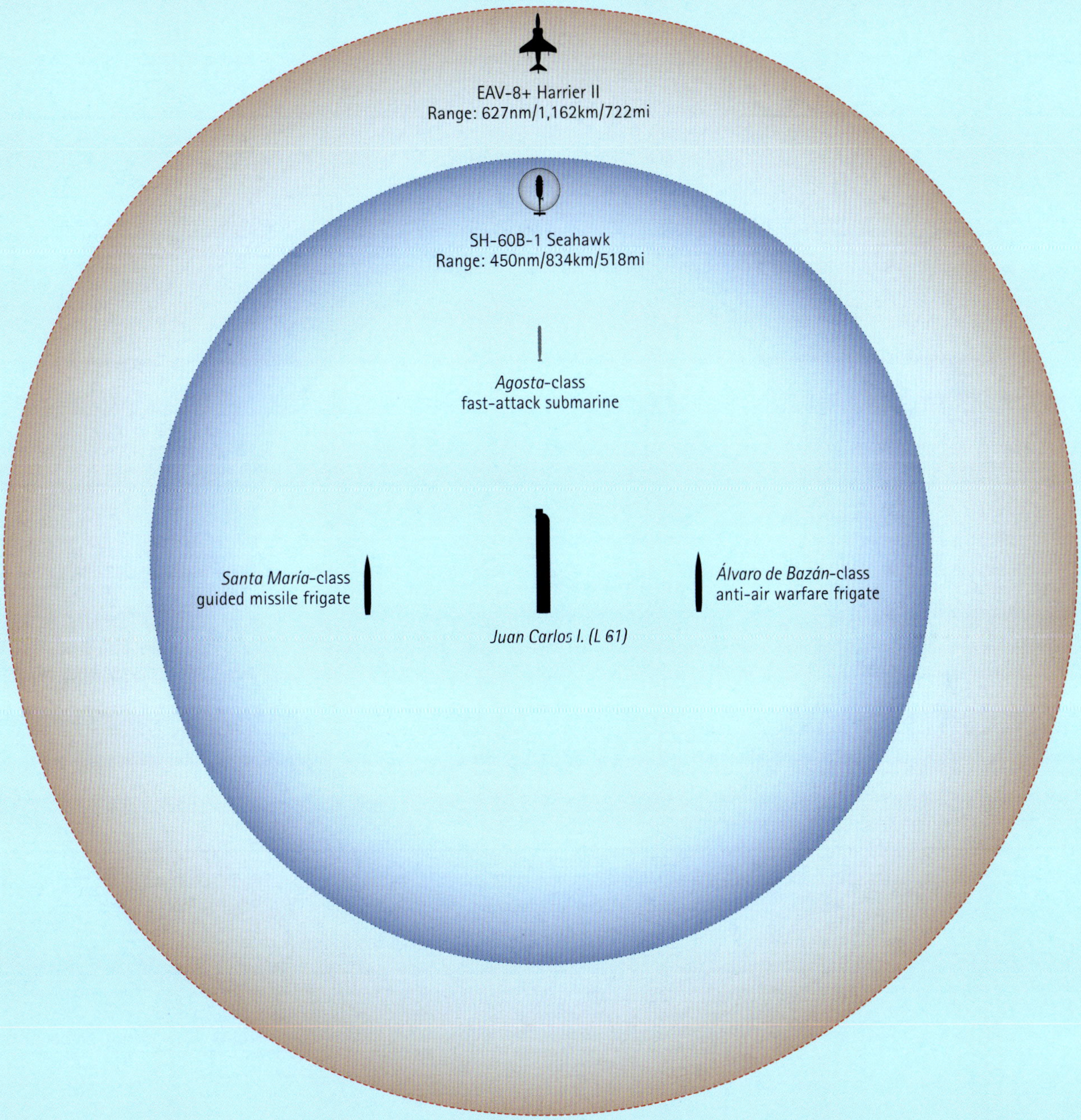

This is a purely schematic presentation of a likely carrier battle group and is not to scale.
In reality, the composition of such a force is dependent on various parameters.

Chapter 8

UNITED KINGDOM

Gabriele Molinelli

'Nemo propheta in patria' is a phrase that can be associated with the naval arm of the Royal Navy, or at least to the fixed wing part of it. The Fleet Air Arm has given birth to naval aviation, and over the years, has introduced key innovations that to this day shape aircraft carriers and air wings around the world. The list, by no means complete, includes the angled deck, the steam catapult and the mirror landing aid.

The Fleet Air Arm has accomplished much, in war as in peace, yet it never enjoyed smooth sailing in policy and budgetary decisions: it was taken into the RAF before returning to the senior service only in the imminence of the second world war. Then it was dramatically dismantled when all large, catapult-equipped carriers were removed from service without replacement, with the last and most famous of all British aircraft carriers, HMS *Ark Royal IV*, bowing out in February 1979.

Naval fixed wing aviation survived in spite of greatly reduced capability, through yet more innovation: Short Take Off and Landing, the Harrier and the *Invincible*-class through-deck cruisers. It went on to allow the UK to recapture the Falklands and avoid a humiliating defeat, but in 2000 was again put under RAF control; in 2006 it was stripped of its Sea Harriers, and in 2010, it was grounded for good when the Harrier GR9 was withdrawn and HMS *Ark Royal V*, in a repeat of a sad fate, was removed from service, with HMS *Illustrious* kept as LPH only. *Illustrious* left service in 2014, and the hopes to see her preserved were shattered during 2016. The 'age of the Invincibles' is now well and truly over as *Illustrious* is towed towards a Turkish yard to be scrapped.

But again, although just as a 40 per cent contribution to a RAF-led 'Joint Force Lightning', fixed wing naval aviation is working towards resurrection, banking its future on two new carriers, HMS *Queen Elizabeth* and HMS *Prince of Wales*, which are the greatest and most capable ever built in Britain. Not yet in service, they are already being imitated across the world. Their twin island arrangement will be present on the new large LHD in build for the Italian navy and a Russian concept for a new super-carrier also has two islands.

At over 65,000 tons, they are aiming for exceptional levels of lean manning through automation: the base ship crew is 679, comparable to the far smaller *Invincible*-class. With air wing, embarked military force and command staff they can comfortably accommodate 1600 men and women. They are meant to support up to 36 F-35 fighters and generate 108 sorties on first-day Surge and then 74 sorties a day for the successive 10 days, followed by at least 20 more days of operations at a rhythm of 36 sorties per day, before needing resupply. After the crew moved on board HMS *Queen Elizabeth*

Royal Navy

Fleet Air Arm

Roundel of Royal Navy

◄ Royal Navy's latest aircraft carrier HMS *Queen Elizabeth* during its maiden voyage. (Crown Copyright)

While work continued to complete HMS *Prince of Wales* at Rosyth, HMS *Queen Elizabeth* embarked on sea trials after leaving the Scottish dockyard in June 2017 and entered her new home in Portsmouth for the first time in August. (Crown Copyright)

contractor sea trials started on 26 June off the coast of Scotland. The trials scheme comprised five weeks at sea, after which the carrier made her first entry into her home port of Portsmouth on 16 August. The Royal Navy's future flagship embarked on its next set of sea trials in October before returning to Portsmouth for official commissioning into service by her namesake, HM Queen Elizabeth II, on 7 December. On 8 September, *Prince of Wales* also had her own naming ceremony.

The impact of the new carriers on worldwide practice might still expand further. To enhance bring-back payload on the STOVL F-35B, the Royal Navy plans to use the innovative technique of short rolling vertical landings, similar to carrier landings but in slow motion and without wires. To guide the aircraft accurately on the unsteady deck, a new system of light signals, the Bedford Array, is being developed, and in the near future, these innovations could be adopted by others as well.

But even as the world continues to build upon Fleet Air Arm expertise and accomplishments, the future of aircraft carrier operations in the United Kingdom remains rife with difficulties to overcome.

Rear Admiral Keith Blount, Assistant Chief of Naval Staff (Aviation, Amphibious Capability and Carriers), is the senior reporting officer for the *Queen Elizabeth*-class carriers programme and responsible for the ships' entry into service. He has repeatedly assured that the arrival of the carriers will fundamentally change the way the Royal Navy operates, bringing the focus back to large task group operations: the carriers will always sail within a task group including escorts and support vessels. Normally it would be easier to believe this, since it is only logical, but the last few years have seen the Royal Navy struggling to put together any kind of supporting force around the amphibious vessels that are now its sole capital ships.

There are some encouraging signs, however. During 2014, the Royal Navy carried out Exercise Deep Blue, embarking a whole ASW squadron of nine Merlin HM.Mk 2 helicopters on HMS *Illustrious* and surrounding her with two Type 23 frigates. The exercise saw British and Dutch submarines trying to get to the carrier while the Merlin squadron worked to keep at least two helicopters on station, around the clock, to ward them off. This was definitely a big effort, but also a reminder of how run down certain Royal Navy capabilities are, if you consider that Cdr Ben Franklin, Commander of the Royal Navy's Maritime Merlin Force has commented: 'Nine Merlins on one carrier is a sight no-one has seen – and one no-one involved will ever forget'. It was the first time for the Merlin force, and many years have passed since the Royal Navy as a whole had practiced a squadron-wide ASW effort.

HMS *Illustrious* went out of service soon after, and it fell on HMS *Ocean*, an amphibious assault ship, to carry out Deep Blue II, in the Mediterranean, during the summer of 2016. Deep Blue II saw the embarkation of even helicopters, adding Sea King ASaC. Mk 7 and Lynx to the Merlins. ASW was again a priority but the exercise added in air attacks, courtesy of 736 Naval Air Squadron (NAS) with its Hawk T.Mk 1 jets, and the AEW effort to contrast them, thanks to the old Kings from 849 NAS.

These training events are fundamental milestones on the way to the regeneration of a capable carrier air wing that is meant to include nine Merlin HM2 for ASW screening and another four or five in AEW configuration to track enemy air movements and provide early warning.

The difficulties to overcome are significant, and within a couple of years both ASW and AEW tasks will be the remit of the Merlin force as the last Sea King ASaC.Mk 7 are withdrawn from service in 2018. The Royal Navy has received a total of 30 Merlin ASW helicopters uplifted to the HM.Mk 2 standard through an upgrade programme that saw the last delivery in July 2016. A further eight Merlin helicopters remain in HM.Mk 1 configuration, grounded and awaiting their fate, while four more have been in storage for years and have been cannibalized. The Royal Navy has been trying for years to secure funding to upgrade some or all of the eight orphaned HM.Mk 1, but the struggle so far has had no success.

The withdrawal of Sea King, however, will leave the Royal Navy short of AEW platforms. Under the CROWSNEST programme, Lockheed Martin as prime contractor will deliver a palletized AEW solution for installation on the Merlin. An updated variant of the Thales Cerberus suite, centered on the Sarchwater radar and already employed by the Sea King Mk7, has been selected and the manufacturing contract has been announced on January 16, 2017. Ten modernised Cerberus suites will be acquired and modifications will be introduced on all 30 Merlin HM.Mk 2 to make it possible to roll on and roll off the AEW kit as needed, with the operation expected to require only a few hours. Operational and training realities suggest that at least 8 helicopters will be AEW roled at any one time, putting a lot of strain on the small fleet.

While fighting a last ditch battle to try and secure the additional airframes that would fundamentally ease the task of providing ASW and AEW coverage to the fleet, the navy is meanwhile planning on the basis of a 30-strong fleet. Of the current three frontline ASW squadrons, 820 NAS, 814 NAS and 829 NAS, only two will remain: as 820 NAS becomes the carrier squadron, 814 and 829 will merge by the end of 2018, to carry out all other duties, including High Readiness flight in support of the Towed Array Patrol Ship, the on-call ASW frigate (these days normally one thing with the FRE, Fleet Ready Escort). The resulting super-squadron will primarily deliver Small Ship Flights for the Type 23 ASW frigates, which is today's 829 NAS task. Any residual capability generated would be available for the carriers or other tasks.

849 NAS, the AEW squadron, will switch from Sea King to Merlin helicopters and CROWSNEST radar kits, while 824 NAS will carry on as the fleet training unit.

The pressures on a fleet of just 30 helicopters faced by the demanding and very specialized tasks of ASW and AEW will be immense, even assuming that Merlin HM.Mk 2 can stick to plans for a Forward Fleet of 25 out of 30 total machines, with the balance undergoing heavy maintenance.

The other key element of the air wing is, obviously, the F-35B. Uncountable pages have been written about the JSF, but in the meanwhile the aircraft has been maturing and the British contingent has been hard at work in the US, taking part in the trials and in the development. In November 2016, the British involvement in the USMC-led third tranche of Development Testing, held on board of the new USS *America*, has been very substantial: the Royal Navy sent an air traffic controller, five engineers, handlers, and maintainers that in the future will be responsible for the safe movement and handling of F-35B on the new carriers. A British team from the Integrated Test Force based at Patuxent River also embarked for the 23-days cruise: this consisted of one RAF test pilot, three flight test engineers, and six maintainers responsible for the detachment's maintenance evaluation.

Ahead of the publication of the SDSR 2015, chancellor George Osborne said the UK would purchase 42 F-35B by 2023, an acceleration compared to the 2010 plan, in order to be able, in the same year, to have two complete operational squadrons of 12 aircraft each.

There is some uncertainty about whether the 42 aircraft quoted will be delivered by 2023, or just ordered. The difference is substantial, considering that a couple of years elapse between order and delivery. The rhythm of the purchases will depend on the decision to be taken at the Main Gate 5 point, scheduled for the 2017 budget cycle. To this day, the UK has firm commitments in place for just 18 aircraft, including those already delivered and the long lead items purchased for a single airframe in Low Rate Initial Production lot 11. The LRIP 11 contract will only be signed next year, so that the single aircraft might well be joined by a few others, but all depends on MG5.

Long term acquisition plans are just as vague. The UK reaffirmed its commitment to 138 F-35 'over the life of the programme', but it is hard to guess which year they have in mind. The MOD Major Projects Portfolio, released in July 2016 but current to September 2015, shows 2026 as Lightning II Project End Date, because that is the year in which the full Block IV hardware and software release is expected to become operational, including all specified British weapons (Meteor, SPEAR 3, ASRAAM Block 6, Paveway IV bunker-buster variant) but it is highly unlikely the UK would order 138 aircraft by then.

In May 2016, Air Cmdr. Harvey Smyth, the commander of the UK's Lightning Force, explained that the RAF would eventually form four frontline and one OCU squadron, all with 12 aircraft, plus No 17 (Reserve) Test and Evaluation Squadron (TES) with three instrumented jets.

The timeline for reaching this goal has not been revealed, but the first two frontline squadrons are meant to be operational by the end of 2023. No 17(R) Squadron is operational since February 2015 and already has all three Instrumented Test aircraft ordered by the UK (BK-1, BK-2 and BK-4), while the training and operational units are building up alongside US Marine Corps squadrons at MCAS Beaufort, in South Carolina. According to 2014 plans, a total of 24 British pilots would be trained by the USMC own training unit, Marine Fighter Attack Training Squadron 501 (VMFAT-501), with the last ones completing their courses in May 2018. After that, an Operational Conversion Unit is expected to begin operations at RAF Marham from July 2019. A squadron identity for the OCU has yet to be chosen and announced.

The first operational squadron will be the RAF's No 617 Squadron, the 'Dambusters' of World War II fame: the build-up has begun at Beaufort and will see the squadron officially standing up in January 2018. Within six months they will start crossing the Atlantic to move into their new home, RAF Marham, where a gigantic infrastructure effort, known as Project ANVIL, is preparing Hardened Aircraft Shelters, hangars, offices and maintenance structures ahead of the F-35's arrival. By December the same year, the squadron should achieve Initial Operational Capability for land-based missions. In the meanwhile, HMS *Queen Elizabeth* will have crossed the Atlantic in the opposite direction to embark No 17(R) Squadron and, probably, a number of USMC aircraft for First of Class flying trials.

No 617 Squadron will conduct its own carrier qualifications to meet IOC (maritime) by December 2020, and the intent is that all pilots graduating from the OCU will be carrier-qualified. That will mark the true rebirth of British naval aviation, and it all should come together for the first operational deployment of HMS *Queen Elizabeth*, planned for 2021.

No 617 Squadron will continue to grow not just in capability but in size over the following few years, until first the OCU and then the second frontline squadron split off from it. The second squadron, which will stand up in 2023 between April and December, will have a Fleet Air Arm identity as 809 NAS, the 'Immortals' which has a phoenix reborn from the flames as symbol. A fitting image for the unit that will bring naval fixed wing aviation back on the scenes after a long absence. Regardless of the squad-

A Merlin HM.Mk 2 of 820 NAS completes the first aircraft landing on HMS *Queen Elizabeth*. Lt Luke Wraith was at the controls for the milestone event on 3 July 2017, soon after the carrier left Rosyth to begin trials in the North Sea. (Crown Copyright)

809 Naval Air Squadron has been resurrected as the first Royal Navy formation to fly the UK's F-35B Lightning II Joint Strike Fighter aircraft. (Crown Copyright)

rons' previous histories, however, the formations will all be jointly manned, with an expected 60:40 balance in favour of the RAF, which is also the budget holder and the controller of the Joint Force Lightning, which sits under RAF Group 1. The Fleet Air Arm fixed wing branch's resurrection, in other words, will only be partial, and there is no going back on the loss of independence that came back in 2000 with the birth of Joint Force Harrier. The only thing to do is hope in a different and better end for this second attempt.

One potential threat to Joint Force Lightning is the possible emergence of a RAF appetite for land-based F-35A, which could go to the detriment of the embarkable Bs. Air Commodore Linc Taylor did nothing to hide the RAF's interest for the A variant when he spoke during the Fairford Royal International Air Tattoo 2016, openly suggesting that a split buy option will be on the table at the SDSR 2020. He explained that: 'The F-35A offers you a greater range and greater payload. There may be space for an 'A' variant, so we will look at 'A' and 'B's in the future'. The statement is as true as it is dangerous for the future of the reborn British naval aviation: the planned force of four squadrons will already struggle to generate and sustain a suitably large air wing, and any reduction to this force could very quickly precipitate the UK into the dreaded 'carriers without aircraft' scenario. An observation that can be made is that four squadrons plus OCU and TES equate to an operational fleet of just 63 aircrafts, less than half of the planned 138 total. While an operational fleet does need a back up and attrition reserve, a 63 to 75 ratio does appear extreme. Is there room for a split buy without reducing the number of F-35B squadrons? Possibly. The RAF is at present so encouraged by the integrated support and maintenance arrangement for the Typhoon fleet that is now planning to stand up eight rather than five frontline squadrons, from a fleet of some 107 Tranche 2 and 3 aircraft plus 30 retained Tranche 1s, originally due to be withdrawn by 2019 but, since the SDSR 2015, expected to run up to 2035. The F-35, also thanks to the vast use of simulation in training, should not require an overly large sustainment fleet, and there should be plenty of room for forming additional squadrons. It is a very delicate issue, however: it might be better to just form extra F-35B squadrons rather than create a second fleet, no matter how closely related and helped by commonality. The risk of a fratricidal battle for resources as occurred between Tornado and Harrier is too high, and availability from a large fleet of a single type is likely going to always beat the combined availability of machines from two smaller fleets.

The other big question in need of an answer is what kind of impact the loss of HMS *Ocean* will have on the carriers and on the UK's amphibious capability. *Ocean* is the only RN amphibious unit designed and built to support an air group of helicopters and launch company-group assault waves mounted in rotary wing transports and with attack helicopter escort. She will be withdrawn from service in 2018, without direct replacement, with her crew reinvested to help the navy man the carriers. Losing her will leave the Royal Marines hundreds of bunks short and without a single hangar due to the LPDs and LSDs having none. The crisis has been well visible on the horizon to anyone with eyes for several years, but the MOD only got around to acknowledging the problem in the SDSR 2010, when 'Carrier Enabled Power Projection' entered the frame. In essence, the carriers will also be the Royal Marines' LPHs. What impact will this have?

We do not yet know how the carriers will alternate out at sea. The SDSR 2015 assured that both will be brought into service and HMS *Prince of Wales*'s crew is being formed, but doubts remain on how the two ships will effectively be used. Considering that putting together even just one Air Wing remains a challenge, is it realistic to expect both ships to be operational at any one time? In theory, the Royal Navy could use one as a Fleet Carrier and the other as LPH, filling the *Ocean*-shaped hole, and the Major General Rob Magowan, commander general Royal Marines, suggests exactly this in his end of 2016 message to the troops. It is however easier to expect that only one carrier at a time will be operational and deployed, at least most of the time, so that she'll have to juggle two trades at once. She'll be a USMC-style LHA, rather than a strike carrier, and Magowan intends to always embark elements of agile Special Purpose Task Groups.

It has emerged that, as part of CEPP, HMS *Prince of Wales* will be fitted with 'enhancements' to better support the amphibious assault role from 2023. It is too late now to apply the changes to *Queen Elizabeth*, so she will be retrofitted later, presumably at the first major docking period. The modifications will probably be relatively limited: extra accommodation for embarked Marines, and arrangement for the storage of their kit and ammunition, first of all. However, a new flight deck organization could also be included, increasing the number of spots from six to 10, with a study already completed to demonstrate the feasibility of 10-helicopter waves. Rear Admiral Blount described CEPP through three example-configurations: Carrier Strike, Expeditionary Strike and Littoral Manoeuvre. The first calls for two embarked squadrons of F-35B (24 aircraft), nine Merlin HM.Mk 2 for ASW and an AEW Flight of four or five CROWSNEST, although the ship can easily embark a third F-35B squadron if ASW helicopters

809 NAS

820 NAS

845 NAS

849 NAS

No 617 Squadron

are not required or are offloaded to other vessels in the task group. In 2014, the MOD said it will deploy a Carrier Strike airwing once every two years as part of the routine carrier generation cycle, while the assumption is that normally a single squadron will be embarked, although the USMC's own F-35Bs could be frequent visitors and increase the number of jets on deck.

The Expeditionary Strike configuration could be the most frequently observed: this integrates one F-35B squadron, a reinforced Royal Marines company group (circa 250 strong) and helicopters for their insertion ashore.

Littoral Manoeuvre is a 'fully amphibious' configuration with at least two company groups of Marines and a large number of helicopters. This mix, and variants of it, can obviously be employed only against low-capability enemies or with air support and cover being provided by the second carrier or by allies.

In addition to the Merlin and Lightning forces, the Carrier Air Wing will routinely draw from RAF Chinook squadrons and from the Army Air Corps's Attack Helicopter Force, which is composed of two regiments: 3 and 4, each with two squadrons of Apache AH.Mk 1 gunships. The two regiments alternate yearly into high readiness and one of the two squadrons is earmarked for embarked operations.

The Royal Marines will embark elements of their Commando Helicopter Force, which is composed of 845 and 846 NAS, equipped with ex-RAF Merlin HC.Mk 3/3A transports which are now being navalised as the HC.Mk 4/4A that features folding tail and rotor, and upgraded with the same glass cockpit used by HM.Mk 2. The CHF also includes 847 NAS, equipped with Wildcat AH.Mk 1 for reconnaissance, artillery direction, escort and light utility. Further Wildcat AH.Mk 1 could be embarked by the AAC, coming from 1st Regiment, composed of 652, 661 and 659 Squadrons.

The RAF Puma HC.Mk 2s could also be embarked if necessary for a major operation although this is not a routine occurrence. Chinook is not a naval helicopter but, unlike Puma, is a regular presence on HMS *Ocean*, even though it can reach the hangar only if the rotor blades are removed. On the new carriers, the aircraft lift is large enough to permit movement of Chinook with spread rotor from the deck to the hangar. The cavernous hangar of the new carriers is able to welcome any type of naval aircraft, including the USMC's MV-22 Osprey, a flexible asset that the Royal Navy hopes to have on board every time.

Future units of Royal Navy carrier air wing

Unit	Aircraft type	Role	Base	Remarks
809 NAS	F-35B	Multirole fighter	RAF Marham	12 aircraft; to stand up in late 2023*
820 NAS	Merlin HM.Mk 2	ASW	RNAS Culdrose	9 helicopters expected
845 NAS	Merlin HC.Mk 4	COD, assault, CSAR	RNAS Yeovilton	12 helicopters in three deployable 'units of action' of four, with at least one expected to be routinely embarked.
849 NAS	Merlin HM.Mk 2	AEW	RNAS Culdrose	Up to 5 helicopters expected to embark, with CROWSNEST palletised radar
No 617 Squadron, RAF	F-35B		RAF Marham	12 aircraft; to stand up in late 2023*

* Based on current plans, a third and fourth F-35B squadron will be formed in the late 2020s.

A Merlin HC.Mk 3 of 845 NAS conducting HI-Line (Heave In) training on the flight deck of a Royal Australian Navy frigate in the Far East during Exercise Jeanne D'Arc 17. The former RAF Merlins are being upgraded to HC.Mk 4 Commando standard and will be part of the *Queen Elizabeth* air wing (Crown Copyrigth 2017)

Two Wildcat AH.Mk 1s, one Merlin HM.Mk 2 and two RAF Chinooks on board HMS *Ocean* during NATO Exercise Trident Juncture 2015. Depending on configuration, all these types will be included in the *Queen Elizabeth* air wing. (Crown Copyright)

A future UK carrier strike air wing

No. of aircraft	Type	Role and remarks
12*	F-35B	Air defence; maximum of 36 for Carrier Strike
4–5	Merlin HM.Mk 2	AEW
9	Merlin HM.Mk 2	ASW
4	Merlin HC.Mk 4	COD, CSAR, assault
8	Apache AH.Mk 1	Attack; for Littoral Manoeuvre mission
3	Chinook HC.Mk 4/5/6	Transport; for Littoral Manoeuvre mission
6	Wildcat AH.Mk 1	Attack; for Littoral Manoeuvre mission
40		A maximum of 40 aircraft can be deployed

The *Queen Elizabeth*-class air wing is designed to be 'scalable' between Carrier Strike and Littoral Manoeuvre missions; in practice, a 'mixed-mission' complement is expected for most deployments.
* Total 36 F-35Bs is dependent on embarking USMC aircraft; maximum 24 UK aircraft.

The future Royal Navy carrier battle group (2021+)

No.	Ship class	Ship name	Fleet	Displacement	Crew
1	*Queen Elizabeth*-class aircraft carrier	HMS *Queen Elizabeth* (R08)		70,600	1,600
2	Type 45 anti-air warfare destroyers			8,500 8,500	191 191
2	Type 23 (*Duke*-class) anti-submarine frigates			4,900 4,900	185 185
1	*Astute*-class nuclear submarine			7,500	98
1	*Tide*-class tanker			37,000	109
					2,559

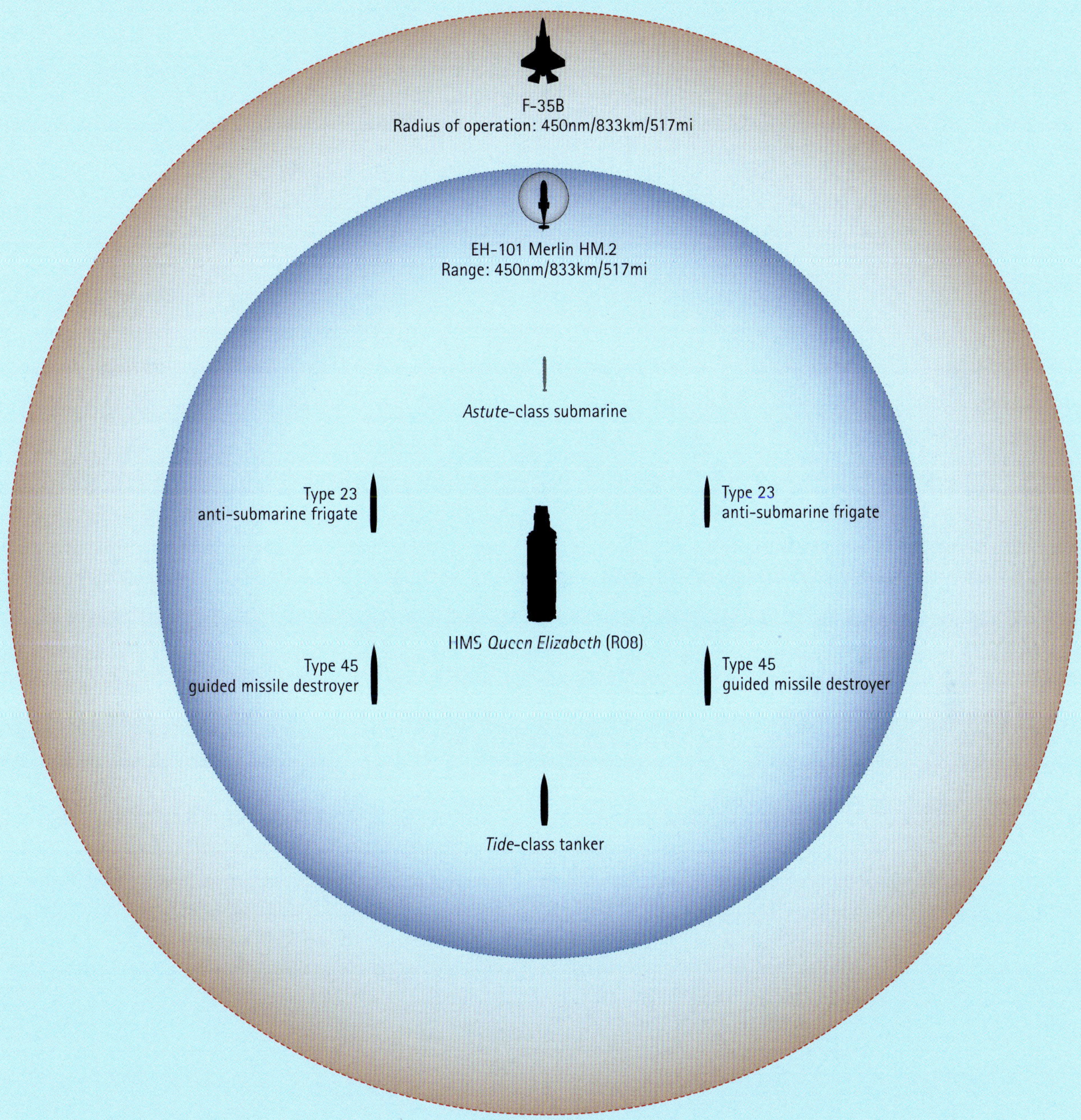

This is a purely schematic presentation of a likely carrier battle group and is not to scale.
In reality, the composition of such a force is dependent on various parameters.

Chapter 9

UNITED STATES

Tom Kaminski

On 8 May 2011 the US Navy marked the 100th anniversary of the birth of Naval Aviation. Although the first naval aviator, Lieutenant Theodore 'Spuds' Ellyson, began his flight training at the Curtiss Aviation Camp on North Island in December 1910, the US Navy recognises the date in 1911 that CAPT Washington Irving Chambers, US Navy, Officer-in-Charge of Aviation, prepared the requisition of the Navy's first aircraft, as the birth date of Naval Aviation. Known as the A-1 Triad, the aircraft was purchased from aviator and inventor Glenn H. Curtiss.

US Naval aircraft have been operating from carrier decks since October 1922 when a Vought VE-7SF was launched from the USS *Langley* (CV 1) for the first time.

Today, the US Navy's aircraft carriers are the ultimate symbol of air-power projection, a flexible force able to react at short notice to support the US president on the international stage and meet aggression or support humanitarian operations. The US Navy's nuclear-powered aircraft carriers stamp America's military might in the minds of any potential adversary, and provide a compelling deterrent to any would-be aggressors. Each supporting an air wing that is the equivalent of many proud air forces, and with its supporting vessels, the Carrier Strike Group (CSG) is the backbone of the US Navy.

Battle groups operate in international waters without needing permission for landing or overflight rights. Each is a self-sustained floating airport that is sovereign US territory. When deployed, they operate with their own ZIP code, post office, hospital, dental clinic, barbershops, athletic facilities and chapels. More than 18,000 meals are prepared daily and each of the crew has e-mail access.

A carrier has approximately 18 levels, including eight above the ship's enormous hangar bay and 10 decks below. The 'island' or superstructure above the flight deck contains the bridge, where the admiral and his staff can watch operations and conduct planning at the task group level.

On a strategic level, the US Navy is continuing to react to the 'pivot to the Pacific'. Vide-Admiral Robert L. Thomas commented: 'We're slowly shifting from a 50/50 mix in the US Navy to a 40 per cent Atlantic, 60 per cent Pacific mix', he added, describing the swing away from traditional areas of operation.

Admiral Harry Harris, the US Pacific Fleet commander, said in 2013: 'Our president and secretary of defence are clear. As a nation, we will rebalance to the Pacific and we will work closely with our allies and partners in the Indo-Asia-Pacific region.'

US Navy

US Naval Aviation insignia (high-visibility variant)

◄ Carrier Strike Group 5 led by USS *Ronald Reagan* (CVN 76). (US Navy/MC2 Nathan Burke)

While this strategy was set in motion under the Barack Obama administration, since President Donald Trump took office in 2017 the importance of the Asia-Pacific area of operations has only increased. In October 2017 the US Navy took the unusual step of deploying three *Nimitz*-class carriers in the Seventh Fleet's area of operations (AOO) simultaneously, underlining its presence in the region unambiguously.

However, recent budgetary restrictions have severely impacted the Carrier Strike Groups (CSG), with intense deployment schedules, and little time for rest and recuperation of assets and personnel.

US Navy F/A-18s and two US Air Force B-1B Lancers fly over the USS *Ronald Reagan* (CVN 76), USS *Nimitz* (CVN 68) and USS *Theodore Roosevelt* (CVN 71) Carrier Strike Groups in the Western Pacific.
(US Navy/Lt jg James Griffin)

US NAVY AIRCRAFT CARRIERS

Nimitz class

The decommissioning of the USS *Enterprise* (CVN 65) in 2012 left the US Navy with a single class of nuclear-powered aircraft carriers. With an overall length of 332.84m (1,092ft), a beam of 40.84m (134ft) and full-load displacement of 92,000 to 106,000 tons, the 10 *Nimitz*-class aircraft carriers are the largest warships in the world, each designed for an approximately 50 year service life with one mid-life refueling. Five of the vessels comprising the USS *Nimitz* (CVN 68), USS *Dwight D. Eisenhower* (CVN 69), USS *Carl Vinson* (CVN 70), USS *Theodore Roosevel*t (CVN 71) and USS A*braham Lincoln* (CVN 72) have completed their Refueling Complex Overhauls (RCOH). The USS *George Washington* (CVN 73) midlife RCOH began in August 2017.

The ships were constructed between 1968 and 2009 by Newport News Shipbuilding Company in Newport News, Virginia, and each is powered by two A4W nuclear reactors Steam produced by the reactors drive four turbines that provide 280,000shp to the ship four propellers enabling the ship to reach maximum speeds in excess of 30 knots. The flight deck is 76.81m (252ft) wide and is equipped with four elevators and four steam powered catapults.

USS *Theodore Roosevelt* (CVN 71) transits the Pacific Ocean. (US Navy/MC3 Anthony J. Rivera)

USS *Nimitz* (CVN 68)

The lead ship of its class is named in honor of Fleet Admiral Chester W. Nimitz. The keel for the US Navy's second nuclear-powered carrier was laid on 22 June 1968 and the carrier was launched on 13 May 1972. Commissioned on 3 May 1975, the ship's RCOH was completed in 2001. Nimitz has been home-ported in Coronado, California, since March 2012. The flagship for Carrier Strike Group 11 (CSG-11) will remain in service until replaced by the future USS *John F. Kennedy* (CVN 79).

USS *Dwight D. Eisenhower* (CVN 69)

The keel of the carrier, which was named to honour America's 34th president and General of the Army, was laid on 15 August 1970. The hull was subsequently launched on 11 October 1975 and the vessel was commissioned on 18 October 1977. A midlife RCOH was completed in Newport News in March 2005. Currently home-ported at Naval Station Norfolk, Virginia, 'Ike' is the flagship for CSG-10.

USS *Carl Vinson* (CVN 70)

Named for the late Georgia Congressman, the keel for the 'Gold Eagle' was laid on 11 October 1975. The vessel was launched on 15 March 1980 and commissioned on 13 March 1982. A 3.5 year RCOH was completed in July 2009. The flagship of CSG-1 is home-ported at Naval Air Station North Island, Coronado, California.

USS *Theodore Roosevelt* (CVN 71)

Named for the 26th president, former Secretary of the Navy and leader of the 'Rough Riders', the keel of the 'TR' was laid on 31 October 1981, just eight months after its predecessor a Fleet Ballistic Missile Submarine (SSBN 600) was decommissioned. Launched on 27 October 1984, the vessel was placed in commission less than two years later on 25 October 1986. Serving as the flagship for CSG-12 and home-ported at Naval Air Station North Island, Coronado, California, CVN 71 completed a Refueling and Complex Overhaul (RCOH) at Newport News Shipbuilding on 29 August 2013.

USS *Abraham Lincoln* (CVN 72)

The keel for the namesake of America's 16th president was laid on 3 November 1984 and the vessel was christened on 13 February 1988. It was placed in commission on 11 November 1989. The previous vessel with this name was a Fleet Ballistic Missile Submarine (SSBN 602). Its homeport was changed from Everett, Washington, to Naval Station Norfolk, Virginia, on 7 August 2012. The carrier began a RCOH at Newport News Shipbuilding in Virginia, on 28 March 2013 that was completed in late 2016.

USS *George Washington* (CVN 73)

Named for the nation's first president, the keel of the 'GW' was laid on 25 August 1986, just 17 months after the nation's first nuclear-powered Fleet Ballistic Missile Submarine (SSBN 598) with the same name was decommissioned. The 'Spirit of Freedom' was launched on 21 July 1990 and the ship was commissioned on 4 July 1992. CVN 73 had been home-ported at Fleet Activities Yokosuka, Japan, since 25 September 2008. In preparation for its RCOH the ship's home port was changed to Naval Station Norfolk, Virginia, in December 2015.

USS *John C. Stennis* (CVN 74)

The keel for CVN 74 was laid on 13 March 1991, the hull was launched on 13 November 1993 and the ship was commissioned on November 11, 1995. Named to honor 'the father of America's modern Navy', an eight-term senator from Mississippi, *Stennis* is home-ported at Naval Base Kitsap in Bremerton, Washington, and is the flagship for CSG-3.

USS *Harry S. Truman* (CVN 75)

The keel of CVN 75 was laid on 30 June 1988 and the vessel was christened at Newport News Shipbuilding and Dry-dock in Virginia, on 7 September 1996. The carrier, which is named to honor the nation's 33rd president, was commissioned on 25 July 1998. CVN 75 is home-ported at Naval Station Norfolk, Virginia, and is the flagship of CSG-8.

USS *Ronald Reagan* (CVN 76)

Named in honor of America's 40th president, CVN 76's construction began at Newport News Shipbuilding when the keel was laid on 12 February 1998. The ship was christened on 4 March 2001 and commissioned on 12 July 2003. The ship completed a homeport changes from NAS North Island in Coronado, California to Fleet Activities Yokosuka, Japan, in October 2015, CVN 76 is the flagship of CSG-5.

USS *George H. W. Bush* (CVN 77)

The keel for the last ship in the *Nimitz*-class was laid on 6 September 2003 and the ship was christened on 7 October 2006. CVN 77 was originally planned as the first ship in a new class that was originally referred to as the CVNX-1, and features several changes over its predecessors. These include a redesigned island structure and modernided aircraft launch and recovery equipment. The ship, which is named in honor of the 41st president, was commissioned on 10 January 2009 and is home-ported at Naval Station Norfolk, Virginia. CVN 77 is the flagship for CSG-2.

Gerald R. Ford class

Originally referred to as the CVNX-1 and then as CVN-21, design of the newest class of aircraft carriers was begun in 1998. The US Navy awarded Northrop Grumman Shipbuilding Newport News a USD 5.1-billion contract to begin detail design and construction of the first ship of the *Gerald R. Ford* class on 10 September 2008. The lead ship in the US Navy's newest class of aircraft carrier features many improvements over the earlier *Nimitz*-class design.

CVN 78 features a larger flight deck design that includes just three aircraft elevators and an improved weapons handling system. Sortie generation is improved by an Electro-Magnetic Aircraft Launch System (EMALS) that replaces earlier C-13 Mod 1 and Mod 2 steam-driven catapults, and an electric motor-based Advanced Arresting Gear (AAG) system replaces the older Mk 7 hydraulic arresting system installed in the Nimitz class. The ships will be capable of generating 160 sorties per day (12-hour fly day) and to surge to 270 sorties per day (24-hour fly day) as compared to the *Nimitz*-class, which has the capability to generate 120 sorties per day or surge to 240 sorties for a 24-hour flight schedule.

Additionally, its island structure has been relocated 30.5m (100ft) further aft and is equipped with the AN/SPY-3 Phased array Dual Band Radar (DBR). New and simplified nuclear propulsion plants and electrical power generation systems are also incorporated, allowing the ship to operate with a smaller crew. Each of the ships will be powered by two A1B nuclear reactors that can generate 300MW of electricity, compared to the 100 MW of the earlier *Nimitz*-class A4W reactors. Increased space for flight deck operations and aircraft maintenance is also provided. The US Navy plans to build 11 Ford-class aircraft carriers by 2058.

On 28 July 2017 pilot Lieutenant Commander Jamie R. Struck, callsign 'COACH', in his F/A-18F 'SD 123' from VX-23 made the first carrier arrested landing using new AAG system aboard USN carrier *Gerald R. Ford* (CVN 78) off the Virgina coast.
(US Navy/Erik Hildebrandt)

USS *Gerald R. Ford* (CVN 78)

Advanced construction of the CVN 78 began in August 2005 and on 16 January 2007 the US Navy formally announced that its next aircraft carrier would be named USS *Gerald R. Ford* in honor of the 38th president who had died just weeks earlier. The ship's keel was laid on 14 November 2009 and it was christened on 9 November 2013 at Newport News Shipbuilding. Pre-Commissioning Unit (PCU) *Gerald R. Ford* was launched on 17 November 2013. The aircraft carrier successfully completed acceptance trials on 26 May 2017 and was subsequently commissioned by President Donald Trump on 22 July.

USS *John F. Kennedy* (CVN 79)

On 29 May 2011, the US Navy announced the second ship of the *Ford* class will be named in honor of the 35th president. It will be the second aircraft carrier to bear the name. Construction of the ship began when the first steel was cut on 25 February 2011. Currently scheduled to be launched in February 2020 and enter service in 2022, CVN 79 will likely be equipped with the new Enterprise Air Surveillance Radar (EASR), which had originally been planned to enter the fleet aboard CVN 80. The previous USS *John F. Kennedy* (CV 67) served from 1967 to 2007.

USS *Enterprise* (CVN 80)

During the deactivation ceremony for the USS *Enterprise* (CVN 65) on 1 December 2012, the US Navy announced that the third ship of the *Ford* class would be named *Enterprise*. The start of construction of CVN 80 is planned for 2018, with the ship entering service in 2027. It will be the ninth ship and the third aircraft carrier to carry the name.

USMC AMPHIBIOUS ASSAULT SHIPS

The largest of all amphibious warfare ships are capable of supporting Vertical/Short Take-Off and Landing (V/STOL), Short Take-Off Vertical Landing (STOVL), Vertical Take-Off and Landing (VTOL) tiltrotor and Rotary Wing (RW) aircraft operations. The ships include General Purpose (LHA) and Multi Purpose (LHD) classes.

These vessels serve as the lead ships of the US Navy's Amphibious Ready Groups (ARG). In addition to the LHA or LHD, the ARG is rounded out with an amphibious transport dock (LPD) and a dock landing ship (LSD).

Wasp class

Based on the earlier *Tarawa*-class LHAs the *Wasp* class featured several modifications that improved their ability to support the AV-8B and to deploy Air Cushion Landing Craft (LCAC).

USS *Wasp* (LHD 1)
The keel for LHD 1 was laid on 28 February 1984 and the tenth ship to bear the name was placed in commission 6 July 1989. Two previous aircraft carriers (CV 7) and (CVS 18) carried the name *Wasp* during World War II. The ship is homeported at Fleet Activities Sasebo, Japan.

USS *Essex* (LHD 2)
Named for the lead ship of the Navy's largest class of aircraft carriers, LHD 2 is actually the fifth ship to bear the name. The previous USS *Essex* (CVS 9) was decommissioned in June 1969. The ship's keel for was laid 20 March 1989 and it was commissioned on 17 October 1992. *Essex* is homeported at Naval Base San Diego, California.

USS *Kearsarge* (LHD 3)
Home ported in Norfolk, Virginia, the keel for the fourth USS *Kearsarge* was laid on 6, February 1990. The previous ship named for this New Hampshire Mountain, was an *Essex*-class aircraft carrier (CVS 33). LHD 3 was commissioned 16 October 1993. *Kearsarge* completed a deployment to the 6th and 5th Fleet areas of responsibility with the 26th MEU (SOC) and VMM-266 in November 2013.

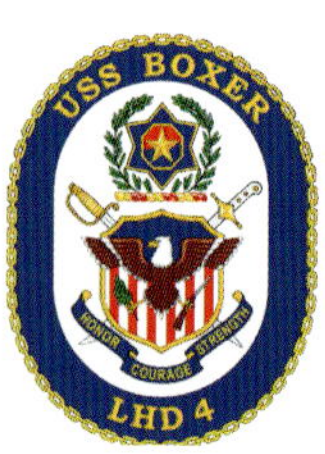

USS *Boxer* (LHD 4)
The keel for the fifth USS *Boxer* was laid on 18 April 1991 and the ship was placed in commission on 11 February 1995. The previous USS *Boxer* (CVS 21) was an *Essex*-class aircraft carrier. *Boxer* is homeported at Naval Base San Diego, California.

USS *Bataan* (LHD 5)

The keel for the second USS *Bataan* was laid on 22 June 1994. The ship was commissioned 20 September 1997 and is currently homeported at Naval Station Norfolk, Virginia. The previous *Bataan* (CVL 29) was an Independence-class light aircraft carrier.

USS *Bonhomme Richard* (LHD 6)

LHD 6 is the second ship named to honor the Flagship of John Paul Jones. Its keel was laid on 18 April 1995 and the ship was placed in commission on 15 August 1998. The previous USS *Bonhomme Richard* (CVA 31) was an *Essex*-class aircraft carrier. LHD 6 is homeported at Naval Station San Diego, California.

Six MV-22 Ospreys line the deck of the multipurpose amphibious assault ship USS *Boxer* (LHD 4) under way off the coast of California.
(US Navy/MC3 Christopher B. Janik)

USS *Iwo Jima* (LHD 7)

The keel for was laid for the seventh ship of the *Wasp*-class on 12 December 1997. The vessel, which is named for the World War II island battle, also honors a previous amphibious assault ship (LPH 2), which was the lead ship in its class. Commissioned on 30 June 2001, *Iwo Jima* has been homeported at Naval Station Mayport, Florida, since August 2014.

USS *Makin Island* (LHD 8)

Named for the battle of Makin Island, which took place in August 1942, LHD 8 is the final ship of the *Wasp* class and the second ship to bear the name. The previous USS *Makin Island* (CVE 93) was a *Casablanca*-class escort carrier. LHD 8's keel was laid on February 12, 2004 and Makin Island was commissioned on 24 October 2009. It is currently home ported at Naval Base San Diego, California.

A landing craft, air cushion (LCAC) enters the well deck of the amphibious assault ship USS *Iwo Jima* (LHD 7) during amphibious squadron and marine expeditionary unit integration training off the coast of North Carolina. (US Marine Corps/Sgt Clemente C. Garcia)

America class

Originally known as LHA Replacement or LHA(R), the *America*-class ships are intended as replacements for the original five *Tarawa*-class LHAs, which have all been decommissioned. The ship's design is based on that of the USS *Makin Island* (LHD 8), but provides additional room for aviation facilities. *America*-class ships are designed to accommodate the Marine Corps' future Air Combat Element (ACE), which includes F-35B and MV-22B. The first two ships, which comprise USS *America* (LHA 6) and USS *Iwo Jima* (LHA 7) are referred to as Flight 0 ships. Key differences from the LHD 8 design include: an enlarged hangar deck, enhanced aviation maintenance facilities, increased aviation fuel capacity, additional aviation storerooms and removal of the well deck. The USS *Bougainville* (LHA 8) will be the first Flight I ship and will reincorporate a well deck to increase operational flexibility.

USS *America* (LHA 6)

The lead ship of a new class, the keel for *America* was laid on 17 July 2009 and the ship was formally commissioned on 11 October 2014. LHA 7 is home ported in San Diego, California, and is the fourth ship to carry the name *America*. Most recently the name was carried by the *Kitty Hawk*-class aircraft carrier USS *America* (CV 66).

The USS *America* (LHA 6), the US Navy's newest class of ship, off the coast of California during F-35B flight operations. (US Navy/Cpl Thor Larson)

USS *Tripoli* (LHA 7)

The keel for the second *America*-class amphibious assault ship was laid down on 22 June 2014. Tripoli is the third ship named for the Battle of Derne, Libya, during the First Barbary War in 1805. The previous USS *Tripoli* (LPH 10) was decommissioned in September 1995. LHA 7 is scheduled to join the fleet in 2018.

USS *Bougainville* (LHA 8)

The Navy awarded a contract to Huntington Ingalls Industries, Ingalls Shipbuilding for the LHA 8 amphibious assault ship in June 2016. The USD 272.5-million contract provided for planning, advanced engineering, and procurement of long lead time material in support of construction. During a ceremony held at Marine Corps Base Camp Lejeune, North Carolina, on 9 November 2016, Secretary of the Navy Ray Mabus announced that the ship would be named USS *Bougainville*. LHA 8 will be the second ship to be named after the island in the northern Solomons. It was the location of a 1943–1944 campaign during which allies secured a strategic airfield from Japan. The first USS *Bougainville* (CVE 100) was a *Casablanca*-class escort carrier that was launched in 1944, and decommissioned in November 1946.

US NAVY AND US MARINE CORPS AIRCRAFT

C-2A Greyhound

First flown in November 1964, the Northrop Grumman C-2A serves as the CVW's carrier on-board delivery (COD) aircraft and is tasked to provide rapid response transportation of fleet essential supplies, repair parts and personnel between shore facilities and deployed aircraft carriers. Grumman Aircraft initially built 19 C-2As and the survivors from the original production batch were phased out of service in 1987. Beginning in 1984, Grumman produced 39 'reprocured' C-2As that are sometimes referred to as the C-2A(R).The new aircraft featured significant airframe and avionics improvements over the original batch.

The C-2A is powered by two 4,600shp (3,400 kW) Allison T56-425 turboprop engines and is capable of delivering payloads up to 10,000lb (4,536kg) at ranges greater than 1,000nm (1,852km). Its 862cu ft (11.89m^3) pressurized cargo bay is capable of carrying cargo as large as aircraft engines.

Although the last of the new Greyhounds was delivered in 1990, the fleet has received numerous upgrades. A service-life extension program (SLEP) that was completed in 2011 provided structural enhancements that increased the aircraft's projected life to 15,000 hours or 36,000 landings. Additionally, the aircraft were completely rewired and a Communication, Navigation, Surveillance/Air Traffic Management (CNS/ATM) upgrade was carried out. Both upgrades were completed in December 2013.

A C-2A assigned to CVW-8 approaches the carrier USS *George H. W. Bush* during operations in the Mediterranean in 2011. (Giovanni Colla)

As part of the CNS/ATM upgrade the aircraft was equipped with a glass cockpit featuring two six-by-eight multi-function displays (MFD), a new navigation suite, transponder, flight management system (FMS), a Terrain-Awareness Warning System (TAWS), Traffic Collision-Avoidance System (TCAS) and upgraded radios. The installation of eight-blade NP2000 propellers was completed in March 2014.

The inventory currently includes 35 C-2As and the fleet flies an average of 9,500 hours annually. The operational fleet of 28 C-2As is currently operated by two Fleet Logistics Support Squadrons. VRC-30 at NAS North Island, California, and VRC-40 at Naval Station Norfolk, Virginia support each deployed Carrier Strike Groups with a detachment of two C-2As. The aircraft operate on a hub and spoke system, typically staging ashore at an airfield in the vicinity of the carrier's operating area and flying daily flight to and from the carrier. During a typical six-month CVW deployment, the two-aircraft COD detachment transports more than a million pounds of cargo, 5,000 passengers and flies approximately 1,000 hours.

Carrier airborne early warning squadron VAW-120 serves as the combined E-2/C-2 Fleet Replacement Squadron (FRS) and operates six Greyhounds. A single C-2A is assigned to air test and evaluation squadron VX-20 at NAS Patuxent River, Maryland.

The Navy announced, in February 2015, that it would replace the C-2A fleet aircraft with a variant of the Bell-Boeing MV-22B tiltrotor. Although the first CMV-22B COD variants will be delivered in 2020, the C-2A is currently scheduled to remain in service until 2028.

E-2C Hawkeye/E-2D Advanced Hawkeye

The Northrop Grumman E-2 airborne early warning aircraft has served as the 'eyes of the fleet' for over 50 years. Tasked as an airborne battle management command and control system, the Hawkeye also provides the fleet with a theater air and missile defense capability (TAMD). First flown under the designation W2F-1 in October 1960, the US Navy received its first E-2A in 1964.

The Hawkeye is the oldest design flying from the US Navy's aircraft carriers but it has undergone many changes since the E-2As made its first deployment in 1965. Today two basic models are operated by the US Navy. These comprise the E-2C and the E-2D, which first flew in September 1972 and August 2007 respectively.

Since entering service, the E-2C has seen numerous upgrades that have significantly enhanced the Hawkeye's capabilities. Beginning in June 1992 the first of 50 Group II aircraft, including 12 that were upgraded from the earlier Group I configuration entered service. The aircraft featured the AN/APS-145 radar, a new identification friend or foe (IFF) system, new displays, navigation and mission computer upgrades.

First flown in April 1998, the Hawkeye 2000 (HE2K) variant is the fifth generation production E-2C and incorporated enhancements in data management, system throughput, operator interfaces, connectivity, and situational awareness that supported the Navy's evolving TAMD mission. It joined the fleet in 2002. In addition to the AN/APS-145 radar, which is capable of detecting and tracking targets and controlling more than 20 airborne intercepts, the Hawkeye 2000 features an improved identification friend/foe (IFF) system, the Joint Tactical Information Distribution System (JTIDS), a global positioning system (GPS) and the Carrier Aircraft Inertial Navigational System (CAINS) II navigation system and an improved commercial, off-the-shelf- (COTS) based mission computer upgrade, a new operator display and improved satellite communications. Additionally, the (AN/USQ-3A) Cooperative Engagement Capability (CEC) system, which is a key component of the TAMD mission, is integrated into the Hawkeye 2000. The CEC allows the Hawkeye 2000 to work in conjunction with the Aegis combat systems installed on Navy warships to protect the fleet. It also features the passive AN/ALQ-217 electronic support measures (ESM) system, which autonomously detects and identifies electronic signal and locates their sources.

The aircraft is powered by two 5,000shp (3,728kW) T56-A-427 turboprop engines and is equipped with eight-blade NP2000 propellers. A Communication, Navigation, Surveillance/Air Traffic Management (CNS/ATM) upgrade that was completed in December 2013 provided the aircraft with a glass cockpit. Sharing commonality with the C-2A, it features two six-by-eight multi-function displays (MFD), a new navigation suite, transponder, flight management system (FMS), a Terrain-Awareness Warning System (TAWS), Traffic Collision-Avoidance System (TCAS) and upgraded radios.

Production of the Hawkeye 2000 variant for the US Navy ended when the last aircraft was accepted in September 2009. Earlier Hawkeye variants including the Group 0 and Group 1 have all been retired.

The crew includes a pilot, co-pilot and three naval flight officers (NFO) that serve as mission system operators and are tasked as combat information center officer, aircraft control officer, and radar officer.

The E-2D Advanced Hawkeye began System Development and Demonstration (SDD) began in 2002 and pilot production started in July 2007. The program received approval to enter full rate production in March 2013. The E-2D achieved initial opera-

An E-2C Hawkeye of VAW-124 is readied for a mission on the deck of USS *George H. W. Bush*. (Giovanni Colla)

tional capability (IOC) in October 2014 and its maiden deployment with carrier airborne early warning squadron VAW-125 aboard the USS *Theodore Roosevelt* (CVN 71) began in March 2015 and concluded in November. The E-2D features the Lockheed Martin AN/APY-9 active electronically scanned array (AESA) radar, which provides 'beyond the strike group' coverage. It is a key component of the Navy Integrated Fire Control – Counter Air (NIFC-CA) system of systems. It works in conjunction with tactical aircraft and surface-combatants equipped with the AEGIS Combat System to detect, track and defeat air and cruise missile threats to the fleet at extended ranges.

The Advanced Hawkeye is also equipped with a digital 'glass' cockpit that features 17in (43.2cm) liquid-crystal display (LCD) panels, which enable the co-pilot to function as fourth tactical mission operator. Powered by two 5,100shp (3,800kW) T56-A-427A turboprops, the E-2D has a gross weight of 57,500lb (25,855 kg), and is 4,000lb (1,814kg) heavier than the E-2C. Upgrades will provide the E-2D with an air-to-air refueling capability that is currently being tested. Northrop Grumman modified the first E-2D at its St Augustine, Florida, facility, under an Aerial Refueling (AR) Engineering and Manufacturing Development contract that was awarded in September 2013. The first of three modified Hawkeyes flew at St Augustine in December 2016.

The US Navy plans to procure 75 E-2Ds and 51 have been ordered including 31 that are being built under a multi-year procurement that began in 2014. The Advanced Hawkeye is expected to fully replace the E-2C by 2025.

The US Navy's active inventory, in late 2016, included 44 E-2Cs, 27 E-2Ds and a single TE-2C that is dedicated to pilot training. Hawkeyes currently equip eight fleet

Sailors prepare to launch an E-2D Hawkeye assigned to VAW-125 from the flight deck of USS *Ronald Reagan*. (US Navy/MC2 Nathan Burke)

An E-2D Hawkeye from VAW-126 prepares to land on the flight deck of the aircraft carrier USS *Harry S. Truman*. (US Navy/MCS Rebekah A. Watkins)

carrier airborne early warning squadrons (VAW) and one Fleet Readiness Squadron. Two E-2Cs are operated by the Naval Aviation Warfare Development Center (NAVAVNWARDEVCEN) at NAS Fallon, Nevada and air test and evaluation squadrons VX-1 and VX-20 at NAS Patuxent River, Maryland, have two and four E-2Ds assigned respectively. The latter unit also has a single E-2C on its books.

F/A-18A/B/C/D Hornet

First flown in November 1978, the F/A-18A was conceived as a multi-role fighter-attack aircraft and developed by McDonnel Douglas and Northrop (now Boeing and Northrop Grumman). Its development can be traced to the Northrop's entry into the USAF's Lightweight Fighter Program, which was known as the YF-17. The first Hornets entered service with strike fighter squadron VFA-125 in February 1981. Operational aircraft were assigned to Marine fighter attack squadron VMFA-314 in January 1983 and the US Navy's VFA-25 in March 1984. The Hornets replaced a variety of US Navy and Marine Corps types including McDonnell Douglas F-4 fighter, RF-4 reconnaissance and McDonnell Douglas A-4 and Vought A-7 attack aircraft. The strike fighter first saw combat over Libya in April 1986 during Operation El Dorado Canyon.

More than 600 single-seat F/A-18As and two-seat F/A-18Bs, which were originally designated TF-18A, were delivered before production switched to the F/A-18C/D in 1987. F/A-18Cs that were delivered beginning in October 1989 were further upgraded and featured a night attack capability.

Two 17,700lb-st (78.7kN) General Electric F404-GE-402 low-bypass turbofan engines power the 'legacy' Hornet, which is equipped with the Raytheon AN/APG-65 or AN/APG-73 radar. Its weapons capabilities include an internal 20mm M61 rotary cannon in the nose and seven weapon stations. The underwing stations can carry 14,000lb

(6,350kg) of ordnance or external fuel tanks including AGM-65 Maverick air-to-ground missiles, AGM-88 High-Speed Anti-Radiation Missile (HARM), AIM-120 Advanced Medium-Range Air-to-Air Missile (AMRAAM), AGM-154 Joint Stand-Off Weapon (JSOW), GBU-31/32/38/54 Joint Direct Attack Munition(JDAM), GBU-10/12/16/24/51 laser-guided bombs, and the GBU-12F/52 dual-mode laser-guided bombs. The Hornet is also capable of launching AGM-84 Harpoon anti-shipping missiles and the AGM-84K Stand-off Land-Attack Missile-Expanded Response (SLAM-ER) as well as unguided general purpose bombs, 2.75in (70mm) Hydra rockets and a variety of other weapons including cluster bombs, and naval mines. Wingtip rails support the carriage of AIM-9 air-to-air missiles.

The Marine Corps received its first single-seat F/A-18As in January 1983 and the fighters initially replaced the service's active duty F-4N/S Phantom IIs. Transition of the last Marine Reserve F-4S squadron to the F/A-18A followed in 1992. The majority of the early Hornets were later replaced by the newer F/A-18Cs.

Replacement of the Grumman A-6E in Marine all-weather attack squadrons began in 1990 when the service began fielding the night-attack variant of the two-seat F/A-18D. The aircraft, which later took on the forward air controller (airborne) [FAC(A)] and tactical air controller (airborne) [TAC(A)] missions were also tasked to conduct tactical reconnaissance when the Advanced Tactical Air Reconnaissance System (ATARS) was introduced in 1999. The two-seat variants are not, however, normally assigned to support CVW deployments.

In an effort to keep the F/A-18A tactically relevant, the US Navy modified 61 aircraft to the A+ configuration, with the AN/APG-73 radar and F/A-18C avionics. A further upgrade brought 54 of those aircraft up to F/A-18C capability under the designation F/A-18A++. Another program, begun in 2014, is upgrading 40 F/A-18Cs to a C+ configuration at a cost of around USD 3 million per aircraft.

The modifications are being incorporated on 23 Lot 10/11 F/A-18Cs that have been stored at Davis-Monthan AFB, Arizona, and seven fighters that are being drawn from the active fleet. The upgrade provides the fighter with a sixth MIL-STD-1553 multiplex bus (MUX Bus), AN/APX-111 combined interrogator/transponder (CIT), Multifunctional Information Distribution System (MIDS), Tactical Aircraft Moving Map Capabilities (TAMMAC), the Multi-purpose Display Group Upgrade (MDGU), which installs new full-colour displays, Joint Helmet-Mounted Cueing System (JHMCS), APG-73 radar, AN/ALE-47 countermeasures dispensing system (CDS) and the SJU-17 Naval Aircrew Common Ejection Seat (NACES).

The F/A-18C+ is also be capable of carrying the latest G4 version of the AAQ-28 Litening targeting pod, which features advanced FLIR CCD/TV and laser imaging sensors and deploying the AIM-9X air-to-air missile. The reactivations began in 2015 when the first four airframes were trucked from Tucson to Boeing's Cecil Field facility in Jacksonville, Florida. Upgrades will be completed in 2019.

The updated strike fighters will ultimately be operated by two Marine fighter attack squadrons and deliveries will be completed in 2020. In addition to upgraded avionics, the aircraft receive structural upgrades that extend the service life from 6,000 hours to 8,000 hours. Each upgrade requires around nine to 18 months to complete. The first two F/A-18C+ aircraft were delivered in October 2015 and April 2016 and both were assigned to Marine fighter attack squadron VMFA-115 at MCAS Beaufort, South Carolina.

Left: US Navy F/A-18Ds are a rare sight on carriers. This example from VX-23 was operating from USS *Dwight D. Eisenhower* (CVN 69) in 2011 to test systems used in the Unmanned Combat Air System Carrier Demonstration (UCAS-D) programme.
(US Navy/MC Seaman Albert Jones)

Right: A single-seat F/A-18C assigned to VFA-87 'Golden Warriors' departs the flight deck of the USS *George H. W. Bush* (CVN 77)
(Rich Cooper)

Additionally around 150 legacy Hornets are being upgraded under a service-life extension program (SLEP) that will enable them to attain 10,000 flight hours. Continued upgrades will provide the Hornets with a new Advanced Capabilities Mission Computer (ACMC), displays and weapons including the AIM-120D and AIM-9X Block II missiles. The F/A-18A++, F/A-18C and F/A-18C+ are all compatible with the AN/ALQ-231 Intrepid Tiger II electronic warfare pod, which was first fielded in 2014.

As of November 2016, the US Navy and Marine Corps combined legacy Hornet fleet included 559 aircraft. The Navy's portion of the fleet comprised 37 F/A-18As, 14 F/A-18Bs, 219 F/A-18Cs and 38 F/A-18Ds as well as two NF/A-18Cs and two NF/A-18Ds that are permanently modified to support test and evaluation efforts. The last F/A-18Cs assigned to the US Pacific Fleet fighter squadrons have been replaced by Super Hornets; however, the Hornet will continue to fill US Navy Carrier Air Wing deployments until 2026.

In November 2016 the Marine Corps fleet included 53 F/A-18As, seven F/A-18Bs, 129 F/A-18Cs and 92 F/A-18Ds. Two Marine Hornet squadrons currently support US Navy CVW deployments as part of the Tactical (TACAIR) Integration Plan.

Because the Marine Corps is not procuring the F/A-18E/F, it will retain the F/A-18C/D until fielding of the Joint Strike Fighter is completed. Hornets will remain in service with the active duty squadrons until 2029 and with the reserves until 2030. Transition of the East Coast Hornet squadrons to the F-35B/C will, however, result in the Marine Corps Hornet fleet being consolidated at MCAS Miramar by 2027.

F/A-18E/F Super Hornet

McDonnell Douglas began developing the single-seat F/A-18E and two-seat F/A-18F in 1987, under the Hornet 2000 program. The Super Hornet first flew in November 1995 and deliveries to strike fighter squadron VFA-122 began during September 1999. The Super Hornet achieved initial operational capability in 2001 and its first deployment aboard USS *Abraham Lincoln* (CVN 72) was carried out by VFA-115 beginning in July 2002. The new model first saw combat in November 2002 when it conducted strikes in Afghanistan in support of Operation Enduring Freedom. Super Hornets assigned to VFA-14 and VFA-41 were the first to field the Shared Reconnaissance Pod (SHARP)

Sailors move an F/A-18E assigned to VFA-113 'Stingers' onto an aircraft elevator aboard the aircraft carrier USS *Theodore Roosevelt* (CVN 71). (US Navy/MC3 Rachael Treon)

and Joint Helmet Mounted Cueing System (JHMCS) in 2002. They were also the first to use the aircraft as a tanker.

The Super Hornet is a significantly larger strike fighter than its predecessor, with more fuel for increased range and its carrier-recovery payload is more than 9,000lb (4,082kg) which provides the ability to bring back costly, unexpended weapons to the deck of the carrier.

The single-seat F/A-18E and two-seat F/A-18F are respectively 4.2ft (1.28m) longer than the single and two-seat legacy Hornets. Additionally, wing span is increased by 4.7ft (1.43m) and the wing area is 25 per cent larger. The internal fuel capacity is increased by 33 per cent, which increases the aircraft's combat range by 32 per cent. The Super Hornet is powered by two 22,000lb-st (97.9kN) General Electric F414-GE-400 engines. Like the legacy Hornet, it is equipped with an internal 20mm M61 rotary cannon. In addition to wingtip stations for AIM-9 Sidewinder missiles, the F/A-18E/F features seven stations under the wing and centerline and can carry the same types of weapons as the legacy Hornets. The Super Hornet's ability to carry a buddy-refueling store allows it to serve as tanker that can escort strike aircraft or as a recovery tanker near the carrier. The Block I versions of the F/A-18E/F featured the AN/APG-73 radar however; the Block II's redesigned nose section accommodates the AN/APG-79 Active Electronic Scanned Array (AESA) radar. Boeing delivered 64 Block I F/A-18Es and 83 Block I F/A-18Fs before production switched to the Block II. AESA radar installations began with the 136th Block II aircraft and it has been retrofitted to the earlier aircraft.

Another view of an F/A-18F operating from USS *George H. W. Bush*. This aircraft wears the markings of VFA-213. (Rich Cooper)

Super Hornets equipped with the AESA radar were initially deployed by VFA-213. The Super Hornet is also equipped with the Distributed Target System (DTS), which automatically transmits and receives targeting information to and from other platforms and ground receivers over the Link 16 network. Additionally, it is capable of carrying the AN/ASQ-228 Advanced Targeting Forward-Looking Infra-Red (ATFLIR) for strike, reconnaissance, and surveillance missions and fielding of an Infra-Red Search and Track (IRST) sensor that was first tested in 2014, will begin in 2017. Installed in the front end of the Super Hornet's FPU-13 Fuel Tank Assembly, the sensor will enable the passive detection of aerial targets at long ranges.

Boeing has delivered more than 550 Super Hornets and the inventory included 287 F/A-18E and 259 F/A-18F models in November 2016. The Navy's Program of Record includes 563 Super Hornets comprising 287 FA-18Es and 259 F/A-18Fs and the type is expected to be in US Navy service beyond 2035. A planned Service Life Extension Plan (SLEP) will extend service life of 563 Super Hornets from 6,000 to 9,000 hours. The first Super Hornets will begin reaching the 6,000-hour limit in 2017.

Although the Navy originally planned to field 20 strike fighter squadrons with the F/A-18E/F, delays associated with the F-35 Joint Strike Fighter program and the need to replace the older legacy Hornets has resulted in the Super Hornet equipping 30 squadrons. Deliveries will continue through 2020 however, the Navy would like to add additional Super Hornets in order to bridge its strike fighter gap until sufficient numbers of F-35Cs are deployed.

EA-18G Growler

Developed by Boeing and Northrop Grumman, the EA-18G combines the two-seat Block II F/A-18F airframe with the sophisticated electronic warfare suite of the ICAP III version of the EA-6B Prowler. Development of the airborne electronic attack (AEA) aircraft, which retains the Super Hornet's General Electric F414-GE-400 engines, began earlier in December 2003 and the prototype first flew on 15 August 2006.

The initial production Growler made its first flight in September 2007 and delivery of operational EA-18Gs to electronic attack squadron VAQ-129 at NAS Whidbey Island, Washington, began in June 2008. The Growler achieved Initial operational capability with VAQ-132 in September 2009 and in 2015 it completely replaced the EA-6B in the electronic attack role when the last US Navy Prowlers were retired. EA-18Gs are assigned to all 10 carrier-based VAQ squadrons and four squadrons are tasked with an expeditionary mission that requires them to support operations from land bases. A Naval Reserve squadron is also tasked with an expeditionary role.

Operating in an expeditionary role VAQ-132 took the EA-18G to war on its initial combat deployment in November 2010. Although it initially operated in Iraq the squadron carried out missions over Libya in March 2011, where it provided electronic attack capability to NATO forces in Operations Odyssey Dawn and Unified Protector. The

Pre-flight inspections on an E/A-18G Growler assigned to VAQ-130 on the flight deck of USS *Dwight D. Eisenhower* during Operation Inherent Resolve.
(US Navy/Petty Officer 3rd Class Robert J. Baldock)

An EA-18G of VAQ-141 returns to the USS *George H. W. Bush* after a mission. (Giovanni Colla)

aircraft's first carrier deployment followed in May 2011 when VAQ-141 was embarked aboard the *USS George H.W. Bush* (CVN-77) as part of CVW-8.

The Growler is operated by a pilot and an Electronic Warfare Officer (EWO). Mission systems include the AN/ALQ-218 receiver, AN/ALQ-227 Communications Countermeasures Set Receiver and up to five AN/ALQ-99 Tactical Jamming System pods can be carried externally. For longer range missions, the aircraft can carry external fuel tanks in lieu of the full configuration of jamming pods. Offensive weapons, used in the Suppression of Enemy Air Defense (SEAD) mission, include the AGM-88 High-speed Anti-Radiation Missile (HARM) missile and its follow-on, the AGM-88E Advanced Anti-Radiation Guided Missile (AARGM), which are both designed to enemy radar and missile sites. Nine weapon stations comprising six under the wings and three on the fuselage provide a capacity of 17,750lb (8,050kg).

The Growler also retains the Super Hornet's AN/APG-79 multi-mode AESA radar and it is capable of carrying the AIM-120 AMRAAM, which provides the aircraft with a self-defense capability.

Although the Growler is equipped with the Multi-mission Advanced Tactical Terminal (MATT) that works in conjunction with the Link 16 tactical datalink, the system is currently being replaced by the new Joint Tactical Terminal – Receiver (JTT-R). In addition, the Growler's ALQ-99 pods will be replaced by the Navy's Next-Generation Jammer (NGJ), which is under development by Raytheon. The NGJ is scheduled to achieve Initial Operating Capability (IOC) in 2021.

In November 2016 the Navy's inventory included 126 EA-18Gs and two NEA-18Gs that were permanently assigned to test duties. Each squadron is equipped with five Growlers. A final batch of ten EA-18Gs was funded in FY2016 bringing total procurement to 160 Growlers. The US Navy expects to operate the EA-18G through 2040.

F-35B/C Lightning II

Intended to fulfill multiple missions, Lockheed Martin developed the Joint Strike Fighter (JSF) in three basic versions that include the USAF's conventional takeoff and landing (CTOL) F-35A, the Marine Corps' short takeoff/vertical landing (STOVL) F-35B and the F-35C carrier-variant (CV) that is operated by the US Navy and Marine Corps. Its development can be traced to the Advanced Short Take-Off/Vertical Landing (ASTOVL), Common Affordable Lightweight Fighter program and the Joint Advanced Strike Technology (JAST) programs. The F-35 is based on the design of the Lockheed Martin X-35, which was selected over the Boeing X-32 as the winner of the JSF competition in October 2001.

The Lightning II will eventually replace the F/A-18, AV-8B and EA-6B, providing the Marines with a single strike, close air support and electronic attack platform and will operate alongside the US Navy Super Hornet. Under current plans, Marines will operate 353 F-35Bs and 67 F-35Cs and the US Navy will acquire 260 F-35Cs.

The F-35B and F-35C are both equipped with the Northrop Grumman AN/APG-81 AESA radar, Lockheed Martin AN/AAQ-40 Electro-Optical Targeting System (EOTS), and the Northrop Grumman AN/AAQ-37 Electro-Optical Distributed Aperture System (DAS). Both variants feature 11 weapons stations, comprising three under each wing, two in each of the two internal weapon bays and one on the fuselage centerline, and will be capable of carrying a podded version of the four-barrel 25mm GAU-22/A cannon. Although the F-35C can carry a payload of 18,000lb (8,165kg), the capacity of the F-35B's centre wing and the outboard internal stations is reduced from 2,500lb

Ordnance is prepared for an F-35B on the amphibious assault ship USS *America* (LHA 6). This event marked the first live ordnance uploaded to the F-35B at sea. (US Navy/Andy Wolfe)

(1,134kg) to 1,500lb (680kg) resulting in a maximum weapons payload of 15,000lb (6,804kg). Additionally, the F-35B's internal weapons bay is slightly smaller than the F-35A/C, which precludes it from accommodating larger 2,000lb weapons including the GBU-31 JDAM.

The F-35B is powered by the Pratt & Whitney F135-PW-600 turbofan engine, a 50in (1.3m) diameter two-stage, counter-rotating shaft-driven lift fan (SDLF) located behind the cockpit, and a three-bearing swivel exhaust nozzle that vectors engine exhaust downward as much as 95 degrees. The STOVL propulsion system increases its empty weight by 3,000lb (1,361kg) when compared to the F-35A and the airframe is rated for +7g rather than +9g like the F-35A. Additionally, the aircraft's fuel load is reduced by 4,750lb (2,155kg) resulting in a reduction in range. On internal fuel, however; the aircraft has a mission radius of 450nm (833km) while carrying two GBU-32 JDAMs and two AIM-120C missiles.

The first of five developmental F-35Bs flew on 11 June 2008 and preparation for STOVL tests began with hover pit testing in Fort Worth on 12 March 2009. It engaged its STOVL propulsion system in-flight for the first time on 8 January 2010.

The Marines received their first production F-35Bs when two examples were delivered to Marine fighter attack training squadron VMFAT-501 at Eglin AFB, Florida, in January 2012 and training started in May 2012. The first operational F-35B was delivered to Marine fighter attack squadron VMFA-121 at MCAS Yuma, Arizona, in November 2012 and the squadron achieved initial operational capability in July 2015. That milestone was met when ten assigned F-35Bs with Block 2B Software, were available for deployment. When it achieved IOC, the F-35B was capable of delivering the

A US Marine Corps F-35B assigned to VMFA-211 prepares to land aboard the amphibious assault ship USS *Essex* (LHD 2) during Exercise Dawn Blitz in October 2017. (US Marine Corps/ Sgt April L. Price)

GBU-32, GBU-12 Paveway II LGB and the AIM-120C on the internal stations. VMFA-121 relocated to Japan in early 2017 and will conduct the F-35B's first shipboard deployment in 2018.

Shipboard suitability testing began on 3 October 2011, when the F-35B executed the first vertical landing aboard the amphibious assault ship USS *Wasp* (LHD 1). A second round of sea trials began when DT-II was conducted aboard the *Wasp* in August 2013. Phase I of operational testing (OT-I) followed on 18 May 2015 when seven F-35Bs operated by VMFAT-501 and VMFA-121 spent 12 days aboard the *Wasp*. The final phase of developmental testing (DT-III) was conducted aboard the USS *America* (LHA 6) in November 2016.

A detachment of Marine operational test and evaluation squadron VMX-1 currently operates four F-35Bs from Edwards AFB, California, but it will relocate to MCAS Yuma, Arizona, when initial operational test and evaluation (IOT&E) is completed in 2018.

A second squadron began the conversion to the F-35B, when VMA-211 received its first Lightning IIs on 9 May 2016. VMFA-314 will be the first Marine squadron to equip with the carrier version when it stands up at MCAS Miramar, California, in 2020.

Ultimately nine active duty Marine Corps squadrons will be equipped with 16 F-35Bs, and five will have ten F-35Bs assigned. Two Marine Reserve squadrons will each have ten F-35Bs assigned and 25 examples will be assigned to each of two fleet replacement squadrons. In addition four active duty Marine squadrons will each be equipped with ten F-35Cs that will support US Navy carrier air wing operations.

The first developmental F-35C flew on 6 June 2010. Modifications that were required to make the aircraft compatible with carrier operations included a larger folding wing, stronger landing gear and a tail hook. Additionally, it is powered by the Pratt & Whit-

An F-35C Lightning II from VFA-125 'Rough Raiders' make an arrested cable landing on the flight deck USS *Carl Vinson* (CVN 70). During October 2017 *Carl Vinson* is conducting fleet replacement squadron carrier qualifications off the coast of Southern California. (US Navy/MC2 Sean M. Castellano)

ney F135-PW-400 turbofan engine. Four development F-35Cs were produced and the CV variant conducted its first arrested landing at sea aboard the USS *Nimitz* (CVN 68) during the initial at-sea Developmental Testing I (DT-I) in November 2014. DT-II was conducted aboard the USS *Dwight D. Eisenhower* (CVN 69) in October 2015 and the F-35C completed its final at-sea Developmental Test (DT-III) period in aboard the USS *George Washington* (CVN 73) in August 2016. All three Lighting II variants will undergo initial operational test & evaluation (IOT&E) at Edwards AFB in 2018.

Known as the 'Grim Reapers', strike fighter squadron VFA-101 serves as the first US Navy fleet replacement squadron (FRS) for the F-35C at Eglin AFB. Activated in 2012, the squadron received its first production F-35C on 22 June 2013 and the 'Grim Reapers' carried out the first Lightning II training sortie in August 2013. It was tasked with training instructor pilots and developing the training syllabus. A second FRS stood up when VFA-125 is reactivated at NAS Lemoore, California, in January 2017. VFA-125 will be tasked with training fleet pilots, while VFA-101 continues to train instructors for the FRS and the Naval Aviation Warfighting Development Center and refine the training syllabus for the CV variant.

Under plans announced in May 2015, VFA-97 will be the first squadron to transition from the Super Hornet to the F-35C at Lemoore in January 2018 and it will achieve IOC with Block 3F software between August 2018 and February 2019. Whereas each operational squadron have ten F-35Cs assigned, the FRS will be responsible for 30 Lightning IIs.

An F-35C assigned to VX-23 aboard the aircraft carrier USS *Dwight D. Eisenhower*. At the time the F-35C Lightning II Pax River Integrated Test Force was conducting follow-on sea trials. (US Navy/MCS Seaman Anderson W. Branch)

A UH-1Y from the 31st Marine Expeditionary Unit (31st MEU) flies ahead of the USS *Ashland* (LSD 48). *Ashland* was assigned to the *Bonhomme Richard* Expeditionary Strike Group and was on patrol in the Seventh Fleet area of operations. (US Navy/MC3 Derek A. Harkins)

H-1 Upgrades

Begun in 1996, the H-1 Upgrades Program was intended to develop replacements for the Bell UH-1N and AH-1W light utility and attack helicopters in service with the Marine Corps. The project was intended to develop new '4BN' and '4BW' versions of the legacy aircraft that shared a common powertrain, featuring new four-blade main and tail rotors. The two new models also shared an integrated avionics system (IAS) that provided glass cockpits, advanced sensors and Top Owl helmet-mounted sight and display (HMSD) systems as well as a common suite of Aviation Survivability Equipment (ASE). The two new models share 84 percent commonality and have 95 percent commonality in their avionics and share the same software.

The program initially included the remanufacture of 100 UH-1Ns and 180 AH-1Ws to the new UH-1Y and AH-1Z configuration but ultimately only a limited number of UH-1N s and AH-1Ws were remanufactured.

In December 2016, the Marines revealed that it plans to begin replacing the oldest UH-1Ys in 2033 and the oldest AH-1Zs in 2035. The replacement rotary-wing aircraft will leverage technology being developed under the US Army-led Future Vertical Lift (FVL) program.

A UH-1Y attached to the 15th Marine Expeditionary Unit's (15th MEU) Aviation Combat Element takes off from the flight deck of the *San Antonio*-class amphibious transport dock ship USS *San Diego* (LPD 22). (US Marine Corps/Lance Cpl Jeremy Laboy)

UH-1Y Venom

The Marines have operated several variants of the UH-1 since receiving their first UH-1Es from Bell Helicopter in 1964. The single-engine Huey was followed by the twin-engine UH-1N, which entered service in 1971. Although the last operational UH-1Ns were retired in December 2014, four HH-1Ns that are assigned to search and rescue (SAR) duties at MCAS Yuma, Arizona will continue to serve until the end of FY 2017 when their mission is taken over by a private contractor.

The first of two UH-1Ns to be upgraded to UH-1Y configuration under the H-1 Upgrades Program flew for the first time in December 2001. Although plans initially called for remanufacturing up to 100 UH-1Ns, in April 2005 the decision was made to produce new airframes and only 10 conversions were carried out. Additionally, the 'UH-1Y Forward' procurement strategy prioritized production of the Venom in order to replace the under-powered UH-1N fleet more quickly. The UH-1Y entered full rate production in 2008.

The Venom achieved initial operational capability with Marine light attack helicopter squadron HMLA-267 in August 2008 and a detachment of three UH-1Ys deployed with Marine medium helicopter squadron HMM-163 (Reinforced) as part of the 13th

Marine Expeditionary Unit (MEU) in January 2009. HMLA-367 later deployed to Afghanistan with nine 'Yankees' and 18 AH-1Ws in October 2009.

Conversion of the last unit was completed in FY 2015 when reserve squadron HMLA-773 retired its UH-1Ns. Procurement of the last of 160 UH-1Ys, including 150 new-builds, occurred in FY 2016. Each of the active duty squadrons operates 12 UH-1Ys and nine are assigned to the reserve force. In December 2016, 136 Venoms were in service with the Fleet Marine Force including five that were assigned to test and evaluation roles.

Fielding of the UH-1Y eliminated many of the UH-1N's deficiencies including power and capacity limitations and range restrictions. The UH-1Y increased top speed by 31 percent, cruise speed by 37 percent and service ceiling by 16 percent to 170 knots, 146 knots and 20,000ft (6,096m) respectively over the UH-1N. In fact, the aircraft's capabilities ultimate resulted in the decision to restructure the production and the mix of the two types within operational squadrons from 18 Vipers and nine Venoms to 15 of the former and 12 of the latter. The revised structure will enable each deployed squadron to field three detachments equipped with five AH-1Zs and four UH-1Ys.

Powered by two 1,800shp (1,342kW) General Electric T700-GE-401C turboshafts, the UH-1Y cockpit features four 8×6in (20.3×15.2cm) MFDs and two 4.2×4.2in (10.7×10.7cm) dual function displays (DFD). It is equipped with a FLIR Systems Brite Star II electro-optical/infrared sensor turret and like the AH-1Z crew is provided with

An AH-1W lands on the flight deck of the amphibious transport dock ship USS *New York* (LPD 21). (US Navy/MCS Seaman Andrew Schneider)

the Top Owl HMDS. Weapons capabilities include the 7.62mm M240 and .50 caliber GAU-16 machine guns and 7.62mm GAU-17 miniguns and 19-shot LAU-61 and 7-shot LAU-68 2.75in (70mm) rocket launchers. ASE is common with the AH-1Z and includes the AN/APR-39 radar warning receiver, AN/AAR-47 missile warning system and the AN/ALE-47 countermeasure dispensing system. Additionally, the UH-1Y is capable of deploying the AN/ALQ-231 Intrepid Tiger II electronic warfare pod, which was first tested in June 2015. Planned upgrades will provide the Venom with an Integrated Aviation Survivability Equipment (IASE) system capable of detecting and defeating advanced threats.

AH-1W SuperCobra/AH-1Z Viper

The Marine Corps have operated numerous variants of the Cobra gunship since it initially borrowed 38 single-engine AH-1Gs from the US Army in 1969. The Marines received its first twin-engine AH-1Js in September 1970 and the AH-1T, which first flew in May 1986, followed. Both variants were powered by versions of Pratt & Whitney's PT6A TwinPac (T400) series engine.

Initially referred to as the AH-1T+, the AH-1W entered operational service in October 1986, when the first examples were delivered to HML/A-169 at Marine Corps Base

An AH-1W is secured on the flight deck as a UH-1Y comes into land on board HMAS *Canberra* during RIMPAC 2016, a US Pacific Fleet-hosted biennial multinational maritime exercise. (Australian Defence Force/POIS Yuri Ramsey)

Camp Pendleton, California. The twin-engine AH-1W is powered by a pair of 1,690shp (1,260kW) General Electric T700-GE-401 turboshafts that drive two-blade main and tail rotors. Its armament includes the AGM-114 Hellfire and AIM-9 Sidewinder air-to-ground and air-to-air missiles, 2.75in (70mm) rockets, and a turreted 20mm M197 three barrel cannon.

Recent upgrades have provided the AH-1W fleet with a Night Targeting System Upgrade (NTSU), which provided a third generation targeting FLIR with laser designator and laser range finder and colour television capability. Additionally 90 Super Cobras received the Tactical Video Data Link (TVDL) that allows the aircraft to transmit/receive sensor video. A new weapons capability was also added when the helicopter was made capable of firing laser-guided Advanced Precision Kill Weapon System (APKWS) 2.75in (70mm) rockets.

Although the service still operates more than 100 AH-1Ws, the Super Cobra is progressively being replaced by the AH-1Z Viper and Bell Helicopter has delivered more than 60 examples to the Marine Corps.

Under the H-1 Upgrades Program, Bell Helicopter produced three AH-1Z prototypes by modifying AH-1W airframes. The first of those aircraft flew in December 2000. Plans then called for remanufacturing up to 180 AH-1Ws to AH-1Z configuration. Low-rate initial production began in October 2003 and in 2008 the decision was made to remanufacture 168 AH-1Ws and to build 58 new aircraft, increasing AH-1Z production to 226 helicopters.

An AH-1Z from VMM-166 (Reinforced) lands on the flight deck of the amphibious transport dock ship USS *New York* (LPD 21). (US Navy/MCS Seaman Andrew Schneider)

The AH-1Z program received approval for to enter full rate production (FRP) in November 2010 and achieved IOC in February 2011. The decision to pursue an all AH-1Z Build New (ZBN) procurement strategy was subsequently made in December 2011. The change was made to address existing attack helicopter shortfalls, and allowed the Marines to retain AH-1W airframes in the inventory rather than removing them from service to support the remanufacture process. Bell delivered the last of 37 remanufactured AH-1Zs in February 2014 and production of new airframes will run through 2022. The versatility proven by the UH-1Y caused the Marines to take another look at its production plans for the two models and as a result planned procurement of the AH-1Z was decreased while UH-1Y numbers were increased. The USMC's program of record currently comprises 189 AH-1Zs including 152 new-builds.

Three of the eight active duty squadrons have transitioned to the AH-1Z and conversion of the 3rd Marine Aircraft Wing (MAW) units at Camp Pendleton, California, will be completed in July 2017. AH-1Zs will subsequently replace the AH-1Ws assigned to HMLA-367 at MCAS Kaneohe Bay, Hawaii before those squadrons assigned to the 2nd MAW begin to transition in 2018. That process will be completed in 2019 and the 4th MAW's squadron will exchange its AH-1Ws for AH-1Zs beginning in FY 2020.

Each of the squadrons is initially operating with 13 AH-1Zs. However, once conversion of all units from the AH-1W is complete, two additional Vipers will be assigned, bringing the complement to 15. In December 2016, 60 AH-1Zs were in service along with 106 AH-1Ws.

A Marine pilot leaves the cockpit of an AH-1Z aboard the amphibious assault ship USS *Boxer* (LHD 4).
(US Navy/MC2 Kenan O'Connor)

Although the AH-1Z initially retained the AH-1W's T700-GE-401, the aircraft have been equipped with the same -401C version that is installed in the UH-1Y. Each of its cockpits features two 8 x 6in (20.3 x 15.2cm) MFDs and a single 4.2 x 4.2in (10.7 x 10.7cm) dual function display (DFD) that are common with the UH-1Y.

The helicopter retained the AH-1W's 20mm M197 cannon and carries the same weapons as the 'Whiskey'. The AH-1Z is, however; capable of carrying 16 Hellfire missiles doubling the AH-1W's payload or flying twice as far with eight missiles. It is equipped with the AN/AAQ-30 Target Sight System (TSS) and is capable of deploying the AN/ALQ-231 Intrepid Tiger II electronic warfare pod. Fielding of the Joint Air-Ground Missile (JAGM) will begin in 2019. Both the AH-1W and the AH-1Z variants have received new weapons in the form of the laser guided advanced precision kill weapon system (APKWS). Plans also call for equipping the Viper with an Integrated Aviation Survivability Equipment (IASE) system that will be common with the UH-1Y.

CH-53E Super Stallion

Capable of lifting 16 tons of cargo or 55 troops the Sikorsky CH-53E serves as the Marine's heavy-lift helicopter. First flown in 1974, the CH-53E entered service in 1981 with Marine heavy helicopter squadron HMM-464 at MCAS New River, North Carolina. Sikorsky's model S-80 was based on the earlier model S-65 that was operated by the US

Marines from the 15th Marine Expeditionary Unit's (15th MEU) Combat Cargo, attach an RQ-21A Blackjack skyhook recovery system to a CH-53E helicopter during an external lift aboard the amphibious transport dock ship USS *San Diego* (LPD 22) in support of Exercise Alligator Dagger 2017. (US Marine Corps/Lance Cpl Jeremy Laboy)

A CH-53E Super Stallion helicopter assigned to VMM-162, 26th Marine Expeditionary Unit (26th MEU), departs the amphibious assault ship USS *Kearsarge* (LHD 3). (US Marine Corps/Cpl Juan A. Soto-Delgado)

Navy and Marine Corps as the CH-53A/D and RH-53D Sea Stallion. The Super Stallion is powered by three 4,380shp (3,266kW) T64-GE-416 or 4,750shp (3,542kW) -419 turboshaft engines that drive seven-blade main and four-blade tail rotors. The heavy-lift helicopter is capable of carrying internal loads weighing up to 30,000lb (13,607kg) or 36,000lb (16,329kg) externally.

The Marines accepted the last of 177 Super Stallions in 1998 but due to attrition within the CH-53E fleet it later received eight additional aircraft that were reclaimed from storage at Davis-Monthan AFB, Arizona. Previously operated by the US Navy, those Super Stallions entered service between August 2005 and July 2008 after being fully overhauled. Unfortunately the fleet had been reduced to 146 CH-53Es resulting in an adjustment of the Primary Mission Aircraft Inventory (PMAI) from 16 to 12 aircraft. The CH-53E fleet has flown nearly 100,000 combat flight hours since the 2003 invasion of Iraq and attrition has claimed 14 aircraft in that time. With a requirement for 193 CH-53Es, the service currently has a shortfall of 47 aircraft. Two US Navy MH-53Es that were stored at Davis-Monthan AFB, Arizona since 2004 were refurbished by Erickson Incorporated at its facility at Rogue Valley International Airport in Medford, Oregon. The Sea Dragons will be assigned to the FRS in FY 2017 allowing two of the squadron's CH-53Es to be returned to the operational fleet. In addition, each CH-53E is being 'reset' as part of an overhaul and upgrade program that will take three years to complete. Work on the reset validation aircraft was completed at MCAS New River, North Carolina, in April 2016. Currently each of the eight active duty squadrons operates 12 CH-53Es and another 12 helicopters are assigned to the FRS. Additionally three CH-53Es are assigned to test and evaluation duties and a Marine reserve squadron is responsible for six more.

Although current plans call for the last CH-53Es to remain in service until 2032, the helicopters began reaching the end of their 6,150-hour design service lives in the 2011-12 timeframe, at a rate of 15 aircraft per year. An ongoing service life extension program (SLEP) that extends it to 10,000 hours will be completed by FY 2020. Additional planned upgrades will provide the helicopter with Integrated ASE, upgraded radios and Link 16 compatibility.

In March 2004 the USMC announced plans to purchase 154 new Stallions. The first of four YCH-53K flight-test aircraft was unveiled on 5 May 2014 and the new heavy-lift helicopter was formally named King Stallion. It carried out its maiden flight at Sikorsky Aircraft's Flight Development Center in West Palm Beach, Florida, in October 2015 and in August 2016 the final test aircraft joined the test program. The program successfully completed initial operational testing phase OT-B1 in October 2016 and expects to receive approve to enter low-rate initial production (LRIP) in mid-FY 2017. It is powered by three 7,500shp T408-GE-400 (GE38-1B) turboshaft engines that provide the CH-53K with three times the payload/range of the CH-53E.

The 88,000lb (33,916kg) King Stallion, which has the same deck footprint as the current CH-53E, is capable of carrying a 27,000lb (12,247kg) external cargo load more than 110nm (204km).

It is equipped with high-lift rotors, a split-torque transmission, composite structures, digital avionics, and fly-by-wire flight controls. The King Stallion is scheduled to achieve initial operational capability (IOC) in June 2019, when four helicopters and

An Aviation Boatswain's Mate (Handling) uses a spotting dolly to move a CH-53E helicopter in the hangar bay on board the amphibious assault ship USS *America* (LHA 6). (US Navy/MCS Seaman Vance Hand)

combat-ready crews are declared to be 'ready for deployment'. The program of record includes 200 CH-53Ks and once fielding is complete, the eight active duty squadrons will each operate 16 King Stallions while two reserve squadrons will each have eight aircraft assigned. Another 21 CH-53Ks will be operated by the FRS.

Those squadrons assigned to Marine aircraft group MAG-29 at MCAS New River, North Carolina, will be the first to transition. Under current plans, HMH-366 will be the first operational unit to field the CH-53K and its conversion will begin in FY 2019 and be complete in FY 2023. The FRS is also scheduled to receive its first King Stallions in FY 2019.

Transition of the units assigned to MAG-16 at MCAS Miramar, California, will follow beginning in FY 2025 and full operational capability is planned for 2029. A second reserve squadron will be activated with CH-53Es in FY 2023 and both will operate eight CH-53Es until they transition to the CH-53K. The last unit deliveries will occur in FY29 but the final production helicopters will completed in 2031.

MH-53E Sea Dragon

Developed from the Sikorsky CH-53E, the MH-53E was intended as a replacement for the RH-53D airborne mine countermeasures (AMCM) aircraft. First flown in December 1981, the Sea Dragon entered operational service in June 1986.

An MH-53E assigned to HM-14 lands at Naval Surface Warfare Center Panama City Division after conducting airborne mine countermeasure training in the Joint Gulf Test Range in the Gulf of Mexico. (US Navy/Ron Newsome)

Two MH-53Es from Marine Medium Tiltrotor Squadron [VMM-263 (Reinforced)], 22nd Marine Expeditionary Unit (22nd MEU), perform an aerial refueling training exercise with a KC-130J tanker aircraft above the multipurpose amphibious assault ship USS *Bataan* (LHD 5). (US Navy/MC3 James Turner)

Sikorsky delivered 50 MH-53Es and the Navy currently operates 28 MH-53Es that are divided between two operational mine countermeasures squadrons and the FRS. Two additional examples were recently withdrawn from storage and overhauled before entering service as trainers with the Marine Corps CH-53E FRS.

Powered by three General Electric 4,750shp (3,542kW) T64-GE-419 turboshaft engines, the MH-53E is capable of detecting and destroying a wide variety of seaborne mines using mine-hunting sonar in conjunction with mechanical, acoustic and magnetic mine sweeping equipment. Mission equipment includes the towed Mk 105 magnetic minesweeping sled, AN/AQS-24A side-scan sonar and the Mk 103 mechanical minesweeping system. In addition to the AMCM role the MH-53E is also tasked with secondary utility and vertical on-board delivery (VOD) missions.

The fleet has undergone, a fatigue-life extension program (FLEP) that extended the aircraft's service life to 10,000 hours and will allow the Sea Dragons to remain in service through 2025. The Navy is currently evaluating its requirement for the AMCM and VOD missions beyond 2025 when the last Sea Dragons are scheduled for retirement.

HH-60H, MH-60R and MH-60S Seahawk

The Navy rationalized its carrier and ship-based helicopter fleets under the now-completed Helicopter Master Plan, which was originally approved in 2002. Under that plan the SH-60B, SH-60F and HH-60H versions of the Seahawk were phased out of the fleet and the MH-60R and MH-60S became the only variants to regularly conduct shipboard operations. The SH-60B completed its final deployments in July 2015 and the last examples were retired in August. Both the SH-60F anti-submarine and HH-60H strike/rescue versions completed their final deployment with the 'Dragonslayers' of helicopter anti-submarine squadron HS-11 as part of CVW-1 in November 2015.

Under today's concept of operations, each CVW deploys with 19 helicopters that operate from the carrier and with the other air-capable ships of the Carrier Strike Group (CSG). The CVW's rotary wing fleet comprises 11 MH-60Rs assigned to a helicopter maritime strike (HSM) squadron and eight MH-60S variants that are flown by the helicopter sea combat HSM squadron.

The two helicopters share a common cockpit, developed by Lockheed Martin that features four 8×10in (20.3×25.4cm) colour multi function displays (MFD) a digital communications suite and flight management systems.

The MH-60S is assigned the roles of anti-surface warfare, plane guard, search and rescue, mine countermeasures, and logistics. Six of the helicopters are normally assigned to the carrier, while two are operated from a logistics ship in support of vertical replenishment duties. Whereas five MH-60Rs typically operate from the carrier, the remaining rotorcraft are detached to the CSG's escort vessels. Eight HSM squadrons are tasked to support individual ship deployments and each of the expeditionary units is nominally assigned ten MH-60Rs.

HH-60H

The HH-60H, which was primarily tasked with strike rescue and special operations missions, completed its final carrier deployment aboard the USS *Theodore Roosevelt* (CVN 71) in November 2015. Its secondary missions included SAR, medical evacuation (MEDEVAC), vertical replenishment (VERTREP) and fleet support. The HH-60H was equipped with the AN/AAS-44 Generation 2 electro-optical/infra-red (EO/IR) sensor, up to four AGM-114 Hellfire missiles, and door-mounted .50 caliber and 7.62mm weapons.

First flown on 17 August 1988, deliveries of the HH-60H began in 1989. Although the Navy originally received 42 HH-60Hs, in late 2016 just 14 examples remained in service including 11 assigned to Naval Reserve helicopter combat support squadron

An HH-60H from HS-15 picks up ordnance from the aircraft carrier USS *Carl Vinson* during a vertical replenishment at sea. (US Navy/MCS Seaman Nicolas C. Lopez)

HSC-85 at NAS North Island and three that are operated by HSC-3, which serves as the FRS. HSC-85 provides support to the US Navy SEAL Teams and other special operations forces. Under current plans, HSC-85 will continue to operate the HH-60H for the foreseeable future.

MH-60R

Developed under the LAMPS Mark III Block II Upgrade program beginning in 1993, the MH-60R was initially assigned the designation YSH-60R. The first example, which was actually an updated SH-60B, performed its initial flight in on 22 July 1999. It achieved initial operational capability in December 2005 and full operational capability was met in 2010. Although the Navy originally planned to modernize its fleet of SH-60Bs to the later configuration, the decision was later made to build new aircraft. Seven remanufactured MH-60Rs were produced before the first newly produced helicopter made its initial flight in July 2005. The helicopters are produced by Sikorsky Aircraft and system integration is carried out by Lockheed Martin at is Owego, New York, facility. The initial aircraft was delivered in March 2006.

After reaching initial operational capability with HSM-41 in December 2005, the MH-60R began its first operational deployment with HSM-71 in January 2009 aboard the USS *John C. Stennis* (CVN 74).

Powered by two 1,800shp (1,342kW) General Electric GE T700-GE-401C turboshafts, the MH-60R is the Carrier Strike group's sole organic air Anti-Submarine Warfare (ASW) asset. The multi-mission helicopter's primary missions include undersea and Anti-Surface Warfare (ASuW) including responding to fast attack craft/fast inshore attack craft threats. Secondary mission areas include SAR, vertical replenishment (VERTREP), Naval Gunfire Support (NGFS), logistics support, personnel transport, medical evacuation (MEDEVAC) and communications relay.

An MH-60R from HSM-71 assigned to the aircraft carrier USS *John C. Stennis* (CVN 74) in a hard right turn. (US Navy/MC2 Kenneth Abbate)

An MH-60R, armed with an unguided rocket pod and Hellfire missiles, from HSM-74 takes off from the flight deck of the aircraft carrier USS *Dwight D. Eisenhower*.
(US Navy/Petty Officer 3rd Class Robert J. Baldock)

The MH-60R features a digital 'glass' cockpit that is common with the MH-60S. Unlike the earlier SH-60B, it is not equipped with a magnetic anomaly detector (MAD) but features the Raytheon AN/AQS-22F Airborne Low-Frequency Sonar (ALFS), which detects submarine threats at three to seven times the range possible with legacy SH-60F's dipping sonar.

Its mission suite includes, sonobuoys, an acoustic processor, Lockheed Martin AN/ALQ-210 electronic support measures (ESM), Raytheon AN/AAS-44C Multi-Spectral Targeting System (MTS) and Telephonics AN/APS-147 or APS-153 Multi-Mode Radar (MMR). First fielded in 2012, the latter system is capable of following ten times the number of automatic target tracks processed by the SH-60B and features an Automatic Radar Periscope Detection and Discrimination (ARPDD) capability. The aircraft's integrated self-defense (ISD) suite includes infrared counter measures (IRCM) and a countermeasures dispensing systems (CMDS) that deploys chaff and flares against radar, infrared and laser threats. The MH-60R is equipped with a Link 16 datalink that is capable of streaming video and tactical plots to ships and other aircraft, which greatly increases its value as a 'netted' surveillance platform.

Four external stores stations provide the capability to carry various combinations of Mk 46 or Mk 54 torpedoes, Hellfire missiles or external fuel tanks. Additionally it is capable of deploying the Advanced Precision Kill Weapon System II (APKWS) using the LAU-61 2.75-inch Digital Rocket Launcher (DRL). Crew-served .50 caliber and 7.62mm machine guns can also be carried.

The MH-60R has completely replaced both the SH-60B LAMPS III and the SH-60F inner-zone antisubmarine warfare helicopters. Today the aircraft is in service with 15 operational squadrons, one Naval Reserve squadron and two Fleet Replacement squadrons. The final batch of 29 MH-60Rs was procured in FY 2016 bringing the total orders to 278. The fleet included 237 aircraft in December 2016 and deliveries will be completed in FY 2018.

MH-60S

Developed from the on the US Army's Sikorsky UH-60L utility helicopter, the MH-60S is powered by a pair of 1,800shp (1,342kW) General Electric GE T700-GE-401C turboshafts and is equipped with cargo doors on both sides of the fuselage. The rotorcraft is tasked with multiple mission areas including anti-surface warfare (ASuW), Strike Warfare, Combat Search and Rescue (CSAR), Vertical Replenishment (VERTREP) and Airborne Mine Counter Measures (AMCM). The MH-60S supports Carrier and Expeditionary Strike Group, Combat Logistics Ship, and Littoral Combat Ship (LCS) deployments.

The first production MH-60S flew on 27 January 2000 and achieved IOC in August 2002. Initially deployed in Block I configuration by Helicopter Combat Support Squadron Five HC-5 aboard combat stores ship USNS *San Jose* (T-AFS 7) in 2002, the combat support version was dedicated to logistics support, VERTREP, SAR, and utility support. The helicopter retains the Black Hawk's 9,000lb (4,082kg) external cargo capacity and is equipped with a rescue hoist.

Intended to provide an organic AMCM capability for the LCS Mine Countermeasures (MCM) Mission Package, equipment planned for the Block 2 version comprised the AN/AES-1 Airborne Laser Mine-Detection System (ALMDS) and the AN/ASQ-235 Archerfish Airborne Mine-Neutralization System. (AMNS), AN/ALQ-220 Organic Airborne Surface Influence Sweep (OASIS), AN/AQS-20A Sonar Mine Detecting Set. The

Pre-flight checks for an MH-60S of HSC-23 on the flight deck of the amphibious assault ship USS *America* (LHA 6). (US Navy/MC2 Christopher Marshall)

An MH-60S assigned to HSC-9 hovers above the water to simulate a rescue swimmer jump during an airpower demonstration rehearsal alongside the aircraft carrier USS *George H. W. Bush*. (US Navy/MC3 Matt Matlage)

AMCM tow system capabilities that involved the latter two systems were cancelled in March 2012. Development of ALMDS and AMNS continued however, and a detachment from HSC-26 deployed the ALMDS to the Persian Gulf in July 2014. Both systems are deployed via a Carriage, Stream, Tow and Recovery System (CSTRS) developed by the Naval Surface Warfare Center Panama City Division, in Florida.

First deployed aboard USS *John C. Stennis* (CVN 74) with HSC-8, in January 2009, the Block 3A MH-60S armed helicopter is equipped with the AN/AAS-44C Multi-Spectral Targeting System (MTS) and can carry eight Hellfire missiles carried on external weapon system wings. Additionally, a fixed forward-firing weapon system, which includes the M197 20mm cannon, capable of firing 680 rounds per minute, can be installed.

Crew-served weapons include the FN Herstal laser-sighted M240D 7.62mm guns that are installed in the port and starboard gunners' windows and laser-sighted GAU-21.50 caliber guns from the port and starboard cabin doors. The MH-60S is also certified to fire 2.75in Hydra unguided rockets from the 19-shot LAU-61C/A pod as well as laser-guided Advanced Precision-Kill Weapon System II (APKWS II) rockets. The Block 3B version adds the Link 16 tactical datalink to the Block 3A capabilities.

Procurement of the MH-60S ended in FY 2015, when the final eight aircraft were ordered. The 275th and final MH-60S was delivered to HSC-28 in January 2016. The operational fleet includes 252 aircraft that are assigned to two fleet replacement squadrons and 16 operational squadrons. The latter include ten that are assigned to each of the CVWs and six that are tasked with expeditionary missions. A number of squadrons also use the helicopter in test and support roles and the MH-60S is assigned to SAR missions at five Naval Air Stations.

Whereas the first 50 aircraft are only capable of performing Block 1 Combat Support Missions, aircraft 51 to 275 add the Block 2 AMCM missions and Block 3 Armed Helo missions with installation of ancillary kits. Ten early Block I aircraft were placed in storage at Davis-Monthan AFB, Arizona during 2014.

RQ-21A Blackjack

Development of the RQ-21A Blackjack Small Tactical Unmanned Aircraft System (STUAS) began in 2010 when Insitu received a contract from the US Navy. The system is organic to Navy Special Warfare, Navy Expeditionary Combat Command and Whidbey Island-class ships. It provides tactical intelligence, surveillance and reconnaissance capabilities. Weighing just 135lb (61kg) when fully loaded, the RQ-21A is equipped with EO/IR sensors, laser rangefinders and illuminators, automatic identification system (AIS) and a communications relay capability. The UAS, which has an endurance of 15 hours, is expected to achieve initial operational capability in 2015.

The RQ-21A provides the warfighter with dedicated day and night intelligence, surveillance and reconnaissance (ISR) coverage, target acquisition, and communication relay via a dedicated and cost effective airborne sensor system capable of delivering actionable intelligence to the tactical commander in real time. The expeditionary nature of the Blackjack, which does not require a runway for launch and recovery,

Marines attached to the 15th Marine Expeditionary Unit's (15th MEU) Unmanned Aerial Surveillance unit launch an RQ-21A aboard the *San Antonio*-class amphibious transport dock ship USS *San Diego* (LPD 22). (US Marine Corps/Lance Cpl Jeremy Laboy)

makes it possible to deploy with minimal footprint from both austere land-based and shipboard environments.

An RQ-21A Blackjack system is comprised of five air vehicles, two ground control systems, and launch and recovery support equipment. At 8ft (2.44m) long, a wingspan of 16ft (4.88m) and endurance up to 16 hours, the air vehicle's open-architecture configuration is designed to seamlessly integrate multi-mission payloads, to include day/night full-motion video cameras, infrared marker, laser rangefinder, communications relay package, Automatic Identification System receivers, as well as the addition of other payloads as required.

The Marine Corps completed its first land-based operational deployment September 2014. Initial Operational Test and Evaluation was completed in January 2015. Initial Operational Capability was declared January 2016, followed by a Full Rate Production decision in fall 2016. Marine Corps RQ-21A land-based and shipboard deployments began in summer 2016.

MQ-25 Stingray

The Navy had planned to field an Unmanned Carrier-Launched Airborne Surveillance and Strike (UCLASS) system, however; in 2015, the Office of the Secretary of Defense conducted a comprehensive Strategic Portfolio Review (SPR) of the department's intelligence, surveillance and reconnaissance (ISR) programs. As a result of that review, the RAQ-25 UCLASS was restructured and the new MQ-25A will be a high endurance unmanned aircraft that will initially take over the air refuelling role that is currently assigned to the F/A-18E/F. When fielded, MQ-25A will deliver a high-endurance organic aerial refueling capability. Additionally, the Stingray carrier-based air refueling system

An artist's impression of the future MQ-25. (US Navy)

(CBARS) will be capable of providing an around the clock, sea-based ISR capability in support of the Carrier Battle Group. ISR capabilities being considered for the maritime domain awareness mission may include signal intelligence (SIGINT), automatic identification system (AIS), and electro-optical/Infrared (EO/IR) sensors.

Ongoing aircraft carrier modifications to prepare Mission Control Spaces and integrate UCLASS architecture and control system and connectivity segments will be adapted for the MQ-25.

The service expects to issue a request for proposals (RFP) in 2017 and the Stingray will enter service in the mid-2020s. In September 2016, Lockheed and Boeing both received USD 43 million contracts to conduct risk reduction activities in advance of the engineering and manufacturing development phase of the program. Northrop Grumman and General Atomics subsequently received USD 35.8 million and USD 43.8 million contracts for the same efforts in October before Northrop withdrew from the competition the following month.

T-45C Goshawk

Developed from the British Aerospace Hawk trainer aircraft, the McDonnell Douglas T-45A was selected as the winner of the VTXTS programme in November 1981. The aircraft was only a portion of the T-45 Training System that included academics, simulators, and logistic support. Although it physically resembles the Royal Air Force variant of the Hawk, a significant amount of structural redesign was required in order

Sailors guide a T-45C Goshawk assigned to Carrier Training Wing (CTW) 1 onto a catapult aboard the aircraft carrier USS *Dwight D. Eisenhower* (CVN 69) during carrier qualifications. (US Navy/MC3 Nathan T. Beard)

to make the T-45A capable of withstanding carrier landings and take-offs. The first of two prototypes flew in April 1988 and the initial production aircraft was delivered in October 1990. Boeing and its McDonnell Douglas subsidiary delivered the first of 83 operational T-45As to the Navy before production switched to the more advanced T-45C in 1997. Equipped with a 'glass' cockpit, the T-45C first flew in October 1997 and was delivered that November. Originally known as the 'Cockpit 21' project, the system was first evaluated in a modified T-45A that first flew in March 1994.

The majority of the Goshawk fleet is divided between four squadrons at NAS Kingsville, Texas and NAS Meridian, Mississippi that are tasked to provide intermediate and advanced pilot training. Boeing delivered the last of 221 T-45 Goshawk trainers to the US Navy at its St Louis, Missouri, facility in October 2009. Surviving T-45As were upgraded to the later configuration under the Required Avionics Modernization Program (RAMP) beginning in 2001. In addition to the cockpit modifications, the RAMP brings the earlier aircraft up to the same airframe configuration as late model T 45Cs. The last T-45A left service in 2015 and the last T-45C conversions was completed by March 2016. T-45Cs stationed at NAS Pensacola support the Undergraduate Military Flight Officer (UMFO) curriculum. The Virtual Mission Training System (VMTS), which entered service in December 2013, equips 15 T-45Cs. The system allows the Goshawk to conduct realistic tactical radar training via the use of a synthetic radar capability. The synthetic radar simulator system, which is monitored by instructors on the ground, generates simulated targets on the T-45C's radar scope and enables the student NFO to direct the pilot to intercept the simulated target. It can also be used to simulate virtual air-to-air and ground-to-air scenarios.

A T-45C Goshawk assigned to Carrier Training Wing (CTW) 2 lands on the flight deck of the aircraft carrier USS *Dwight D. Eisenhower* (CVN 69) during carrier qualifications. (US Navy/MC3 Jameson E. Lynch)

AV-8B, TAV-8B Harrier II

Developed jointly by McDonnell Douglas and British Aerospace beginning in 1976, the AV-8B was planned as a replacement for the Marine Corps' McDonnell Douglas A-4M Skyhawk and AV-8A Harrier fleets.

Its design utilized the basic structure of the earlier AV-8A, but incorporated a new cockpit and larger all-composite supercritical wing and composite horizontal stabilizers. Fuselage modifications included a revised intake design, which increased airflow at low speeds, and lift improvement devices (LIDs) that added two removable ventral strakes and a retractable dam to the lower fuselage.

Flight testing began in November 1978, when the first of two YAV-8B prototypes took to the air in St. Louis, Missouri. The AV-8B entered operational service with Marine attack training squadron VMAT-203, at MCAS Cherry Point, North Carolina, in January, 1984 and Marine attack squadron VMA-331 achieved initial operational capability (IOC) with the Harrier II in August 1985.

The first of 16 two-seat TAV-8Bs flew for the first time on 21 October 1986 and VMAT-203 received its first aircraft in July 1987.

Development of a Night Attack variant of the AV-8B, featuring a GEC Forward Looking Infrared (FLIR) navigation system and new night vision goggles (NVG) compatible wide-angle Head-Up Display (HUD) and colour head-down cockpit displays, began in 1985. The first of 66 production aircraft was delivered to VMA-214 in September 1989.

An AV-8B assigned to Marine Medium Tiltrotor Squadron 161 (Reinforced) lands on the flight deck of USS *America* (LHA 6). (US Navy/MC2 Ramon Go)

A US Marine Corps AV-8B separates from a KC-10 Extender after receiving fuel during a mission in support of Combined Joint Task Force-Operation Inherent Resolve over Iraq in February 2017. (US Air Force/Senior Airman Tyler Woodward)

Plans for a radar–equipped variant were first announced in 1987 and development of began in 1990. A prototype first flew in September 1992 and operational fielding of the AN/APG-65-equipped AV-8B+ began in August 1993 when VMA-542 at MCAS Cherry Point received its first aircraft.

Although production ended in April 1993, when the last of 27 new build aircraft was delivered, 74 earlier Day Attack models were also upgraded to the later configuration. The advanced variant also retained the FLIR and night attack capabilities incorporated on the Night Attack variant.

Harriers are tasked with conducting numerous missions including close air support (CAS), interdiction, armed over-watch and non-traditional intelligence, surveillance and reconnaissance (ISR) using the AN/AAQ-28 Litening II targeting pod. The ability of the AV-8B+ to carry the AIM-120 AMRAAM air-to-air missiles also allows the aircraft to conduct self-escort and MEU air defense missions.

The AV-8B is currently in service with five operational squadrons and an FRS assigned to the 2nd and 3rd MAWs. The operational squadrons operate a mix of Night Attack variants and radar-equipped models. Each squadron has a Primary Mission Aircraft Authorized (PMAA) strength of 16 Harrier IIs and the FRS is assigned a mix of 17 AV-8Bs and 16 TAV-8As.

The squadrons are regularly tasked to provide detachments that are attached to a Marine Expeditionary Unit/Aviation Combat Element (MEU/ACE) aboard Navy

A total of 16 two-seat TAV-8Bs are available to train Harrier II pilots.
(U.S. Navy)

amphibious vessels. Marine Harrier IIs made their combat debut in 1991 during Operation Desert Storm and most recently saw action against ISIL in support of Operations Inherent Resolve in Iraq and Syria and Odyssey Resolve in Libya.

Recent upgrades have made the Harrier compatible with the G4 version of the AN/AAQ-28 Litening II targeting pod and added a video downlink capability that allows the Harrier to transmit live video from the pod to the joint terminal attack controllers/forward air controllers (JTAC/FAC) via the Remote Operated Video Enhanced Receiver (ROVER) ground station.

Weapons carriage was improved through the incorporation of the BRU-70/A Digital Improved Triple Ejector Rack (DITER), which increases the aircraft's smart weapon carriage capability from four weapons to as many as ten 500lb (227kg) GBU-38 Joint Direct Attack Munitions (JDAM).

Along with full integration of the AN/ALE-47 countermeasure dispensing system, the AV-8B has also been equipped with the AN/ALQ-231 Intrepid Tiger II (IT II) electronic warfare pod, which provides the aircraft with an electronic attack capability.

Under current plans the last AV-8Bs will be retired in 2026 and in December 2016 the inventory comprised 111 AV-8Bs and 16 two-seat TAV-8B trainers.

MV-22B, CMV-22B Osprey

First flown in March 1989, the Bell Helicopter/Boeing MV-22B formally entered the USMC inventory in May 1999, when deliveries to Marine medium tiltrotor training squadron VMMT-204 began. Marine medium tiltrotor squadron VMM-263 subsequently achieved IOC with the Osprey in June 2007.

Transition of the last CH-46E squadrons was completed in 2015 and the Osprey now serves as the medium-lift platform for the Marine Corps. Although the tiltitrotor suffered through a lengthy and contentious development it has proven to be a very capable platform and has greatly increased the Marines capability. In November 2015 the Osprey fleet achieved its 300,000th flight hour milestone.

An MV-22B Osprey assigned to VMM-161 (Reinforced) 'Greyhawks' lands on the flight deck of the amphibious assault ship USS *America* (LHA 6) during Exercise Alligator Dagger 2017.
(US Navy/MCS Seaman Vance Hand)

Deployed operationally to Iraq by VMM-263 in October 2007, the tiltrotor aircraft subsequently completed its first deployment with the same squadron, as part of an MEU in November 2009. The Osprey has also supported Special-Purpose Marine Air-Ground Task Crisis Response (SP-MAGTF CR) Africa since April 2013 when six aircraft were deployed to Moron AB, Spain.

The current program of record (POR) includes a fleet of 360 aircraft that will be fielded by 18 active, and four reserve squadrons and a single FRS by 2020, however a Requirements Based Analysis will likely increase the POR to 380 aircraft providing sufficient airframes to equip the planned standup of VMM-362 and VMM-212 at Miramar and New River in FY 2018 and FY 2019.

In December 2016 the fleet comprised 216 aircraft including 11 that were supporting test and evaluation efforts, 24 that were assigned to the FRS and 12 that were tasked with Presidential support. Each operational squadron has 12 Ospreys assigned. Transition of the two reserve CH-46E squadrons to the Osprey began in 2013 and will be complete in FY 2018, when VMM-774 achieves full operational capability (FOC).

The first of two squadrons moved from MCAS Miramar to MCAS Kaneohe Bay, Hawaii in 2016 when VMM-268 relocated. It will be followed by VMM-363 in FY17.

Deliveries of the current production Block C aircraft, which feature a new weather radar and improved aircraft survivability equipment (ASE), began in 2010. Under current plans, the operational squadrons will operate a mixed fleet of Block B and Block C aircraft. Although early Block A variants continue to serve with the FRS, the last examples will be upgraded to Block B configuration in FY 2017. Planned upgrades include Integrated Aircraft Survivability Equipment (IASE) and enhanced networking capabilities. The first 24 IASE systems were fielded beginning in 2016 and retrofits for the fleet will follow in 2017.

Upgrades also include a V-22 Aerial Refueling System (VARS), which is currently under development. The system will provide the Marine Air Ground Task Force (MAGTF) with an organic tanker capability when it achieves IOC in mid-FY 2018. Full operational capability is planned for FY 2019. The Osprey is also being made compatible with the AN/ALQ-231 Intrepid Tiger II (IT II) electronic countermeasures pod. The Osprey is capable of carrying a ramp mounted M240D 7.62mm or GAU-16 .50 caliber machine guns as well as the Interim Defensive Weapon System (IDWS), which features a turreted 7.62mm mini-gun. Enhanced weapon system developments will, however; provide the Osprey with all-axis, stand-off and precision weapons capabilities. The integration of laser-guided 2.75in (70mm) Advanced Precision Kill Weapons System (APKWS) rockets, missiles and heavy guns could allow the Osprey to conduct a wide range of offensive and defensive combat missions.

Naval Surface Warfare Center (NSWC) Dahlgren has explored the use of forward firing rockets, missiles, fixed guns, a chin mounted gun. It has also looked at the use of a 30mm gun along with gravity drop rockets and guided bombs that could be deployed from the MV-22B. Armament requirements for the Osprey are currently being defined by the NSWC. If the initiatives stay on track, integration of new weapons could begin as early as 2019.

The Osprey is powered by two 6,150shp (4,586kW) Rolls-Royce T406-AD-400 (AE1107C) turboshaft engines that drive 38.1ft (11.6m) diameter rotors. The tiltrotor has a combat radius of 425nm (787km) when carrying 24 Marines or 12,500lb (5,670kg) of cargo. The Osprey has a maximum internal cargo capacity of 20,000lb (9,072kg) and can carry sling loads weighing up to 15,000lb (6,804kg) externally. It has a top speed of 280 knots (519km/h) and a cruise speed of 266 knots (493km/h) and its internal air refueling capability makes it capable of self-deployment.

Marines assigned to the 26th Marine Expeditionary Unit (26th MEU), and Sailors unload a MV-22B Osprey aircraft assigned to Marine Medium Tiltrotor Squadron (VMM)162 (Reinforced), aboard the amphibious assault ship USS *Kearsarge* (LHD 3) in the Atlantic Ocean (US Marine Corps/Lance Cpl Alexis C. Schneider)

An MV-22B assigned to Marine Medium Tiltrotor Squadron (VMM 162) takes off from the flight deck aboard the amphibious assault ship USS *Iwo Jima* (LHD 7). (US Navy/MCS Seaman Joe J. Cardona Gonzalez)

In February 2015, the US Navy announced that it will replace its existing fleet of Northrop Grumman C-2A Greyhound carrier on board delivery (COD) aircraft with a specialized variant of the Bell-Boeing MV-22B tiltrotor. Under the terms of a Memorandum of Understanding (MOU) between the Navy and the Marine Corps, the former will acquire four V-22s annually beginning in FY 2018 and running through 2020.

The decision to acquire the Osprey was partially based on the results of a six-day military utility assessment (MUA) of the tiltrotor in the COD role aboard the aircraft carrier USS *Harry S Truman* (CVN 75). During the MUA, Marine Corps MV-22Bs transported passengers and cargo between the carrier and land bases and demonstrated its ability to conduct the COD mission with no modifications and no adverse impact to cyclic flight operations aboard the ship.

Assigned the designation CMV-22B the COD variant, which utilizes the baseline MV-22B airframe, will be equipped with an extended range fuel system that will allow the Osprey to fly a distance of 1,150nm (2,130km) without aerial refueling. It will also feature a high-frequency radio and public address system that is required to support over-the-horizon communications.

Design work on the COD variant began in March 2016, when the Bell-Boeing Joint Program Office received a USD 151 million engineering services contract.

Deliveries will begin in 2020 and planned procurement includes 44 CMV-22Bs by 2024. The service plans to complete the recapitalization of its COD capability by 2026. The Osprey may also replace the MH-53E in the Vertical On-board Deliver (VOD) mission.

CARRIER AIR WING ASSIGNMENTS AND UNITS

USS *Harry S. Truman* (CVN 75) – CSG-8 with Carrier Air Wing One (CVW-1/AB)

Squadron	Nickname	Aircraft	MoDex
VFA-11	'Red Rippers'	F/A-18F	1xx
VFA-211	'Fighting Checkmates'	F/A-18F	2xx
VFA-136	'Knighthawks'	F/A-18E	3xx
VFA-81	'Sunliners'	F/A-18E	4xx
VAQ-137	'Rooks'	EA-18G	5xx
VAW-126	'Seahawks'	E-2D	60x
HSC-11	'Dragonslayers'	MH-60S	61x
HSM-46	'Grandmasters'	MH-60R	7xx
VRC-40 Det 1	'Rawhides'	C-2A	xx

USS *Carl Vinson* (CVN 70) – CSG-1 with Carrier Air Wing Two (CVW-2/NE)

Squadron	Nickname	Aircraft	MoDex
VFA-2	'Bounty Hunters'	F/A-18F	1xx
VFA-137	'Kestrels'	F/A-18E	2xx
VFA-192	'Golden Dragons'	F/A-18E	3xx
VFA-34	'Blue Blasters'	F/A-18C	4xx
VAQ-136	'Gauntlets'	EA-18G	5xx
VAW-113	'Black Eagles'	E-2C	60x
HSC-4	'Black Knights'	MH-60S	61x
HSM-78	'Blue Hawks'	MH-60R	7xx
VRC-30 Det 2	'Providers'	C-2A	xx

USS *Dwight D. Eisenhower* (CVN 69) – CSG-10 with Carrier Air Wing Three (CVW-3/AC)

Squadron	Nickname	Aircraft	MoDex
VFA-32	'Swordsmen'	F/A-18F	1xx
VFA-86	'Sidewinders'	F/A-18E	2xx
VFA-131	'Wildcats'	F/A-18C	3xx
VFA-105	'Gunslingers'	F/A-18E	4xx
VAQ-130	'Zappers'	EA-18G	5xx
VAW-123	'Screwtops'	E-2C	60x
HSC-7	'Dusty Dogs'	MH-60S	61x
HSM-74	'Swamp Foxes'	MH-60R	7xx
VRC-40 Det 4	'Rawhides'	C-2A	xx

USS *Ronald Reagan* (CVN 76) – CSG-5 with Carrier Air Wing Five (CVW-5/NF)

Squadron	Nickname	Aircraft	MoDex
VFA-102	'Diamondbacks'	F/A-18F	1xx
VFA-27	'Royal Maces'	F/A-18E	2xx
VFA-115	'Eagles'	F/A-18E	3xx
VFA-195	'Dambusters'	F/A-18E	4xx
VAQ-141	'Shadowhawks'	EA-18G	5xx
VAW-125	'Tigertails'	E-2D	60x
HSC-12	'Golden Falcons'	MH-60S	61x
HSM-77	'Sabrehawks'	MH-60R	7xx
VRC-30 Det 5	'Providers'	C-2A	xx

Carrier Air Wing Seven (CVW-7/AG)

Squadron	Nickname	Aircraft	MoDex
VFA-143	'Pukin' Dogs'	F/A-18E	1xx
VFA-103	'Jolly Rogers'	F/A-18F	2xx
VFA-83	'Rampagers'	F/A-18C	3xx
VFA-25	'Fist of the Fleet'	F/A-18E	4xx
VAQ-140	'Patriots'	EA-18G	5xx
VAW-121	'Bluetails'	E-2C	60x
HSC 5	'Nightdippers'	MH-60S	61x
HSM-72	'Proud Warriors'	MH-60R	7xx
VRC-40 Det 3	'Rawhides'	C-2A	xx

USS *George H. W. Bush* (CVN 77) – CSG-2 with Carrier Air Wing Eight (CVW-8/AJ)

Squadron	Nickname	Aircraft	MoDex
VFA-31	'Tomcatters'	F/A-18E	1xx
VFA-213	'Black Lions'	F/A-18F	2xx
VFA-87	'Golden Warriors'	F/A-18E	3xx
VFA-37	'Ragin Bulls'	F/A-18C	4xx
VAQ-131	'Lancers'	EA-18G	5xx
VAW-124	'Bear Aces'	E-2C	60x
HSC-9	'Tridents'	MH-60S	61x
HSM-70	'Spartans'	MH-60R	7xx
VRC-40 Det 2	'Rawhides'	C-2A	xx

USS *John C. Stennis* (CVN 74) — CSG-3 with Carrier Air Wing Nine (CVW-9/NG)

Squadron	Nickname	Aircraft	MoDex
VFA-41	'Black Aces'	F/A-18F	1xx
VFA-14	'Tophatters'	F/A-18E	2xx
VFA-97	'Warhawks'	F/A-18E	3xx
VFA-151	'Vigilantes	F/A-18E	4xx
VAQ-133	'Wizards'	EA-18G	5xx
VAW-117	'Wallbangers'	E-2C	60x
HSC-14	'Chargers'	MH-60S	61x
HSM-71	'Raptors'	MH-60R	7xx
VRC-30 Det 4	'Providers'	C-2A	xx

USS *Nimitz* (CVN 68) – CSG-11 with Carrier Air Wing Eleven (CVW-11/NH)

Squadron	Nickname	Aircraft	MoDex
VFA-154	'Black Knights'	F/A-18F	1xx
VFA-147	'Argonauts'	F/A-18E	2xx
VFA-146	'Blue Diamonds'	F/A-18E	3xx
VMFA-323	'Death Rattlers'	F/A-18C	4xx
VAQ-142	'Gray Wolves'	EA-18G	5xx
VAW-121	'Bluetails'	E-2D	60x
HSC-8	'Eightballers	MH-60S	61x
HSM-75	'Wolfpack'	MH-60R	7xx
VRC-30 Det 3	'Providers'	C-2A	xx

Unassigned with Carrier Air Wing Fourteen (CVW-14/NK)

No squadrons assigned; currently deactivated (latest until 1 October 2025).

USS *Theodore Roosevelt* (CVN 71) — CSG-12 with Carrier Air Wing Seventeen (CVW-17/NA)

Squadron	Nickname	Aircraft	MoDex
VFA-22	'Fighting Redcocks'	F/A-18F	1xx
VFA-113	'Stingers'	F/A-18E	2xx
VMFA-312	'Checkerboards'	F/A-18C	3xx
VFA-94	'Mighty Shrikes'	F/A-18F	4xx
VAQ-139	'Cougars'	EA-18G	5xx
VAW-116	'Sun Kings'	E-2C	60x
HSC-6	'Screamin Indians'	MH-60S	61x
HSM-73	'Battlecats'	MH-60R	7xx
VRC-30 Det 1	'Providers'	C-2A	xx

MARINE CORPS STRUCTURE AND THE AMPHIBIOUS READY GROUP

Established by an act of the Second Continental Congress on 10 November 1775, the US Marine Corps serves as America's Expeditionary Force in Readiness. The Marine Aviation Centennial was formally celebrated on 22 May 2012, which marks the day that Marine Corps 1st Lt Alfred A. Cunningham reported to Greenbury Point, Annapolis, Maryland, for flight training.

In 2010 the US Marine Corps began a Force Structure Review (FSR) that evaluated the posture and capabilities of the service and recommended changes that would refine its future organisation and return it to its expeditionary roots. Released in March 2011, the final report called for a reduction in the size of the Marine Corps from 202,000 to approximately 186,800 active-duty personnel beginning in 2015 after US troops returned from Afghanistan. Interestingly, the Corps had only recently completed an expansion as part of the 'Grow the Force' plan, which was begun in 2006. In addition to expanding the size of the active-duty force to 202,000 Marines, it provided for three balanced Marine Expeditionary Forces (MEF). As part of that move, the Marines added two infantry battalions that resulted in expansion in other areas, including aviation. The Marine Aviation Transition Strategy (MATS) added 5,000 aviation personnel and four new aviation squadrons were formed. Additionally, numerous other units were relocated and/or re-equipped with new aircraft types.

As a result of the FSR, the USMC is being restructured into an expeditionary middleweight force that will allow it to fill a void that exists between the special operations (SOF) and conventional forces. It will be larger than the SOF but lighter and more expeditionary than conventional US Army units. Key actions resulting from the FSR will tailor Marine Divisions (MARDIV), Marine Aircraft Wings (MAW) and Marine

USS *Bataan* ARG

HSC-26 'Chargers'

VMM-365 (Rein) 'Blue Knigths'

The amphibious assault ship USS *Bataan* (LHD 5) pulls alongside the dry cargo and ammunition ship USNS *Washington Chambers* (T-AKE 11) during a replenishment-at-sea. On deck can be seen the variety of an ARG: AV-8B, CH-53, SH-60 and MV-22. (US Navy/MC2 Mutis A. Capizzi)

USS *America* ARG

HSC-23 'Wild Cards'

VMM161 (Rein) 'Grey Hawks'

Logistics Groups (MLG) and will trim fixed-wing aviation by 16 per cent. As a result, the number of flying squadrons will be reduced from 70 to 61 while the number of unmanned air system (UAS) squadrons will grow from four to five. Additionally, the Marine Reserve Division, MLG and MAW headquarters will be placed in cadre status and their functions will be consolidated with the Marine Reserve Force Headquarters.

The Marine Corps' combined arms task forces integrate air, ground and support units into rapidly deployable Marine Air-Ground Task Forces (MAGTF) that are capable of operating independently or as part of a larger combined joint task force. These modular organisations can be tailored to meet the scale of individual operations as dictated by a particular situation.

Responsibility for the ground and aviation forces assigned to the respective Atlantic and Pacific Fleet Marine Force (FMF) is assigned to the Marine Forces Command (MARFORCOM) and Marine Force Pacific (MARFORPAC). When deployed, these forces, which are considered to be part of the US Navy's operating forces, are organised as MAGTFs and formed in three sizes. Each includes a Command Element (CE), Ground Combat Element (GCE), a Logistics Combat Element (LCE) and an Aviation Combat Element (ACE).

The largest of the Marine Corps' major warfighting units is the Marine Expeditionary Force (MEF). Led by a three-star lieutenant general, each of the three numbered MEFs can comprise as many as 50,000 personnel. The MEF is composed of one or more MARDIV, MLG and MAW. As part of the service's expeditionary mission, the latter are designed to operate from a combination of ships and from austere airfields.

Designed for smaller-scale contingency operations, the Marine Expeditionary Brigade (MEB) is a mid-size MAGTF and comprises a reinforced infantry regiment, a composite Marine Aircraft Group (MAG) and Combat Logistics Regiment (CLR). A one-star brigadier general leads the MEB and 8,000 to 22,000 personnel can be assigned.

Serving as the smallest MAGTF, the Marine Expeditionary Units (MEU) are designed for persistent forward deployment. Each of the seven MEUs is under the command of a full colonel and consists of a Reinforced Medium Helicopter or Tiltrotor Squadron – HMM(R) or VMM(R) – a Battalion Landing Team (BLT) and a Combat Logistics Battalion (CLB) and has 1,700 to 2,800 personnel. They are normally deployed on a rotational basis with a US Navy Amphibious Ready Group (ARG) that generally includes an amphibious assault ship (LHA/LHD), a dock landing ship (LSD) and an amphibious transport dock (LPD).

In addition to the previously mentioned designated MAGTFs, when required, Special Purpose MAGTFs (SP-MAGTF) can be formed. These non-standing organisations are temporarily assigned to conduct specific missions.

The primary mission for the MEU and the ARG as a whole is to support the Marines on the ground. In total, the ARG includes over 4,000 sailors and Marines. While a US Navy CVW is broadly 'aircraft-centric' in its approach, the MEU is focused on the mission of the Marines. The nature of the MEU means that it can be deployed closer to the action and it naturally provides a great deal more lifting capacity. The amphibious assault ship always works in support of the MEU and the ARG and with their respective commanders

A typical ACE deploys with up to 10 MV-22Bs (VMM), four CH-53Es (HMH), six AV-8Bs (VMA), four AH-1W/Zs and four UH-1Ys (both from an HMLA). The AH-1s and UH-1s are sometimes embarked on board an accompanying amphibious transport dock, providing more space on board the assault ship for the MV-22s, which are heavier and require more deck space than the predecessor CH-46E. A detachment from a US Navy Helicopter Sea Combat Squadron (HSC) is directly assigned to the LHD/LHA, usually with four MH-60S helicopters for logistics support. Whether based around a VMM or HMH, a composite squadron can include a maximum of 36 aircraft, although 28 is more usual. In addition, refuelling and transport support can be provided by land-based USMC KC-130 aircraft

An MV-22B Osprey takes off from the flight deck of USS *America* (LHA 6) in November 2016. The demonstration was the first shipboard Marine Corps F-35B integration demonstration alongside other ACE assets. (US Marine Corps/Cpl Thor Larson)

The aircraft carrier USS *Carl Vinson* (CVN 70), the guided-missile destroyer USS *Wayne E. Meyer* (DDG 108) and the guided-missile cruiser USS *Lake Champlain* (CG 57) with Japan Maritime Self-Defense Force destroyers in the Philippine Sea in March 2017. The *Carl Vinson* Carrier Strike Group was on a western Pacific deployment as part of the US Pacific Fleet-led initiative to extend the command and control functions of US Third Fleet. (US Navy/MC3 Matt Brown)

A *Nimitz*-class air wing

No. of aircraft	Type	Role and remarks
12	F/A-18E/F Super Hornet	One squadron; multirole fighter
12	F/A-18E/F Super Hornet	One squadron; multirole fighter
12	F/A-18E/F Super Hornet	One squadron; multirole fighter
10	F/A-18C Hornet	One squadron; multirole fighter
5	EA-18G Growler	Electronic attack
4	E-2C/D Hawkeye	AEW
2	C-2A Greyhound	COD
8	MH-60S Seahawk	Multirole helicopter
10	MH-60R Seahawk	Multirole helicopter
75		

A *Nimitz*-class carrier battle group (CSG-5, September 2017)

No.	Ship class	Ship name	Fleet	Displacement	Crew
1	*Nimitz*-class aircraft carrier	USS *Ronald Reagan* (CVN 76)	Pac	100,000	5,700
Up to 3	*Ticonderoga*-class guided missile cruiser	USS *Antietam* (CG 54) USS *Chancellorsville* (CG 62) USS *Shiloh* (CG 67)	Pac Pac	6,800 6,800 6,800	400 400 400
Up to 6	*Arleigh Burke*-class guided-missile destroyer, drawn from nine-ship Destroyer Squadron 15		Pac Pac Pac	8,315–9,200 8,315–9,200 8,315–9,200	303–323 303–323 303–323
1	*Los Angeles*-class submarine			6,927	129
1	*Supply*-class fast combat support ship			49,600	235
					Around 8,173–8,233

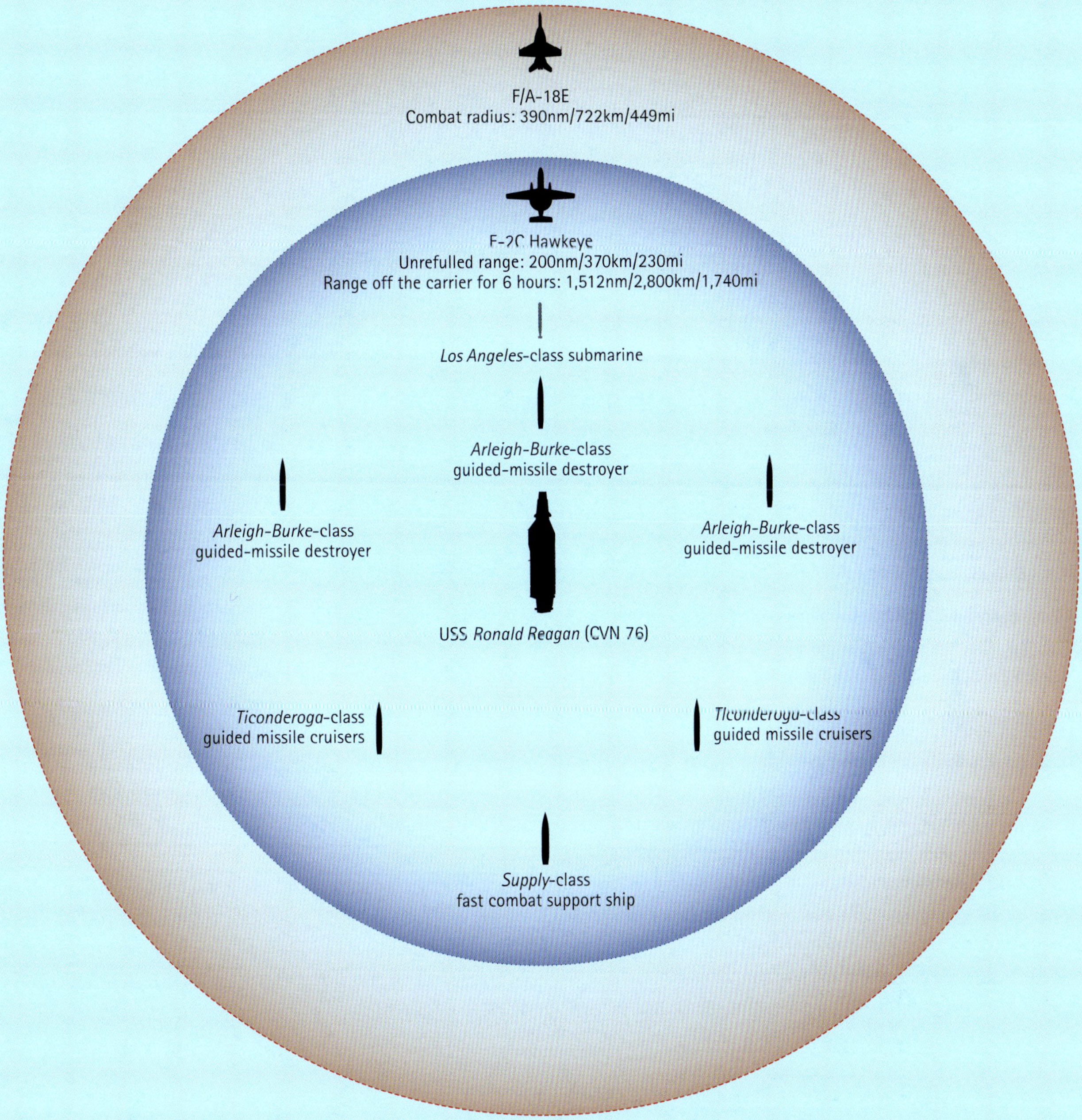

This is a purely schematic presentation of a likely carrier battle group and is not to scale.
In reality, the composition of such a force is dependent on various parameters.

USS *Gerald R. Ford* (CVN 78) transits the Atlantic Ocean in preparation for a practice underway replenishment in August 2017. The carrier was conducting test and evaluation operations.
(US Navy/MC3 Mathew R. Fairchild)

Initially, at least, the *Ford*-class carriers are expected to embark Carrier Air Wings that are similar to the *Nimitz*-class. Aircraft-handling changes relate primarily to modifications to better accommodate and operate the F-35C. However, delays to the Joint Strike Fighter mean that integration activities have been deferred pending initial operational capability for the CV version of the Lightning II.

Above all, the improvements in the ship design are intended to allow the embarked air wing to operate with fewer personnel and to maximise the sortie generation rate of its strike aircraft by 33 per cent compared to the Nimitz. According to the US Navy, the *Ford*-class CVN will be capable of embarking an air wing of 75+ aircraft, compared to a nominal 60+ for the *Nimitz*-class. However, the exact composition of the *Ford*-class CVN is dependent on CVW assignments and availability, and is therefore uncertain at the time of writing.

Future *Gerald R. Ford*-class carrier battle group (2020 onwards)

No.	Ship class	Ship name	Fleet	Displacement	Crew
1	*Gerald R. Ford-class*	USS Gerald R. Ford (CVN 78)		100,000	4,297

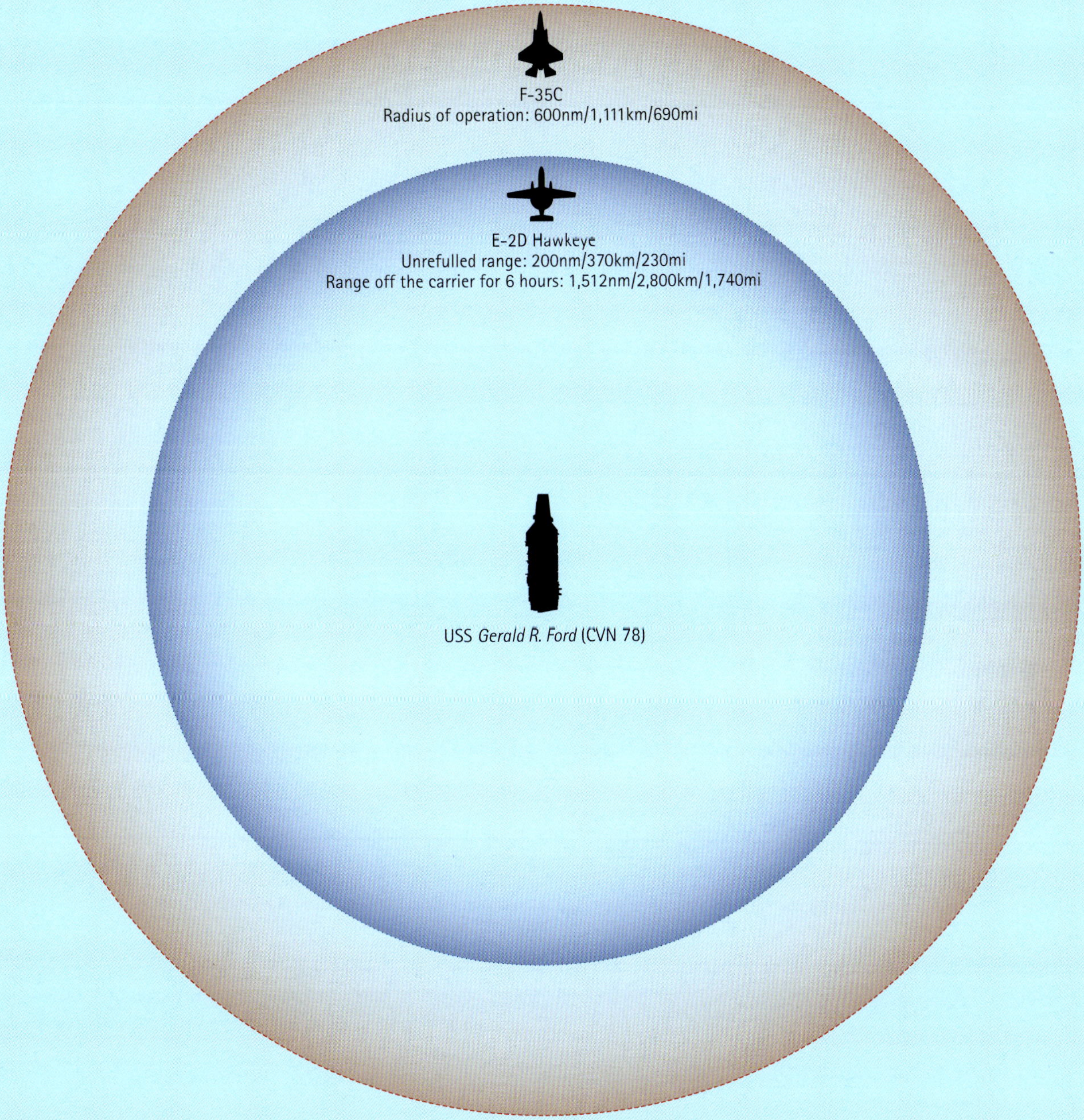

This is a purely schematic presentation of a likely carrier battle group and is not to scale.
In reality, the composition of such a force is dependent on various parameters.

Amphibious dock landing ship, USS *Carter Hall* (LSD 50), fleet replenishment oiler, USNS *Kanawha* (T-AO 196), amphibious assault ship USS *Bataan* (LHD 5), and dry cargo and ammunition ship, USNS *Washington Chambers* (T-AKE 11) sail together while executing a replenishment-at-sea. The *Carter Hall* and the *Bataan* Ready Group were deployed in the Fifth Fleet area of operations.
(US Navy/Naval Air Crewman (Helicopter) 2nd Class Kyle Hecht)

A *Wasp*-class air wing

No. of aircraft	Type	Role and remarks
6	AV-8B Harrier II	Multirole fighter
4	AH-1Z Viper	Attack/CAS
4	CH-53E Super Stallion	Heavy transport
12	MV-22 Osprey	Medium transport
5	RQ-21 Blackjack	ISR
3	UH-1Y Venom	Multirole helicopter
34		

Organised within a VMM squadron

Typical current *Wasp*-class expeditionary strike group (Bataan Amphibious Ready Group)

No.	Ship class	Ship name	Fleet	Displacement	Crew
1	*Wasp*-class amphibious assault ship	USS *Bataan* (LHD 5)	Atl	41,006	1,108*
1	*San Antonio*-class amphibious transport dock	USS *Mesa Verde* (LPD 19)	Atl	24,443	111**
1	*Harpers Ferry*-class amphibious dock landing ship	USS *Carter Hall* (LSD 50)	Atl	16,360	419***
					1,638******

* plus 1,687 Marines
** plus 500 Marines
*** plus 418 Marines
**** plus around 2,800 Marines = grand total of around 4,450

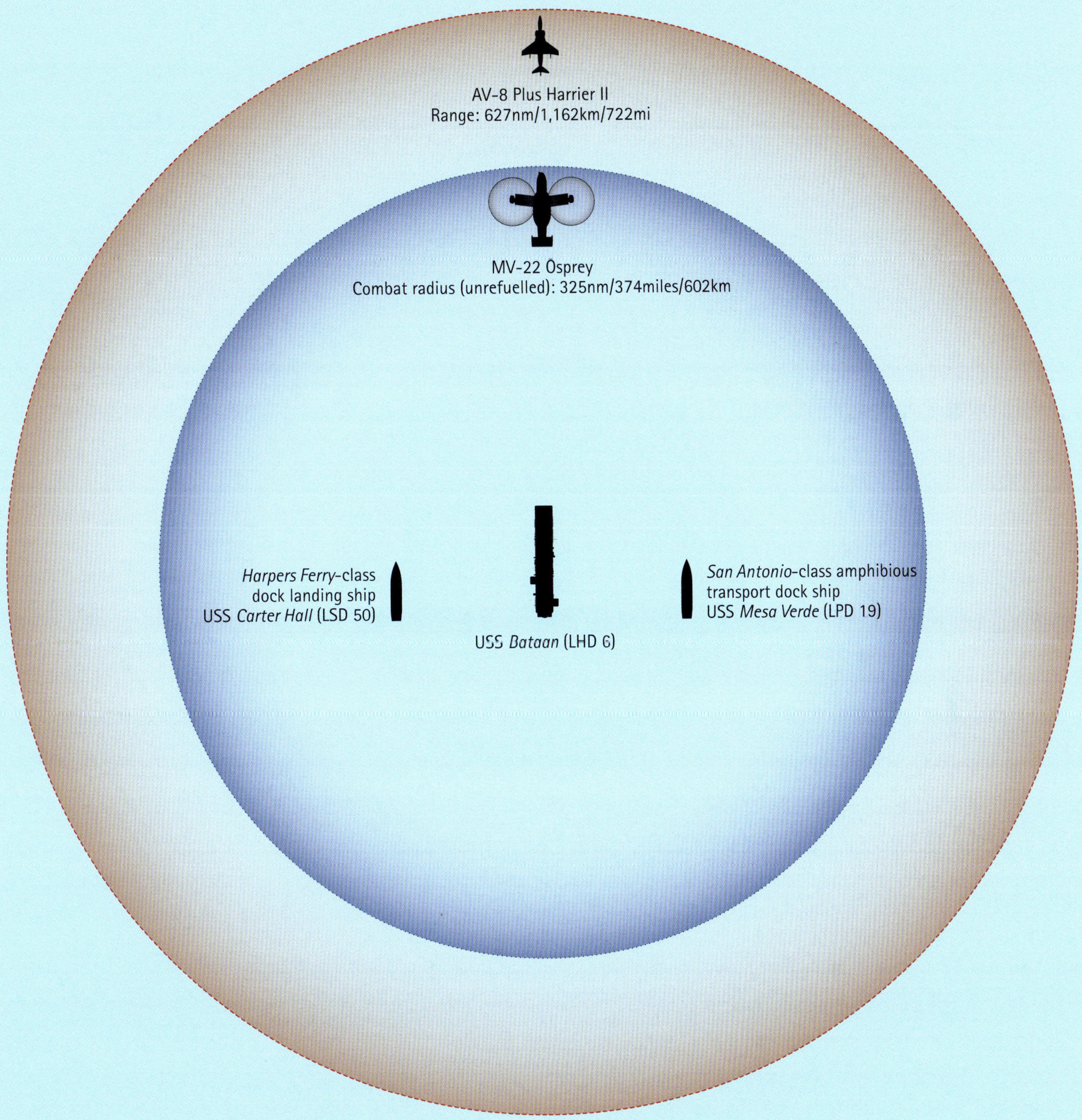

This is a purely schematic presentation of a likely carrier battle group and is not to scale.
In reality, the composition of such a force is dependent on various parameters.

The expeditionary base USS *Lewis B. Puller* (ESB 3), left, the amphibious assault ship USS *America* (LHA 6), the amphibious dock landing ship USS *Pearl Harbor* (LSD 52) and the *Arleigh Burke*-class guided-missile destroyer USS *Howard* (DDG 83), back, in formation while participating in a photo exercise during Alligator Dagger 2017. (US Navy/MC2 Alexander Ventura II)

An *America*-class air wing

No. of aircraft	Type	Role and remarks
10	F-35B Lightning II	Multirole fighter
3	AH-1Z Viper	Attack/CAS
4	CH-53E Super Stallion	Heavy transport
12	MV-22 Osprey	Medium transport
5	RQ-21 Blackjack	ISR
3	UH-1Y Venom	Multirole helicopter
36		

Organised within a VMM squadron

Typical current *America*-class expeditionary strike group (America Amphibious Ready Group)

No.	Ship class	Ship name	Fleet	Displacement	Crew
1	*America*-class amphibious assault ship	USS *America* (LHA 6)	Pac	45,693	1,059*
1	*San Antonio*-class amphibious transport dock	USS *San Diego* (LPD 22)	Pac	25,000	361**
1	*Harpers Ferry*-class amphibious dock landing ship	USS *Pearl Harbor* (LSD 52)	Pac	16,088	419***
					1,839****

* plus 1,894 Marines
** plus 699 Marines
*** plus 418 Marines
**** plus around 2,800 Marines = grand total of around 4,450

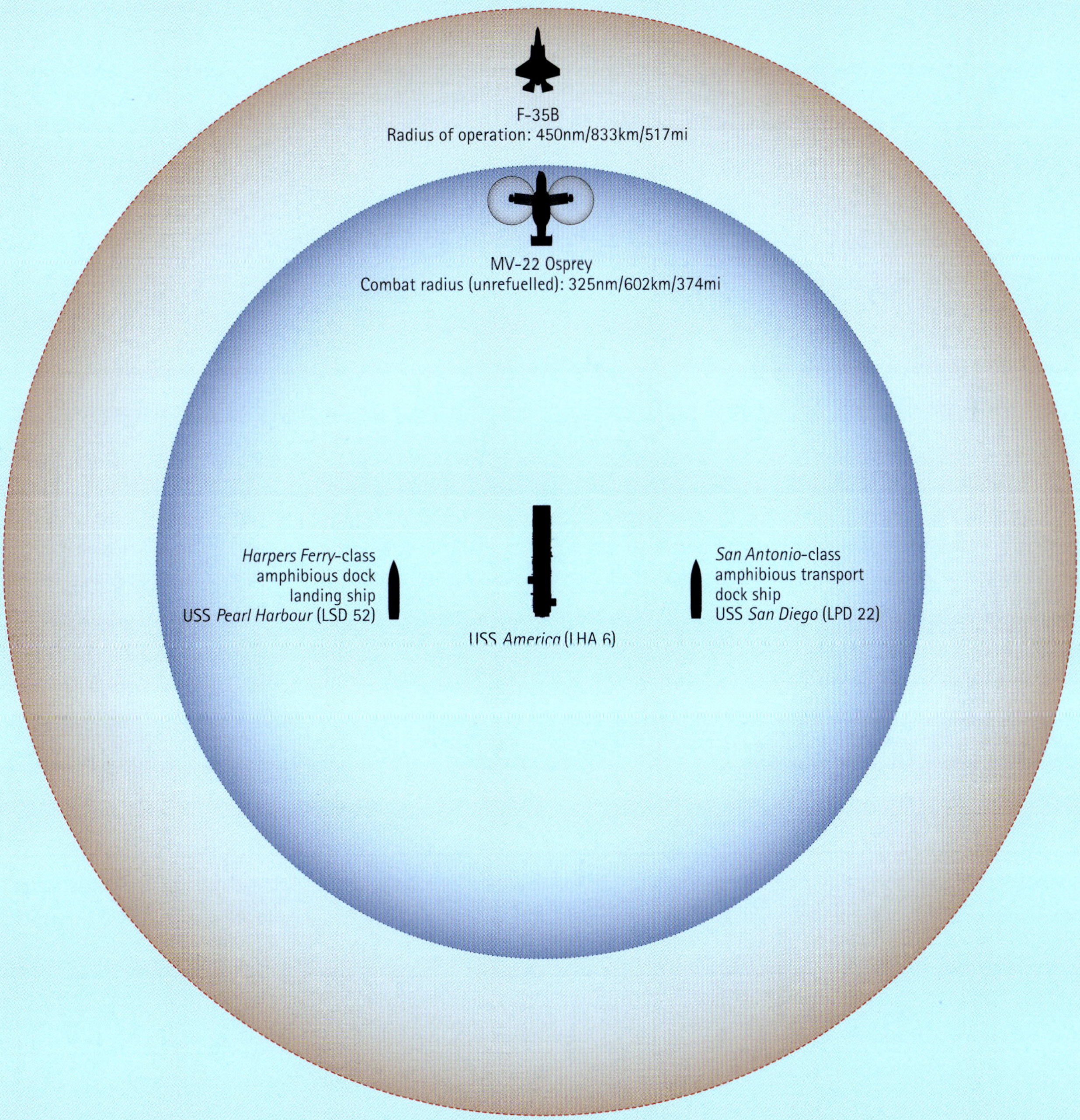

This is a purely schematic presentation of a likely carrier battle group and is not to scale.
In reality, the composition of such a force is dependent on various parameters.

APPENDIX I: SHIP CLASSES

The following pages show the world's current aircraft carriers as defined for the purposes of this book, including the Brazilian carrier, the immediate fate of which remained uncertain as of late 2017. Also included are the forthcoming Chinese, UK and US carriers.

Besides basic technical data, this appendix includes an artwork for each class, to demonstrate the relative sizes of these warships.

With the exception of the US Navy Carrier Air Wings, the composition and total number of aircraft within an air wing typically vary due to mission requirements.

Brazil | *São Paulo*

A plan was developed to modernise the *São Paulo* between 2015 and 2019, at a cost of more than USD 200 million. However, budget restrictions meant that work never began and in February 2017 the Marinha do Brasil announced it would decommission the carrier. According to a statement from Brazil's Directorate of Communications and Information Technology of the Navy: 'After several attempts to recover the operational capacity of the *São Paulo*, the Admiralty concluded that a modernisation programme would require high financial investment, contain technical uncertainties and would require a long completion period.'

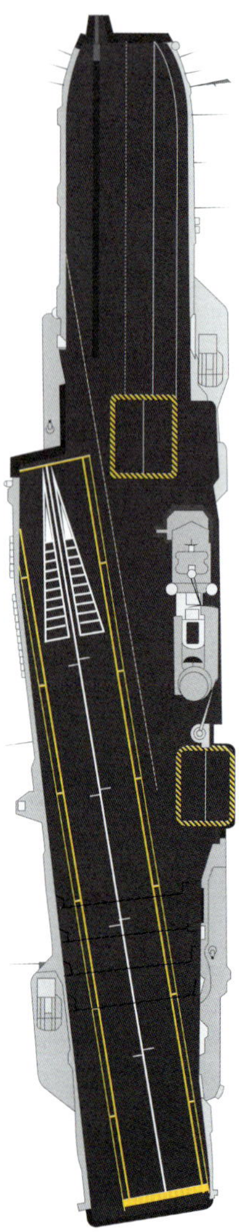

Top view of NAeL *São Paulo* (A12)
(Drawing by James Lawrence)

Clemenceau-class	
Name	*São Paulo* (ex-*Foch*)
Pennant number	A12
Laid down	15 February 1957
Launched	23 July 1960
Commissioned	15 July 1963
General characteristics and specifications	
Displacement	24,200 tonnes standard, 32,800 tonnes fully loaded
Length	265m (869.4ft)
Beam	31.7m (104ft)
Draught	8.6m (28.2ft)
Propulsion	Six Indret boilers, four steam turbines, 93MW (126,000hp), two propellers
Speed	32kt
Range	7,500nm at 18kt
Complement	1,920 (582 air group); 984 if only helicopters are carried
Sensors and weapons	
Combat system	SICONTA Mk 4
	DRBV 23B air search radar (to be replaced by a BAE Artisan derivative radar)
	DRBV 15 air and surface search radar
	NRBA 50 landing approach radar
	DRBI 10 3D height finder radar
	DRBC 32C fire control radar (installed but inoperative)
	DRBN 34 navigation radar
Armament	Three Simbad launchers for Mistral anti-aircraft missiles

China | *Liaoning*

Today's *Liaoning* began as the younger, sister vessel of the in-service Russian carrier *Admiral Kuznetsov*, and had been left unfinished after the fall of the Soviet Union and fallen into a state of disrepair. Despite various concerns, the Ukrainian government sold the partially completed empty hull albeit with the engines already installed for about USD 20 million in 1998. She arrived in China in 2002, and rebuild started in 2004. Renamed as *Liaoning*, she was handed over as the Type 001 carrier with the pennant number 16 to the PLAN on 23 September 2012.

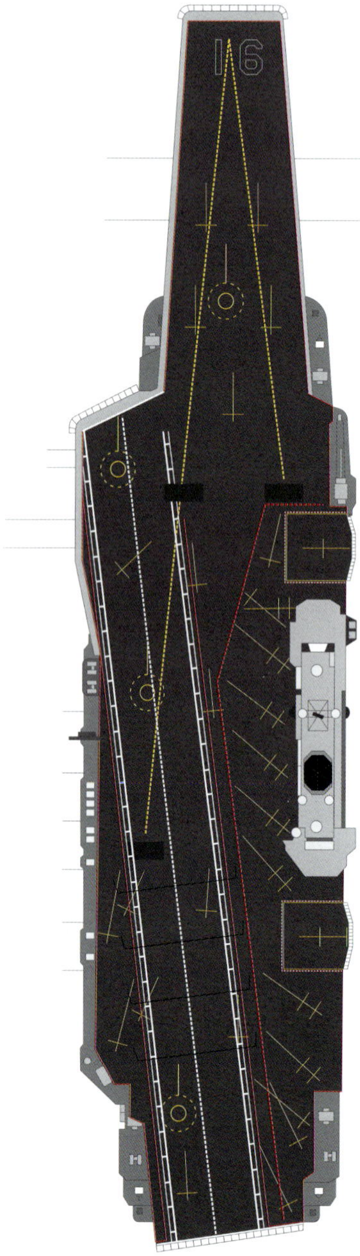

Top view of *Liaoning* (16)
(Drawing by James Lawrence)

Type 001 class (formerly Project 1143.5 Orel/*Kuznetsov*-class)*	
Name	*Liaoning* (ex-*Varyag*, ex-*Riga*)
Pennant number	16
Laid down	6 December 1985
Launched	6 December 1988
Commissioned	25 September 2012 (as *Liaoning*)
General characteristics and specifications	
Displacement	53,000-55,200 tonnes standard, 58,600-67,500 tonnes fully loaded
Length	304.5m (999ft)
Beam	70m (229.7ft)
Draught	10.5m (34.4ft)
Propulsion	Eight KVG-4 boilers, four TV-12-4 turbines, 147MW (200,000hp), four propellers
Speed	32kt
Range	3,850nm at 32kt
Complement	1,960 (626 air group)
Sensors and weapons	
	Fregate MAE-3/Type 381B Top Plate air search radar
	Type 346 Dragon Eye air search and fire control radar
	Mineral ME/Band Stand fire control radar (x2)
Armament	Three HHQ-10 18-cell launchers for anti-aircraft missiles, three 30mm Type 1130 CIWS

* General characteristics for *Varyag* as originally designed.

China | Type 002

This warship is officially the first indigenous carrier class designed and developed for the Chinese Navy. It closely follows its sister-ship *Liaoning* and construction of this heavily improved *Kuznetsov*-class design allegedly began January 2014 with lay-down in Dalian in March 2015. There is still some uncertainty concerning its true designation, but it seems likely it will be officially designated as the Type 002 aircraft carrier. Launch of the vessel occurred on 26 April 2017 and it might be named *Shandong* (CV-17).

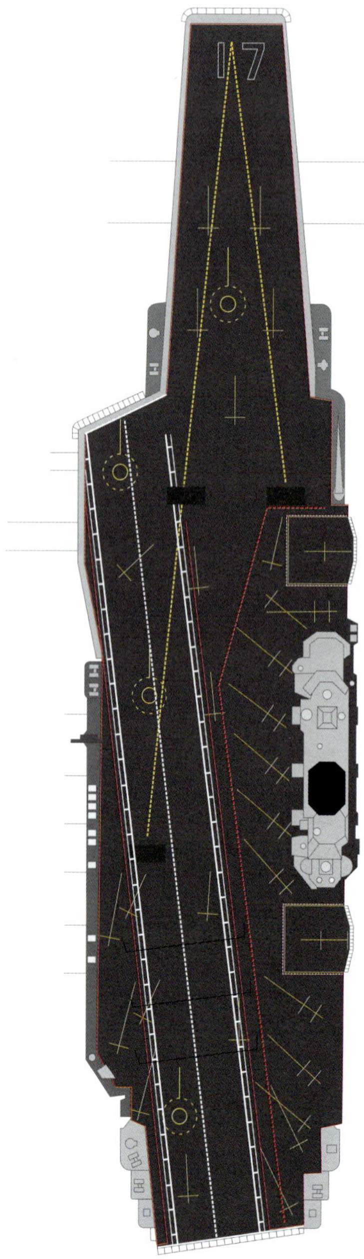

Top view of *Shandong* (17)
(Drawing by James Lawrence)

Type 002 class (formerly Project 001A)	
Name	Not yet known; rumours suggest *Shandong*
Pennant number	Not yet know; rumours suggest 17
Laid down	10 March 2015
Launched	26 April 2017
Commissioned	Expected around 2020
General characteristics and specifications	
Displacement	55,000 tonnes standard (estimated), 70,000 tonnes fully loaded (estimated)
Length	304.5m (999ft)
Beam	70m (229.7ft)
Draught	10.5m (34.4ft)
Propulsion	Not yet known
Speed	
Range	
Complement	
Sensors and weapons	
	Fregate MAE-3/Type 381B Top Plate air search radar (still unconfirmed)
	Type 346 Dragon Eye air search and fire control radar (still unconfirmed)
	Mineral ME/Band Stand fire control radar (x2)
Armament	Three HHQ-10 18-cell launchers for anti-aircraft missiles, three 30mm Type 1130 CIWS

France | *Charles de Gaulle*

The combination of the carrier *Charles de Gaulle*, the Rafale M multirole fighter and the E-2C Hawkeye airborne early warning aircraft provide the French Navy with an extremely powerful, coherent and efficient power-projection tool equipped with the latest combat aircraft, precision weapons, satellite communication systems, tactical datalinks and command and control networks. However, with only a single carrier active, France loses its carrier-borne aviation capability whenever the vessel is undergoing refit or pre-deployment training.

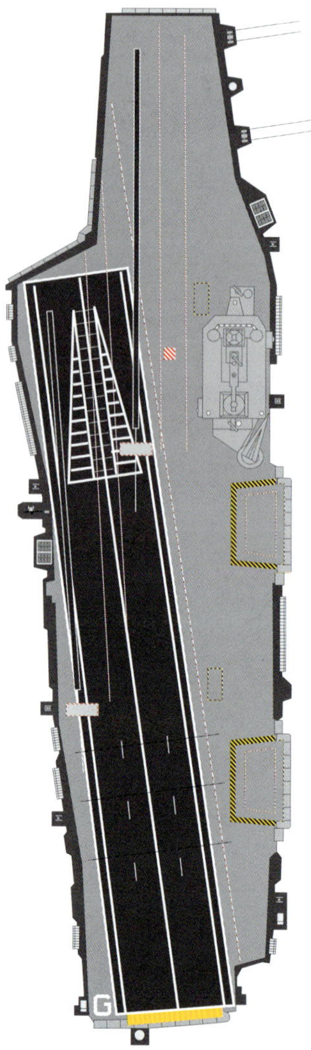

Top view of *Charles de Gaulle* (R91)
(Drawing by James Lawrence)

Charles de Gaulle-class	
Name	*Charles de Gaulle*
Pennant number	R 91
Laid down	14 April 1989
Launched	7 May 1994
Commissioned	18 May 2001
General characteristics and specifications	
Displacement	37,680 tonnes standard, 43,182 tonnes fully loaded
Length	261.5m (857.9ft)
Beam	64.4m (211.3ft)
Draught	9.4m (30.8ft)
Propulsion	Nuclear, two PWR Type 15 reactors, two GEC Alsthom 61 turbines, 61MW (83,000hp), two propellers
Speed	27kt
Complement	1,862 (542 air group)
Sensors and weapons	1,960 (626 air group)
Combat system	
	SENIT 8-05
	DRBJ 11B 3D air search radar
	DRBV 26D Jupiter air search radar
	DRBV 15C Sea Tiger Mk 2 air and surface search radar
	Scanter 6000 surface search radar (x2)
	DRBN 34A navigation radar
	Arabel 3D fire control radar
Armament	Four Sylver A43 octuple launchers for Aster 15 anti-aircraft missiles
	Two Sadral sextuple launchers for Mistral anti-aircraft missiles
	Four 20F2 20mm guns

India | *Vikramaditya*

The Indian Navy is currently looking at acquiring a future naval fighter. Any such aircraft inducted in the coming years will have to at least be able to launch from the roughly 200m (656ft) flight deck of a STOBAR (short take-off but arrested recovery) aircraft carrier – either INS *Vikramaditya* or the new INS *Vikrant* – there is no clarity on whether the navy will build its second indigenous carrier in the CATOBAR (catapult take-off but arrested recovery) configuration or choose to remain with STOBAR.

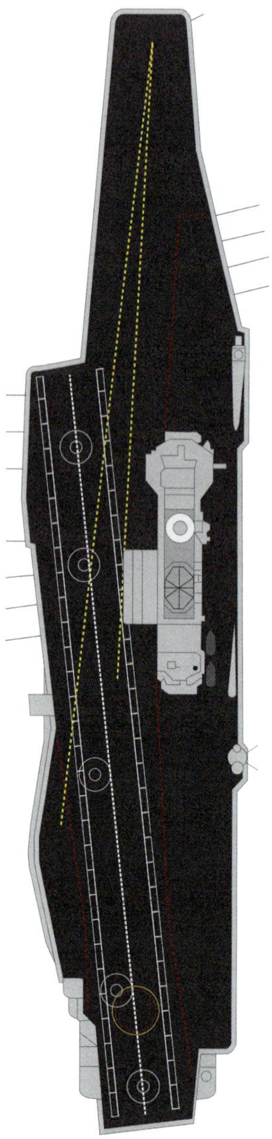

Top view of *Vikramaditya* (R33)
(Drawing by James Lawrence)

Modified *Kiev*-class (Project 1143.0)	
Name	*Vikramaditya* (ex-*Admiral Gorshkov*, ex-*Baku*)
Pennant number	R 33
Laid down	17 February 1978
Launched	1 April 1982
Commissioned	16 November 2013 (as *Vikramaditya*)
General characteristics and specifications	
Displacement	46,129 tonnes fully loaded
Length	283m (928.5ft)
Beam	51m (167.3ft)
Draught	10m (32.8ft)
Propulsion	Eight KVG-4 boilers, four GTZA-674 turbines, 147MW (200,000hp), four propellers
Speed	29kt
Range	13,800nm at 18kt
Complement	1,326
Sensors and weapons	
Combat system	Lesorub E
	Podberyozovik-ET2 Flat Screen 3D air search radar
	Fregat MAE-3 Top Plate 3D air and surface search radar
	Strut Pair surface search radar (x 2)
	DRBI-10 tri-dimensional air search radar
	EL/M-2221 fire control radar
	Bridgemaster E navigation radar
Armament	Three octuple launchers for Barak LR/8 anti-aircraft missiles
	Four AK-630 30mm CIWS

Italy | *Cavour*

While its predecessor the carrier *Giuseppe Garibaldi* was conceived as a helicopter carrier and the AV-8B+ Harrier II was integrated later on, the *Cavour* was always planned as a 'true' aircraft carrier, to operate with the new F-35B. The carrier is also the centerpiece for the application of the Sea Basing Concept. This involves the creation of an 'advanced base' in the open seas, made up of a mobile and versatile group of ships of different types that can also be employed in concert with other armed forces, at national and international level.

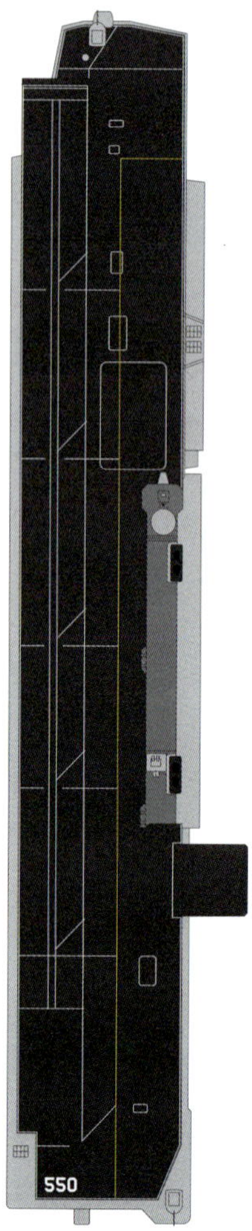

Top view of *Cavour* (C550)
(Drawing by James Lawrence)

Cavour-class	
Name	*Cavour* (ex-*Andrea Doria*)
Pennant number	C 550
Laid down	17 July 2001
Launched	20 July 2004
Commissioned	10 June 2009
General characteristics and specifications	
Displacement	21,160 tonnes standard, 27,900 tonnes fully loaded
Length	244m (800.5ft)
Beam	39m (128ft)
Draught	8.7m (28.5ft)
Propulsion	Four LM2500 gas turbines, 88MW (118,000hp), two propellers
Speed	28kt
Range	7,000nm+ at 16kt
Complement	1,202 (203 air group)
Sensors and weapons	
Combat system	Horizon derivative
	MM/SPY-790 multifunction radar
	MM/SPS-798 air search radar
	MM/SPS 791 surface search radar
	MM/SPN-753(V)10 navigation radar (x 2)
	MM/SPN-720 precision approach radar
	AN/SPN-41A precision approach and landing system
	NA-25XP fire control radar (x 2)
Armament	Four Sylver octuple launchers for Aster 15 anti-aircraft missiles
	Two 76mm (3in) Super Rapid Strales guns
	Three 25mm KBA anti-aircraft guns

Russia | *Admiral Kuznetsov*

The debut combat deployment of the aircraft carrier *Admiral Kuznetsov* between October 2016 and February 2017 was not without incident but did allow Russian Navy Aviation to evaluate and test its recently delivered MiG-29KR/KUBR multi-role fighters, as well as its newly modernised Sukhoi Su-33 ship-borne fighters.

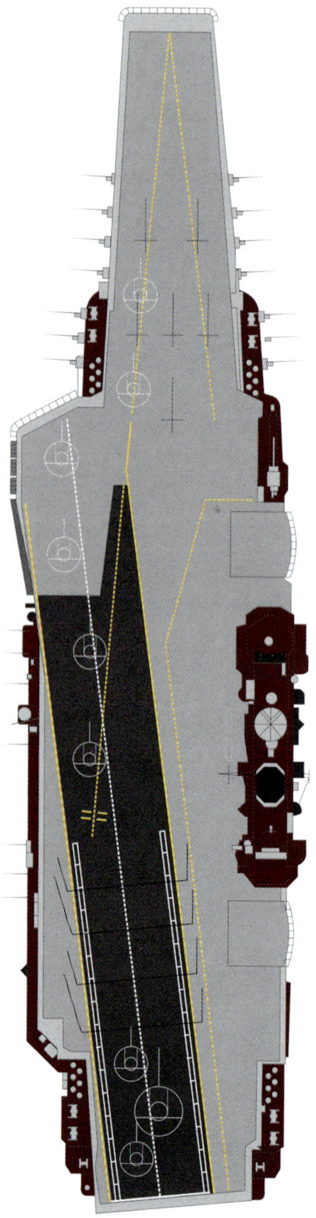

Top view of *Admiral Kuznetsov* (063)
(Drawing by James Lawrence)

Project 1143.5 Orel/*Kuznetsov*-class	
Name	*Admiral Kuznetsov* (ex-*Tbilisi*, ex-*Leonid Brezhnev*)
Pennant number	063
Laid down	1 April 1982
Launched	16 December 1985
Commissioned	25 December 1990
General characteristics and specifications	
Displacement	46,637 tonnes standard, 59,439 tonnes fully loaded
Length	302.3m (991.8ft)
Beam	72.5m (237.9ft)
Draught	19.14m (30ft)
Propulsion	Eight boilers, four turbines, 147MW (200,000hp), four propellers
Speed	29kt
Range	3,850nm at 29kt
Complement	1,960
Sensors and weapons	
	Sky Watch 3D air search radar
	Top Plate B air and surface search radar
	Strut Pair surface search radar (x 2)
	Palm Front navigation radar (x 3)
	Cross Sword fire control radar (x 4)
	Hot Flash fire control radar (x 8)
	Fly Trap B aircraft control radar (x 2)
Armament	Twelve 3M45 SS-N-19 Shipwreck anti-ship missiles
	Four sextuple launchers for Kinzhal SA-N-9 Gauntlet anti-aircraft missiles
	Eight Kashtan CADS-N-1 CIWS (each with one 30mm gun)
	Eight 9M311 SA-N-11 Grison anti-aircraft missiles
	Six AK-630 30mm CIWS

Spain | *Juan Carlos I*

The Harrier II remains a centerpiece of the Spanish Navy's force-projection capability, operating from the carrier *Juan Carlos I*, which replaced the now-withdrawn *Príncipe de Asturias*. However, the future of Spanish fixed-wing carrier-borne aviation will rely upon a future order for the F-35B to replace the Harrier once this type is withdrawn in around 2025.

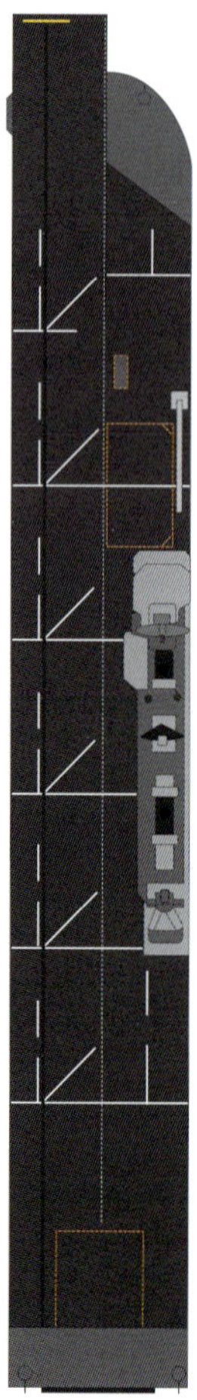

Top view of *Juan Carlos I* (L61).
(Drawing by James Lawrence)

Juan Carlos I-class	
Name	*Juan Carlos I*
Pennant number	L 61
Laid down	20 May 2005
Launched	10 March 2008
Commissioned	30 September 2010
General characteristics and specifications	
Displacement	27,514 tonnes fully loaded
Length	230.8m (757.2ft)
Beam	32m (105ft)
Draught	7m (23ft)
Propulsion	Two LM 2500 gas turbine, 19.8MW (26,550hp): two MAN diesels, 15.7MW (21,080hp); two propellers
Speed	21kt
Range	9,000nm at 15kt
Complement	296
Sensors and weapons	
Combat system	SCOMBA
	Lanza air search radar
	Aries surface search and navigation radar (x 3)
	DRBV 15C Sea Tiger Mk 2 air and surface search radar
	Visionmaster navigation radar
Armament	Four 25mm guns
	Two 12.7mm (0.5in) machine guns

United Kingdom | *Queen Elizabeth* class

The two new Royal Navy carriers are inextricably linked to the UK's procurement of the F-35 Lightning II. The first tranche of 48 aircraft will be of the F-35B variant, which will be jointly operated by the Royal Air Force and Royal Navy and capable of operating from both land and the *Queen Elizabeth*-class aircraft carriers.

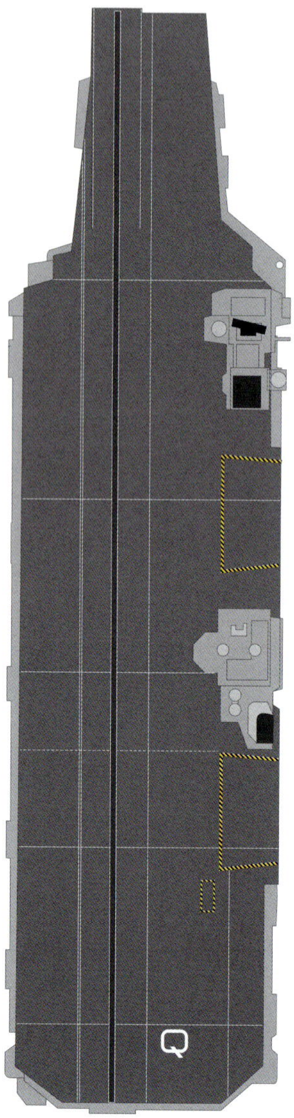

Top view of *Queen Elizabeth* (R08)
(Drawing by James Lawrence)

Queen Elizabeth-class	
Name	HMS *Queen Elizabeth*
Pennant number	R 08
Laid down	7 July 2009
Launched	17 July 2014
Commissioned	7 December 2017
Name	HMS *Prince of Wales*
Pennant number	R 09
Laid down	26 May 2011
Launched	-
Commissioned	
General characteristics and specifications	
Displacement	65,000 tonnes fully loaded
Length	282.9m (928.1ft)
Beam	38.8m (127.3ft)
Draught	11m (36.1ft)
Propulsion	Two MT 30 gas turbines, 70MW (93,870hp), four diesel generators, four induction motors, two propellers
Speed	26kt
Complement	1,586 (853 air group)
Sensors and weapons	
Combat system	CMS-1
	Type 1046 air search radar
	Type 997 air and surface search radar
	SPN-720 precision approach radar
	Visionmaster navigation radar
Armament	Three Phalanx Block 1B 20mm CIWS

United States | *Nimitz* class

The retirement of the USS *Enterprise* in 2012 left the US Navy with a fleet of 10 nuclear-powered aircraft carriers and for the first time in its history all of the ships were built to the same design: the *Nimitz*-class.

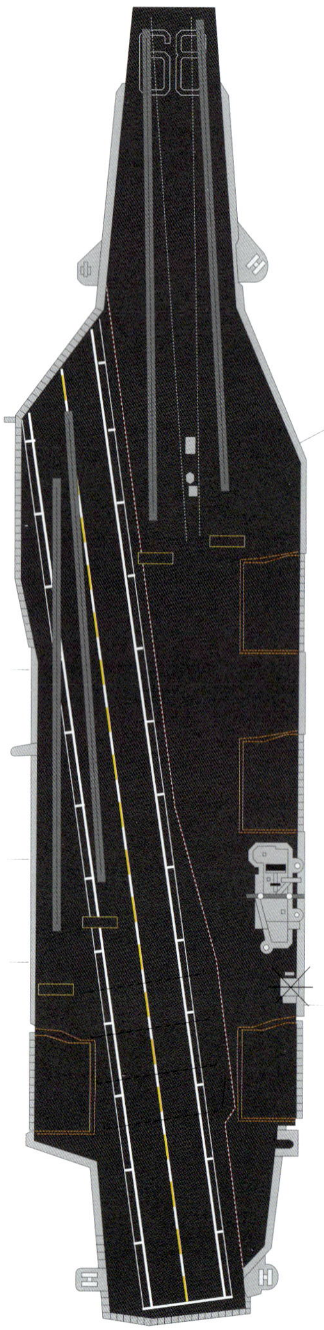

Top view of *Nimitz*-class
(Drawing by James Lawrence)

Nimitz-class			
Name	USS *Nimitz*	Name	USS *George Washington*
Pennant number	CVN 68	Pennant number	CVN 73
Laid down	22 June 1968	Laid down	25 August 1986
Launched	13 May 1972	Launched	21 July 1990
Commissioned	3 May 1975	Commissioned	4 July 1992
Name	USS *Dwight D. Eisenhower*	Name	USS *John C. Stennis*
Pennant number	CVN 69	Pennant number	CVN 74
Laid down	15 August 1970	Laid down	13 March 1991
Launched	11 October 1975	Launched	13 November 1993
Commissioned	18 October 1977	Commissioned	9 December 1995
Name	USS *Carl Vinson*	Name	USS *Harry S. Truman*
Pennant number	CVN 70	Pennant number	CVN 75
Laid down	11 October 1975	Laid down	29 November 1993
Launched	15 March 1980	Launched	7 September 1996
Commissioned	13 March 1982	Commissioned	25 July 1998
Name	USS *Theodore Roosevelt*	Name	USS *Ronald Reagan*
Pennant number	CVN 71	Pennant number	CVN 76
Laid down	13 October 1981	Laid down	12 February 1998
Launched	27 October 1984	Launched	4 March 2001
Commissioned	25 October 1986	Commissioned	12 July 2003
Name	USS *Abraham Lincoln*	Name	USS *George H. W. Bush*
Pennant number	CVN 72	Pennant number	CVN 77
Laid down	3 November 1984	Laid down	6 September 2003
Launched	13 February 1988	Launched	8 October 2006
Commissioned	11 November 1989	Commissioned	10 January 2009

General characteristics and specifications	
Displacement	74,086 tonnes (CVN 68-70), 75,160 tonnes (CVN 71) standard; 92,955 tonnes (CVN 68-70), 97,933 tonnes (CVN 71), 103,637 tonnes (CVN 72-77) fully loaded
Length	332.9m (1,092.2ft)
Beam	40.8m (133.9ft)
Draught	11.3m (37.1ft) (CVN 68-70), 11.8m (38.7ft) (CVN 71), 11.9ft (39ft) (CVN 72-76), 21.1m (39.7ft) (CVN 77)
Propulsion	Nuclear, two A4W/A1G reactors, four turbines, four propellers
Speed	30kt
Complement	5,750 (2,480 air group)
Sensors and weapons	
	SPS-48E/G 3D air search radar
	SPS-49A(V)1 air search radar
	SPQ-9B air search radar
	SPS-67(V)1 surface search radar
	SPN-41, SPN-43C carrier controlled approach radar
	SPS-73(V)12, Furuno 9000 navigation radar
	Mk 9 fire control radar (x 4)
Armament	Two GMLS Mk 29 launchers for RIM-162D ESSM anti-aircraft missiles
	Two GMLS Mk 49 launchers for RIM-116 RAM anti-aircraft missiles
	Two 20mm Vulcan Phalanx Mk 15 CIWS
	Four 25mm Mk 38 Chain Guns (CVN 68, 70, 72, 76)

United States | *Gerald R. Ford* class

The USS *Gerald R. Ford* is the first of a new class of carriers designed to operate with a smaller crew than the previous *Nimitz*-class ships. The design features include new nuclear reactor and propulsion, a redesigned island, EMALS, advanced arresting gear, improved weapons movement and an enhanced flight deck.

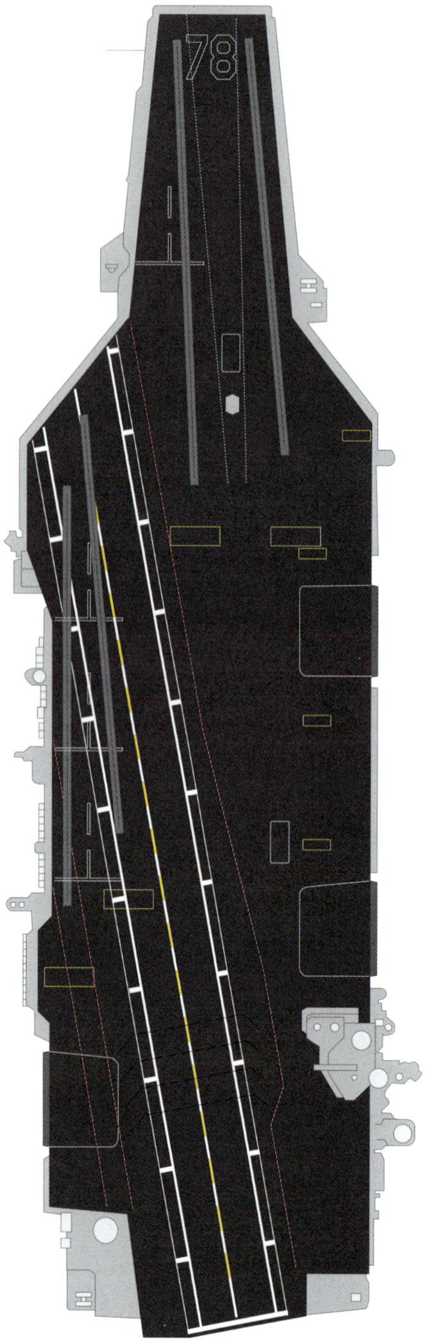

Top view of *Gerald R. Ford*-class (Drawing by James Lawrence)

Gerald R. Ford-class	
Name	USS *Gerald R. Ford*
Pennant number	CVN 78
Laid down	14 November 2009
Launched	17 November 2013
Commissioned	22 July 2017
Name	USS *John F. Kennedy*
Pennant number	CVN 79
Laid down	22 August 2015
Launched	–
Commissioned	–
Name	USS *Enterprise*
Pennant number	CVN 80
Laid down	–
Launched	–
Commissioned	–
General characteristics and specifications	
Displacement	101,605 tonnes fully loaded
Length	332.8m (1,091.9ft)
Beam	40.8m (133.9ft)
Draught	12.4m (40.7ft)
Propulsion	Nuclear, two A1B reactors, four propellers
Speed	30kt
Complement	4,550
Sensors and weapons	
Combat system	CEC
	Dual Band Radar/SPY-3 3D air search radar (CVN 78)
	SPY-4 Volume Search Radar 3D radar (CVN 78)
	Enterprise Air Surveillance Radar 3D radar (CVN 79)
	SPS-73(V)12 navigation radar
	SPY-3 fire control radar (CVN 78)
	SPQ-9B fire control radar (CVN 79)
	SPN-46 precision approach radar
Armament	Two GMLS Mk 29 launchers for RIM-162D ESSM anti-aircraft missiles
	Two GMLS Mk 49 launchers for RIM-116 RAM anti-aircraft missiles
	Three 20mm Vulcan Phalanx Block 1B Mk 15 CIWS

United States | *Wasp* class

USS *Makin Island* (LHD 8) was delivered to the Navy in April 2009 and is the first US Navy amphibious assault ship to be equipped with both gas turbines and an auxiliary propulsion system (APS) instead of steam boilers. The APS uses two induction-type auxiliary propulsion motors powered from the ship's electrical grid rather than relying on main propulsion engines to power the ship's shaft, which are less efficient at lower speeds.

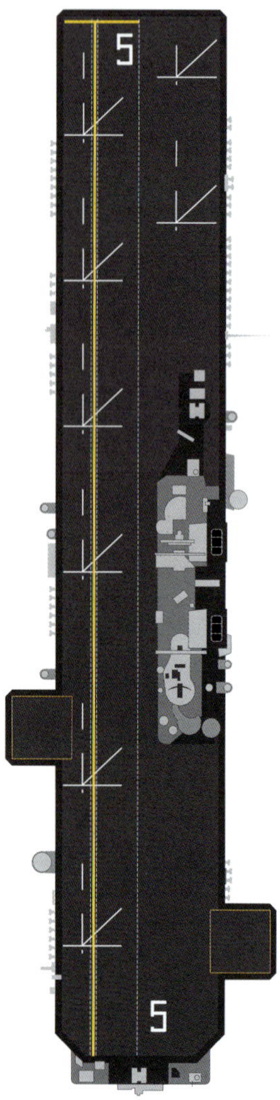

Top view of *Wasp*-class
(Drawing by James Lawrence)

Wasp-class			
Name	USS *Wasp*	Name	USS *Bataan*
Pennant number	LHD 1	Pennant number	LHD 5
Laid down	30 May 1985	Laid down	16 March 1994
Launched	4 August 1987	Launched	15 March 1996
Commissioned	29 July 1989	Commissioned	20 September 1997
Name	USS *Essex*	Name	USS *Bonhomme Richard*
Pennant number	LHD 2	Pennant number	LHD 6
Laid down	16 February 1989	Laid down	29 March 1995
Launched	4 January 1991	Launched	14 March 1997
Commissioned	17 October 1992	Commissioned	15 August 1998
Name	USS *Kearsarge*	Name	USS *Iwo Jima*
Pennant number	LHD 3	Pennant number	LHD 7
Laid down	6 February 1990	Laid down	12 December 1997
Launched	26 March 1992	Launched	4 February 2000
Commissioned	16 October 1993	Commissioned	30 June 2001
Name	USS *Boxer*	Name	USS *Makin Island*
Pennant number	LHD 4	Pennant number	LHD 8
Laid down	26 March 1991	Laid down	14 February 2004
Launched	13 August 1993	Launched	22 September 2006
Commissioned	11 February 1995	Commissioned	24 October 2009

General characteristics and specifications	
Displacement	41,302 tonnes (LHD 1-4), 41,006 tonnes (LHD 5-7), 42,300 tonnes (LHD 8) fully loaded
Length	258.2m (847.1ft)
Beam	32.3m (106ft)
Draught	8.1m (26.6ft)
Propulsion	Two boilers, two turbines, 52.2MW (70,000hp) (LHD 1-7); two LM 2500+ gas turbines, 52.2MW (70,000hp), two Alstom variable speed electric motors, 7.46MW (10,000hp) (LHD 8), two propellers
Speed	22kt
Range	9,500nm at 20kt
Complement	1,123
Sensors and weapons	
Combat system	MTACCS
	SPS-48E 3D air search radar
	SPS-49A(V)9 3D air search radar
	Mk 23 TAS air search radar
	SPQ-9B air search radar (LHD 7-8)
	SPS-67 surface search radar
	SPS-73 navigation radar (x 2)
	SPN-35B (LHD 1-7), SPN-35C (LHD 8) and SPN-43C carrier controlled approach radar
	Mk 95 (x 2), SPQ-9B (LHD 8) fire control radar
Armament	Two GMLS Mk 29 launchers for RIM-7P Sea Sparrow anti-aircraft missiles
	Two GMLS Mk 49 launchers for RIM-116 RAM anti-aircraft missiles
	Two 20mm Vulcan Phalanx Mk 15 CIWS
	Three 25mm Mk 38 Bushmaster guns
	Four 0.5in (12.7mm) machine guns

United States | *America* class

USS *America* (LHA 6), along with the future USS *Tripoli* (LHA 7) and USS *Bougainville* (LHA 8) are LHD variants optimised for aviation capability. The propulsion plant and electrical distribution and auxiliary systems designed and built for USS *Makin Island* are also used aboard USS *America* and USS *Tripoli*, the first ships in the LHA Replacement Program.

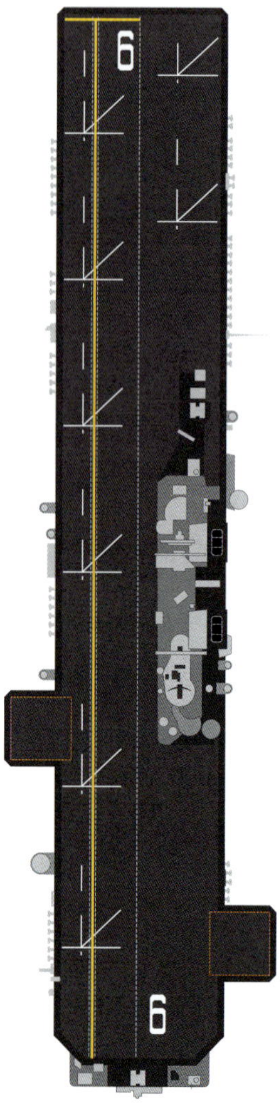

Top view of *America*-class.
(Drawing by James Lawrence)

America-class*	
Name	USS *America*
Pennant number	LHA 6
Laid down	17 July 2009
Launched	4 June 2012
Commissioned	11 October 2014
Name	USS *Tripoli*
Pennant number	LHA 7
Laid down	23 June 2014
Launched	1 May 2017
Commissioned	–
Name	USS *Bougainville*
Pennant number	LHA 8
Laid down	–
Launched	–
Commissioned	–
General characteristics and specifications	
Displacement	44,447 tonnes fully loaded
Length	260.7m (855.3ft)
Beam	32.3m (106ft)
Draught	8.8m (28.9ft)
Propulsion	Two LM 2500+ gas turbines, 52.2MW (70,000hp), two auxiliary propulsion motors, 7.46MW (10,000hp), two propellers
Speed	22kt
Range	9,500nm at 20kt
Complement	1,102
Sensors and weapons	
Combat system	CEC USG-2A
	SPS-48E(V)10 (LHA 6), SPS-48G(V)1 (LHA 7) 3D air search radar
	SPS-49A(V)1 3D air search radar
	SPQ-9B air search radar
	surface search radar
	SPN-35C, SPN-41A (LHA 6) SPN-41B (LHA 7) and SPN-43C carrier controlled approach radar
	SPS-73 navigation radar (x 2)
Armament	Two GMLS Mk 29 launchers for RIM-162D ESSM anti-aircraft missiles
	Two GMLS Mk 49 launchers for RIM-116 RAM anti-aircraft missiles
	Two 20mm Vulcan Phalanx Mk 15 CIWS
	Three 25mm Mk 38 Chain Guns
	Seven twin 0.5in (12.7mm) machine guns

* A class of five ships total is planned.

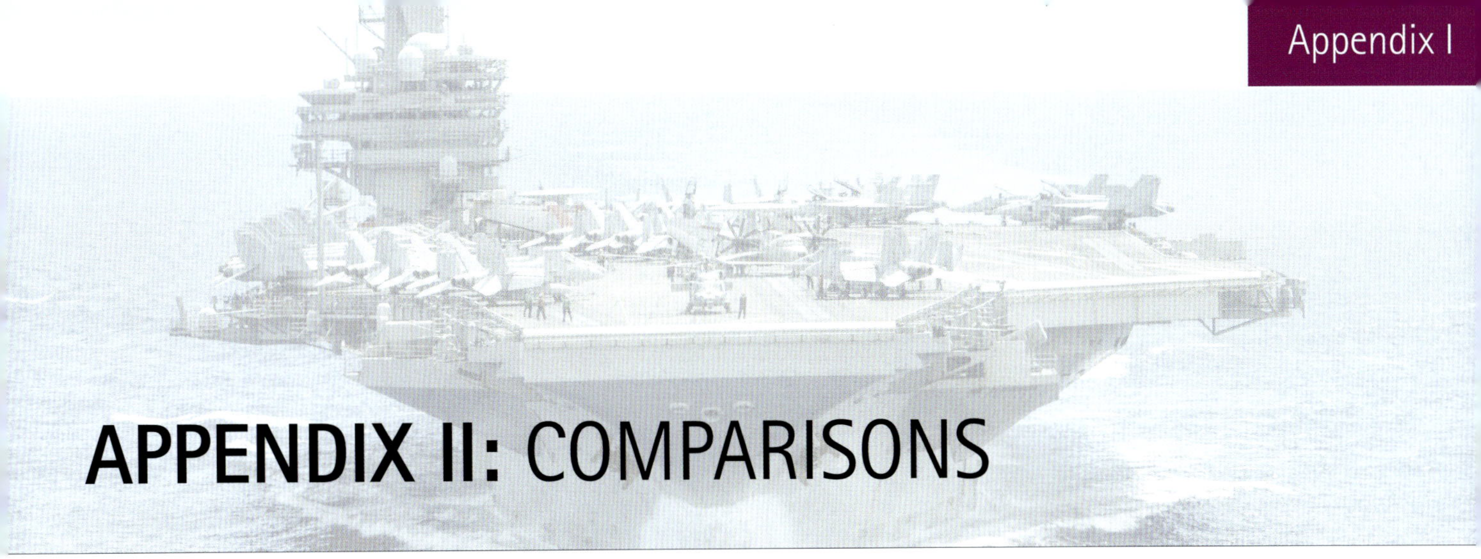

APPENDIX II: COMPARISONS

The most obvious use of an aircraft carrier and its group is the mission of 'force projection'. It is difficult to make a direct comparison between the different classes, since the role, number of aircraft and size of a carrier group depends on a multitude of operational factors and requirements. Clearly, carrier operations are expensive. For this reason, only a few countries are able to effectively operate a carrier group.

These two comparisons provide an overview of aircraft carriers and their air wings in 2017. A graphic of the world's active aircraft carriers, clearly shows the US dominance that is ensured for years to come.

Meanwhile, the size of the carrier and its aircraft launch and recovery capabilities dictate to a considerable degree the different sizes of the air wings embarked on these warships.

ALL THE WORLD'S AIRCRAFT CARRIERS (2017)

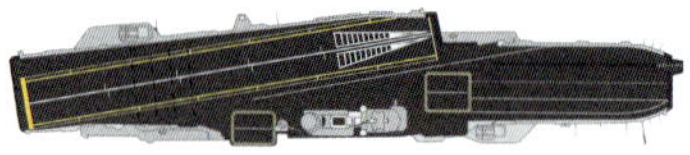

Brazil | *São Paulo* (A12)

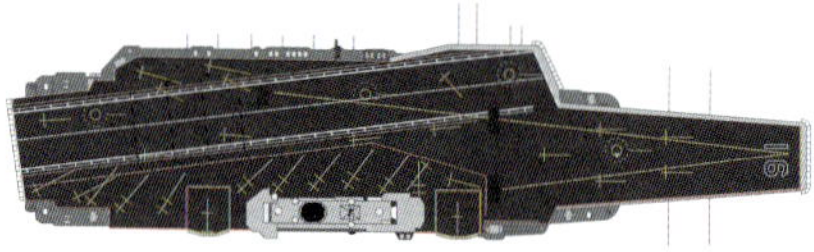

China | *Liaoning* (CV-16)

China | *Shandong* (CV-17)

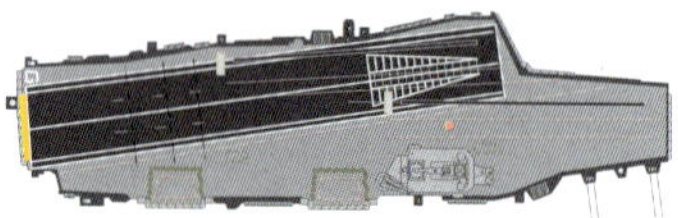

France | *Charles de Gaulle* (R91)

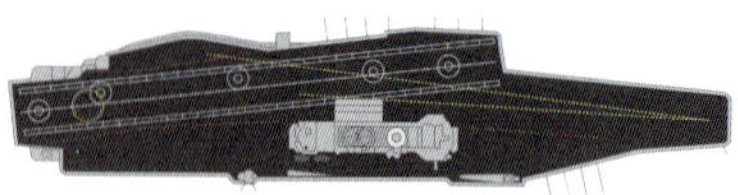

India | *Vikramaditya* (R33)

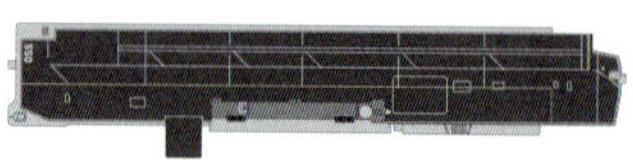

Italy | *Cavour* (C550)

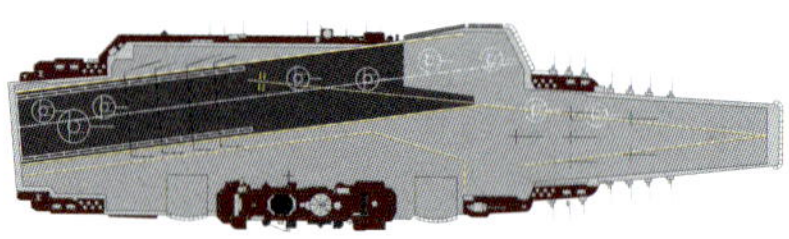

Russia | *Admiral Kuznetsov* (063)

Spain | *Juan Carlos I* (L61)

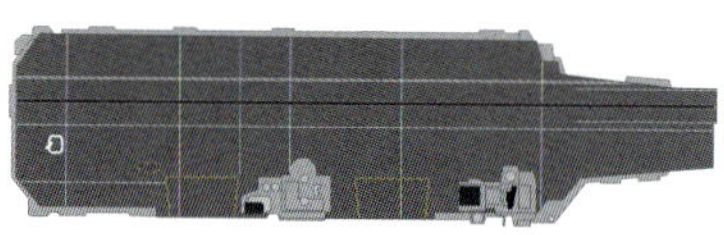

United Kingdom | *Queen Elizabeth* (R08)

USA | *Nimitz*-class

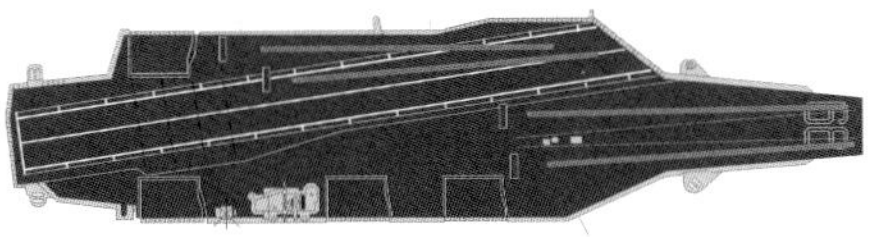

USS *Nimitz* (CVN 68)

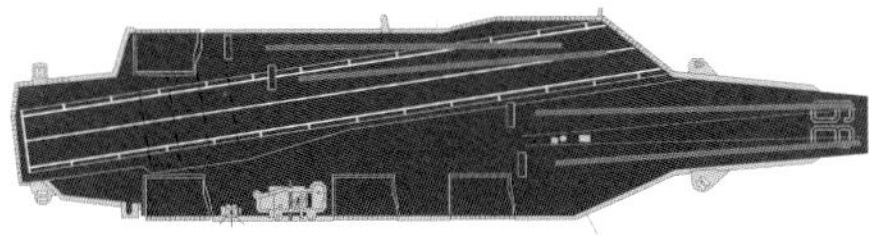

USS *Dwight D. Eisenhower* (CVN 69)

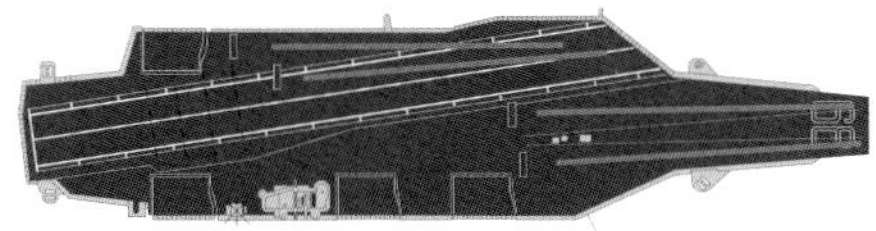

USS *Carl Vinson* (CVN 70)

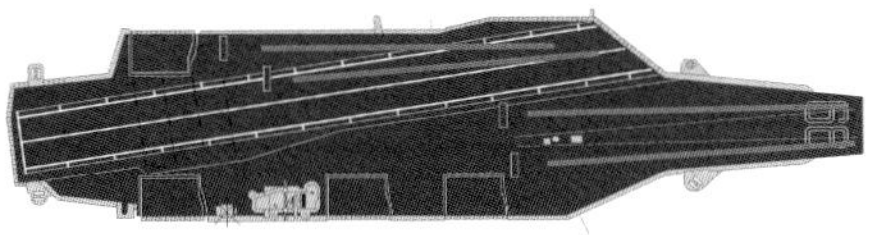

USS *Theodore Roosevelt* (CVN 71)

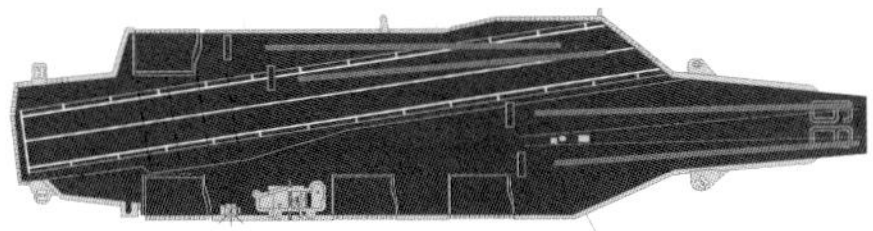

USS *Abraham Lincoln* (CVN 72)

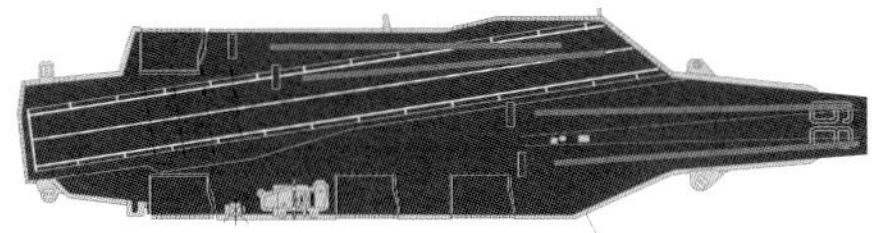

USS *George Washington* (CVN 73)

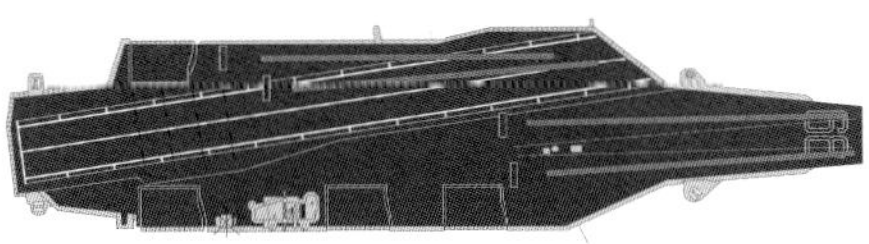

USS *John C. Stennis* (CVN 74)

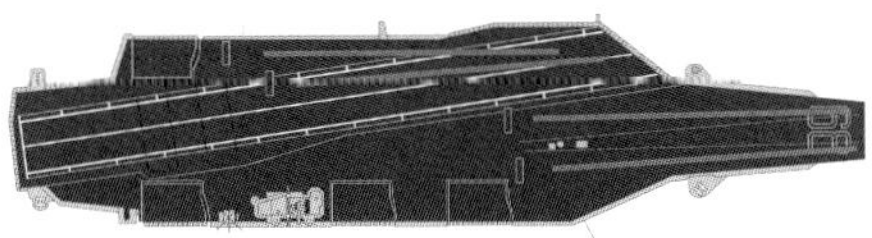

USS *Harry S. Truman* (CVN 75)

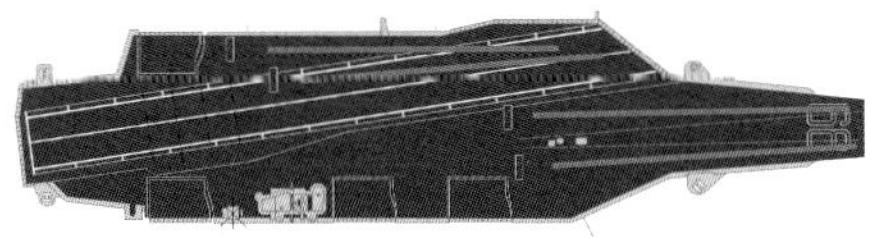

USS *Ronald Reagan* (CVN 76)

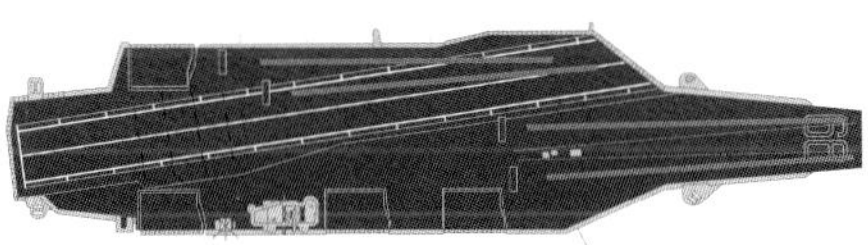

USS *George H. W. Bush* (CVN 77)

USA | *Gerald R. Ford*-class

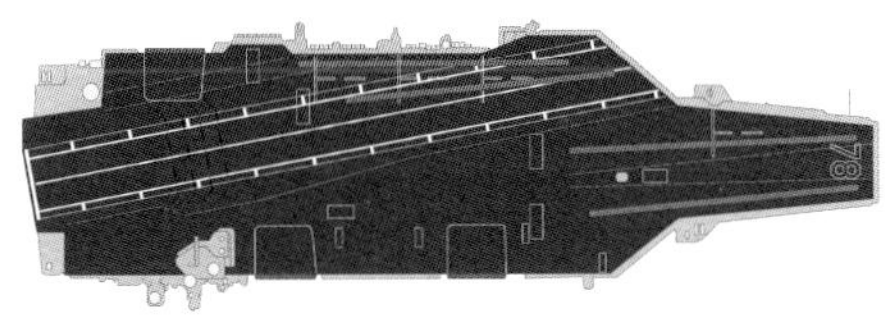

USS *Gerald R. Ford* (CVN 78)

USA | *Wasp*-class

USS *Wasp* (LHD 1)

USS *Essex* (LHD 2)

USS *Kearsarge* (LHD 3)

USS *Boxer* (LHD 4)

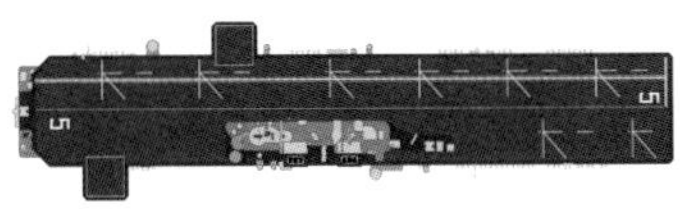

USS *Bataan* (LHD 5)

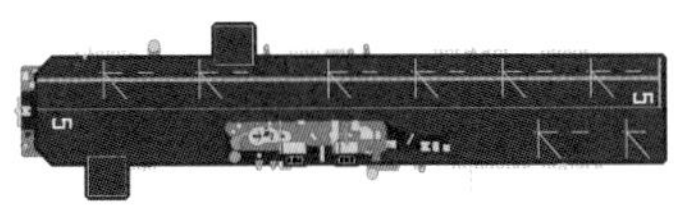

USS *Bonhomme Richard* (LHD 6)

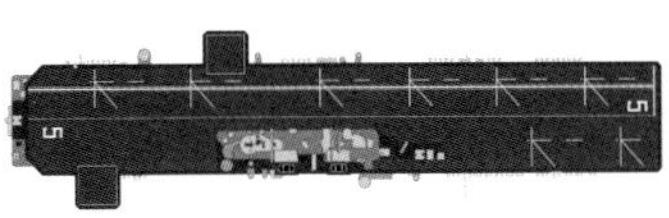

USS *Iwo Jima* (LHD 7)

USS *Makin Island* (LHD 8)

USA | *America*-class

USS *America* (LHA 6)

CURRENT AIR WINGS OF THE WORLD (2017)

Brazil

	6–8	AF-1
	2–3	AF-1A
	3	UH-15A
	3	UH-15B
	3	SH-16

France

	24	Rafale M
	2	E-2C Hawkeye
	2	NH90 Caïman
	2	AS365N Dauphin

China

	20–24	J-15
	2	Z-8JH
	2	Z-9D
	2	Z-18
	2	Z-18F
	2	Z-18J
	2	Z-18S

India

	18	MiG-29K and KUB
	2–3	Chetak
	2–4	Ka-28
	2–4	Ka-31
	1–2	Sea King Mk 42B

Italy

	10	AV-8B+ Harrier II
	6	EH/SH/UH-101
	6	SH/UH-90

Spain

	6	EAV-8B+ Harrier II
	4	SH-3D Sea King
	2–3	AB.212+

Russia

	9–10	Su-33
	4	MiG-29KR and KUBR
	4	Ka-27 and Ka-27PS
	2	Ka-29
	1–2	Ka-31
	1	Ka-52K

United Kingdom

	12	F-35B
	4–5	Merlin HM.Mk 2
	9	Merlin HM.Mk 2
	4	Merlin HC.Mk 4
	8	Apache AH.Mk 1
	3	Chinook HC.Mk 4/5/6
	6	Wildcat AH.Mk 1

United States | *Nimitz* class

12	F/A-18E/F Super Hornet
12	F/A-18E/F Super Hornet
12	F/A-18E/F Super Hornet
10	F/A-18C Hornet
5	EA-18G Growler
4	E-2C/D Hawkeye
2	C-2A Greyhound
8	MH-60S Seahawk
10	MH-60R Seahawk

United States | *Wasp* class

6	AV-8B+ Harrier II
4	AH-1Z Viper
4	CH-53E Super Stallion
12	MV-22 Osprey
5	RQ-21 Blackjack
3	UH-1Y Venom

United States | *America* class

10	F-35B Lightning II
3	AH-1Z Viper
4	CH-53E Super Stallion
12	MV-22 Osprey
5	RQ-21 Blackjack
3	UH-1Y Venom

COMMISSIONED SQUADRON LITHOGRAPHS
We Proudly Serve:
AIR SHOWS
AIR RACERS
LAW ENFORCEMENT
USNAVY
USAF
MARINES
US COAST GUARD
US ARMY
AVIATIONGRAPHIC.COM
Phone: +39.338.487.3171
Email: info@aviationgraphic.com
Address: Via Enrico Lai 35, 09128 Cagliari - ITALY
FULLY CUSTOMIZABLE LITHOGRAPHS WITH LOGO AND TEXT.
PERSONALIZE YOUR SQUADRON LITHOS WITH YOUR AIRCRAFT.
YOU CHOOSE THE CONTENTS, WE MAKE THE FINE ART PRINTS!
* FREE PREVIEWS AND HEAVY DISCOUNTS FOR BULK ORDERS *
www.aviationgraphic.com
We are on FACEBOOK
Join our community!